SECRETS OF
Marie Antoinette

SECRETS OF
Marie Antoinette

✦

Olivier Bernier

DOUBLEDAY & COMPANY, INC.
GARDEN CITY, NEW YORK
1985

BOOK DESIGN BY M FRANKLIN-PLYMPTON

Library of Congress Cataloging in Publication Data
Marie Antoinette, Queen, consort of Louis XVI,
    King of France, 1755–1793.
    secrets of Marie Antoinette.
      1. Marie Antoinette, Queen, consort of Louis XVI,
King of France, 1755–1793. 2. France—History—Louis XVI,
1774–1793. 3. France—Queens—Correspondence.
I. Bernier, Olivier. II. Title.
DC137.1.M37 1985   944′.035′0924 [B]
ISBN: 0-385-19156-1
Library of Congress Catalog Card Number: 85-1683

ACKNOWLEDGEMENTS

The author wishes to thank the Staatsarchiv, Vienna and the New York Public Library.

He owes a particular debt of gratitude to Mr. Robert Rainwater, Keeper of Prints at the New York Public Library, who has generously and frequently shared his knowledge.

SECRETS OF
Marie Antoinette

INTRODUCTION

I

On a cold morning in April 1770, a young girl surrounded by ladies in the richest of court dress stood shivering and naked at the center of a little wooden pavilion on an island in the middle of the Rhine: it was the Archduchess Marie Antoinette's introduction to the French court and its etiquette. Soon she was dressed again, this time in French clothes; her Austrian ladies curtsied and left, and she found herself amid people she had never seen before in her life, but whom she had carefully been coached to treat according to their rank and office. As for her family, her friends, her servants even, she knew she would never see them again: this was an age when queens did not travel. At least as she walked out, she could take pleasure in the splendid carriages which had been ordered specially for her reception; their panels were covered with gold-embroidered blue or red velvet, while, at the four corners, bouquets of gold flowers trembled in the wind. She could also hope that the comtesse de Noailles, her chief attendant,* would prove pleasant, lively, sympathetic.

* The comtesse de Noailles, as *dame d'honneur*, was the chief of the new Dauphine's ladies; next came the *dame d'atours*, who was in charge of the Princess's wardrobe, then the twelve *dames du palais*, or ladies in waiting.

As she quickly discovered, however, Mme de Noailles was a dry, uninteresting woman whose main interest was the complex, subtle etiquette, that first preoccupation of all French courtiers; and far from sympathizing with the homesick girl, she thought it her duty to ignore all feeling; so during those long hours in the swaying carriage, the Archduchess was taught all about the rules of precedence, was told who was entitled to a kiss on the cheek, who merely to a nod, and was generally treated as if she had been an old lady whose only interest in life was the table of ranks. Of course there were interruptions: every town she entered greeted the future Queen of France with parades, speeches, banquets, fireworks and more speeches, and it was noticed that Madame la Dauphine,* as she was now called, listened, responded, smiled, and curtsied with such grace that she won all hearts.

It was a brave effort; but then, only a few days earlier, the fourteen-year-old Archduchess had been thoroughly briefed by her formidable mother, the Empress Maria Theresa; indeed, the two had shared the same bedroom for a week just so that the girl could be prepared for her new life. Then, when the time came to leave her beloved Vienna, Marie Antoinette had received a long detailed set of instructions† which she was urged to read and reread frequently; meanwhile, away at Versailles, the Austrian Ambassador, Florimond, comte de Mercy-Argenteau (called Mercy, for short), stood ready to advise the young Princess. More than just a successful marriage was at stake, after all: the wedding of the Dauphin of France to an Archduchess of Austria was the living symbol of the alliance between the two countries,

* The heir to the throne, in France, was called the Dauphin; his wife was the Dauphine. Although she had yet to meet her future husband, Marie Antoinette had already been married in Vienna by procuration (her brother standing in for her husband) and was thus entitled to be known as Mme la Dauphine.

† See page 31–34.

an alliance which was the foundation of Maria Theresa's foreign policy, one of the great achievements of her reign. If Marie Antoinette failed to charm the King, the Dauphin, and the Court, the French might be tempted to revert to their old friendship with Frederick II of Prussia, a man Maria Theresa referred to, in private, as the Devil.

That Marie Antoinette might dislike her husband and be miserable at Versailles hardly seemed worth considering. This was a political union, not a love marriage. *Bella gerant alii, tu, felix Austria, nube* (Others wage wars; you, happy Austria, marry)—so went the motto. Not for nothing had Maria Theresa given birth to half a dozen daughters; in an age when royal weddings were an important form of politics, it was her policy to extend her sway by that most peaceful of weapons, the nuptial alliance. Already in 1770 one Archduchess was married to the King of Naples while another had become Duchess of Parma: all over Europe, Bourbons and Habsburgs were to be linked by marriage so as to guarantee the safety and prosperity of Austria.

Of course Marie Antoinette was fully aware of all this; the Empress had not wasted her time during those nights spent with her daughter. Marie Antoinette had been made to understand that she would play an important role; but she also took pride in having been chosen to sit on the most glamorous throne in Europe. It was one thing to reign over scenic but underdeveloped Naples or tiny Parma, as her sisters did, quite another to be Queen of France. This had been impressed on her in Vienna, and she felt properly grateful to her mother, who had chosen her for the position. Unfortunately one thing the Empress had never mentioned was that she would have a duty not just to the Empress but also to her new country. The French, Marie Antoinette felt, were lucky to get a daughter of the great Maria Theresa. Of course she must be gracious and dignified in public: that was how a mighty Princess should always appear; but beyond that, she felt all the freer to indulge herself since she was just emerging from a strictly regulated education.

Such behavior was no less than the Empress feared. Like Queen Victoria, she distrusted her children and often, one cannot help feeling, disliked them, although she was a spectacularly conscientious mother. The strictest discipline was observed in the Schönbrunn nurseries. The Empress saw her children every day, kept abreast of their lessons, their physical and mental development, even their carefully regulated amusements. She praised their progress in drawing, singing, and dancing, and liked showing them off. This was most unusual in the eighteenth century, a time when children, who were considered subhuman, were normally neither seen nor heard.

It is in fact one of the paradoxical aspects of Maria Theresa's character that this proud Habsburg Empress, this courageous and effective ruler, reminds one, in her dealings with her children, of nothing so much as a caricatural Jewish mother. Blending pride in her brood with devastating putdowns, constant whining with anxious queries about the children's health, and a cold-eyed appraisal of their talents with fervent protestations of love, Maria Theresa produced in her sons and daughters reactions which seem oddly out of place in her time: rebellious, resentful, yet dependent, they belong more to our century than hers. The key to this peculiar development may well be the fact that the Empress seldom meant what she said, that she set impossible standards and coupled harsh criticism with declarations of affection. "Spare the [verbal] rod, spoil the child" might well have been her motto—but with a difference: because she was a uniquely conscientious sovereign, she always put the needs of the State before those of her family. As a result, while she expected her children to be moral, literate, and hardworking, she also made it clear that even the most sacred principle must give way to political needs.

Still, difficult though the Empress might have been, her children were brought up in much closer proximity to her than was considered normal, partly at the behest of her husband, Francis of Lorraine. A kind man with a huge appetite for food and women, Francis turned out to be the perfect consort. He made his wife an Empress, thus preserving the Imperial crown for the House of Habsburg, since the Holy Roman Empire allowed only male sovereigns; but this august position gave him practically no power. The Empire, which was composed of several hundred independent states, existed only in theory, and there was little the Emperor could do except for conferring titles; his was, in fact, a purely ceremonial role.

Maria Theresa, on the other hand, as the only living child of Charles VI of Habsburg, had inherited all the dynasty's possessions: Hungary with a good piece of today's Romania, Upper and Lower Austria, Bohemia and Moravia (today's Czechoslovakia), Carinthia, Carniolia, the duchy of Milan, the kingdom of Naples (soon lost but replaced by Tuscany), and the Austrian Netherlands (today's Belgium). She ruled these extensive but disparate lands herself with the help, from the 1750s on, of Chancellor Kaunitz. As for Francis, he had little to do except appear on great Court occasions, sleep with the Empress, and enjoy the revenue from Tuscany which was his for life. He collected precious objects, chased (in secret) after women, and spent time with his children. Unlike Maria Theresa, who was both busy and hypercritical, he was a kind, encouraging, often present parent who created a warm family atmosphere in which the children could feel loved and appreciated. It was Marie Antoinette's great misfortune that the Emperor died in 1765 when she was only nine years old. After that, she was left to the care of a devoted but incompetent governess who helped her fake her homework so that the Empress would not realize how backward the little girl was.

In one other, very important respect, Maria Theresa's children differed from those of just about all other European royalty: although they appeared at court on ceremonial occasions, they spent most of their time in an etiquette-free environment. Precedence, as a result, meant nothing to them: indeed, the Empress preferred to lead an essentially bourgeois life. She was quite prepared, when duty called, to put on splendid clothes and hold court; more, she made access to her official presence singularly difficult because she insisted not only on the right degree of nobility, but also on a strictly moral behavior, while preserving the old Spanish etiquette, the stiffest of all. These, however, were rare occasions. Most of the time, she resided at Schönbrunn, just outside Vienna, and lived more like a rich middle-class housewife than a mighty Empress. Not unnaturally, her children grew up to think that this blend of complete informality with the occasional pompous display was the norm. A life in which they were surrounded, all day and most of the night, with courtiers, and were constantly expected to perform so that privacy became the rarest of pleasures would have seemed intolerable and mad to them—but that in fact was just the way the other European ruling families lived.

Because the family was so large—Francis and Maria Theresa had eleven children in all—Marie Antoinette grew up surrounded by brothers and sisters who were, of course, her equals, whereas most royal children saw practically no one but their attendants, who were their inferiors. This had a double result. First, the family unit became central to the children's development, thus creating a fierce, lasting loyalty which, no matter where they lived, made them always consider the family's interests, and therefore Austria's, as paramount; second, once away from their siblings, the Archdukes and Archduchesses had a tendency to make friends with certain, sometimes unsuitable courtiers whom they trusted as if they had been members of the family. The girls in particular tended to have close women friends on whom they depended utterly. Unfortunately, this group living did not teach discrimination: it was enough for someone to be appealing; discretion and reliability were then assumed. But since sovereigns were usually surrounded by ambitious, greedy flatterers, the consequences of this easy friendliness often proved disastrous.

Another curious result of this system of education was, perhaps, the one Maria Theresa would have least expected. She had, from the very beginning, made it plain to her children that they had a lifelong duty to the State. They would marry to serve Austria, they must always remain good Austrians on whatever throne they might sit, they must rule in such a way as to ensure the welfare of their people only inasmuch as it did not conflict with Austria's; but, she told the girls, a wife must always obey her husband. Further, she must please him, must change her tastes to conform to his, while, of course, influencing him so as to make him a faithful and, if possible, subservient ally of the Habsburg Monarchy. The Archduchesses listened to all this, but they also looked at their parents and noticed that it was their mother, not their father, who ruled, while it was their father who adapted himself to his wife's preferences. When they left home to marry foreign rulers, they promptly applied what they had learned and more: at Naples, Parma, and Versailles, it was soon noticed, the husband did the wife's bidding.

These contradictions were magnified, in Marie Antoinette's case, by the instructions her mother gave her as she left and by the letters she received once she reached her new family. On the one hand she was told to observe the rules in effect at the French Court, to show herself as French as the natives, and never to let people realize that she thought her own country superior to France; on the other hand, she was enjoined never to forget that she was an Austrian first. She had been taught that sexual morality was important, that loose women were despicable and outside the pale, and she believed it; but then, when she was asked to be amiable to the King's official mistress and vociferously refused the request, she was promptly and repeatedly scolded by her indignant mother: if the mistress complained, the King would be annoyed, and that in turn might affect the alliance. This kind of perfectly consistent inconsistency does have a name: hypocrisy, a failing widely attributed to Maria Theresa. Frederick II took the greatest pleasure in describing how during the negotiations leading to the partition of Poland, Maria Theresa, who knew that this was an immoral act, started crying every time the subject came up; but, he added truthfully, "the more she cried, the more she took."

II

The Court in which the Archduchess Marie Antoinette found herself at the end of her travels could not have been more different from her native Schönbrunn, and she was singularly ill-prepared for it. Among many other awkward facts, for instance, the Empress had thought it best not to mention that the sixty-year-old King had a young, beautiful, and low-born mistress, the comtesse du Barry. When, on her first evening at Court, the Dauphine saw a ravishingly pretty young woman sitting with the royal family, she asked what Court office the lady held. "She amuses the King, Madame," the comtesse de Noailles answered. "In that case, I want to be her rival," Marie Antoinette innocently replied. Luckily it was a charming error, but the confrontation might have had very awkward consequences.

It is only fair to say, however, that the Court of Versailles was quite awe-inspiring enough to daunt the best prepared of foreigners. Little had changed since Louis XIV, a century earlier, had decided to make it the most splendid in Europe and had set down, once and for all, its incredibly complex and demanding etiquette. Unlike England or Austria, where the great aristocratic families periodically retreated to their country estates, the French nobility lived at Versailles the year round. Exile to one's own château was thought the worst of catastrophes. And the routine of the Court, centered around the King's person, was glittering, intricate, and dangerous.

Whether he resided at the great golden palace of Versailles, at Fontainebleau, or at Compiègne, the King, along with the royal family, was on show day and night. His official *lever* was an important and lengthy public ceremony at which courtiers were allowed in at various stages according to the kind of *entrées* they had; and moving up from one category to the next was ardently desired, since the longer you spent with the King, the better he knew you and the more likely you were to obtain favors from him. The same ritual prevailed, in reverse, for his *coucher;* and all the day's occupations, except for interviews with the ministers, took place in front of a crowd. To shy or impatient members of the royal family, however, the worst ordeal of the day was the meal they had to take in public. Seated alone at a table, facing a crowd of courtiers and visitors from Paris,* they had to eat while being watched as they chewed every bite. Then, too, Court dress was worn most of the day and night; it looked superb, of course, but was both heavy and uncomfortable. And every step, every bow, every word almost was determined by the sacrosanct etiquette.

That too was the work of Louis XIV. In codifying its rules, he had two principal goals in mind: first, through its complex workings, he transformed the Monarch into a demigod whose least bodily functions were almost wor-

* Any decently dressed person was allowed into the palace.

shiped. Indeed, the King came rather before the Deity: it was noticed that at Mass, during the elevation, the courtiers looked, not at the Host, but at the King; and this attitude extended even to the royal dinner, before whose passage all present bowed or curtsied. Then, because the nobles found themselves busy arguing abstruse points of precedence, the length of cloaks worn as a sign of mourning, or the exact placement of the cushions in the Chapel, they had no time left to think of revolting against the government as their ancestors had so often done. All in all, the Sun King's invention proved a success, but by the eighteenth century, it had become rather too much of a good thing. Penned up in the great hives of the royal palaces, idle and greedy, the courtiers spent their lives intriguing against whoever was in power, mistress or minister, and trying desperately to get the King's ear.

Aside from sheer boredom—life at Court entailed hours of waiting, every day—there was good reason to seek the King's favor: all the good things of life were in his gift. If you yearned to be created a Duke or a Marshal of France, if you needed a pension or a sum of money to pay your debts, if you wanted your younger son to be made a bishop, your eldest son to have the reversion of your Court office, if you wanted to become a minister, you had to look to the King. He appointed and fired his ministers, who were responsible to him alone; he made war and peace, considered all tax revenue as his private possession to be spent exactly the way he wanted, he gave—or took away—the great Court offices which were considered the most desirable of prizes, and of course he could order anyone jailed at the Bastille or exiled to any locality in France. Finally, as Maria Theresa constantly reminded her daughter, the continuation, the closeness of the Franco-Austrian alliance depended on him alone.

This system obviously imposed the most enormous and unceasing burden on the person of the Monarch, who must find time and energy for both display and the tasks of government. Louis XIV, who sometimes does indeed seem more than human, found the challenge exhilarating, but Louis XV spent most of his life struggling to keep up with his many duties. A shy and intensely private man, he loathed the display to which he was condemned while still conscientiously going through the obligatory routine. By 1770 he had been on the throne for fifty-five years* and was markedly more sure of himself, but even so he escaped the palaces as often as he could and retreated to smaller châteaux—Choisy, La Muette, Bellevue, Marly—where etiquette could almost be ignored.

Marie Antoinette, as she met her new grandfather-in-law,† knew nothing of this. What she saw, as she jumped out of the carriage and ran to kneel at the King's feet, was an athletic, remarkably handsome man who looked much younger than his age. She noticed immediately that he was gracious, kind, welcoming, yet amazingly majestic, that he could make her feel at ease, that he seemed, indeed, just the person described by the Empress. As for the fifteen-year-old Dauphin, whom she met at the same time, he made a very different impression. Heavyset, awkward, decidedly not good-looking, this gruff, silent, and rather ill-mannered young man was anything but appealing. Still, she set out to charm him, and to everyone's surprise she succeeded. Within days the Dauphin's manners improved and he became markedly more pleasant.

Neither the relatively informal meeting, however, nor the sumptuous wedding ceremonies which followed within days could give the Dauphine any understanding of the situation at Court; since clearly she could not function in a state of ignorance, both Mercy (the Austrian Ambassador) and

* He became King in 1715 at the age of five.
† The Dauphin, son of an earlier, deceased Dauphin, was Louis XV's grandson.

some of her new relatives proceeded to give her the information she needed; and what she discovered was a picture very different from the one painted by the Empress.

First, and most shocking, she was told that Louis XV had an official mistress, the comtesse du Barry, an entrancing young woman with abundant blond hair, a dazzling complexion, huge blue eyes, and a perfect figure. Mme du Barry was cheerful, kind, easygoing, and extremely sexy. She was also a former kept woman, the illegitimate daughter of a monk and a seamstress who had slept with a great many men before ending up in the King's bed. She had been introduced to the King by his valet some two years earlier, had proved to be more than the one-night stand which all expected, and had finally been married to the brother of her former pimp, the comte du Barry, who was sent back to his distant province from the altar without being given a chance to sample the new comtesse's charms. Now a proper lady, she could be presented at Court and thus became part of life at Versailles. That this woman of little virtue wanted to make herself agreeable to the new arrival only horrified Marie Antoinette the more: The Dauphine came, after all, from the most puritanical Court in Europe, so it was bad enough to find an official mistress prominently displayed; but one who was not a member of a noble family, who had in fact been little better than a streetwalker, was too much for an innocent fifteen-year-old to swallow. Even more provoking, she was promptly told that Mme du Barry was at the head of the anti-Choiseul faction at Court, and the duc de Choiseul, the Foreign Minister, was the very man who had arranged her marriage and on whom, her mother had said, she could always rely. Thus within days the situation became simple: on one side there was Good, personified by the duc; on the other, Evil in the shape of "that woman." Above it all, splendid yet intimidating, stood the King whose weakness for the "creature" was both deplorable and incomprehensible.

Naturally this was a gross oversimplification, even in some ways the reverse of the truth; but an unprepared foreign teenager could not be expected to see this, especially since she promptly fell under the sway of three of the most prejudiced, sour, and unpleasant women at Versailles. Mesdames de France, as they were called, were the King's daughters: Adélaïde, who was thirty-eight; Victoire, thirty-seven; and Sophie, thirty-six. Long past the marrying age, Mesdames were unattractive, bad-tempered, interfering old maids who hated almost everyone, resented almost everything, including their own powerlessness, and were determined to use the Dauphine as a convenient tool. In order to do so, however, they had to suppress, in appearance at least, the dislike they automatically felt for her: because the Franco-Austrian alliance had been warmly defended by Mme de Pompadour in the late 1750s, and because Mesdames hated all the King's mistresses, they were rabidly anti-Austrian. This placed them in a very awkward position: not only did they need to influence the Dauphine so as to turn her against Mme du Barry, they were also paradoxically supporters of the Choiseul party, even though he was pro-Austrian, because he was the favorite's avowed enemy. Of course this involved them in a web of inconsistencies; but they forged ahead nonetheless, so with a valiant effort they gave Marie Antoinette a warm welcome.

The bewildered girl, who hardly knew where to turn, was delighted. Since the Dauphin was too childish, silent, and weak to provide her with a lead, and the King was too remote, she turned to Mesdames, safe in the knowledge that she was following her mother's instructions.* The reason for the prudish Empress's recommendation was simple

* See page 36.

enough: in a Court where every man had a mistress and every woman a lover, Mesdames, alone, trod the stony path of sexual virtue. That, unfortunately, was their only merit, while their love of intrigue represented a great danger for the Dauphine. Within months, as a result, Marie Antoinette started willfully ignoring Mme du Barry, to the lady's distress and the King's annoyance, while Maria Theresa came to repent at leisure the endorsement given in haste.

Mesdames also harmed the Dauphine in other, more permanent ways: they taught her to look at politics not in terms of what might be good for the country, but solely as a means for advancing friends and harming enemies; and they further showed her that the way to do this was by backstairs intrigue, a lesson which Marie Antoinette learned quickly and well. Then, too, they surrounded themselves with their own tiny circle of friendly ladies by whom in fact they were completely dominated. What the comtesse de Narbonne was for Madame Adélaïde, Mmes de Lamballe and de Polignac were to be eventually for Marie Antoinette. Of course as soon as the Empress became aware of all this, she wrote frantic letters denouncing Mesdames to her daughter, but it was too late and the harm had already been done.

In the short run, too, Mesdames did much to hurt the Dauphine. Not unnaturally, since she was only fourteen, Marie Antoinette was still very childlike, and Mesdames encouraged her in this when she desperately needed to grow up as soon as possible, while, by turning her against Mme du Barry, they made her life difficult and often unpleasant. The duc de Choiseul who, although rabidly anti-du Barry himself, could have advised Marie Antoinette on other points, soon found himself out of office; and the new ministry, although not Mme du Barry's creation, was certainly friendly to her and thus was despised by the Dauphine.

Why Choiseul should have so violently opposed Mme du Barry has never been quite clear since, at the beginning at least, the favorite showed him nothing but good will. His reasons may, in fact, have been a blend of the personal and the political: personal because his sister, the duchesse de Gramont, had tried hard to become the King's mistress and failed; political because he probably feared Mme du Barry would, in time, come to have more influence on Louis XV than he himself. On both counts, unfortunately, he failed to see reality and as a result started a war to the death with the favorite, thus incidentally confirming Marie Antoinette's own prejudice.

When on December 31, 1770, Choiseul was suddenly and unexpectedly dismissed, the best-informed people assumed that it had been Mme du Barry's doing. In fact they could not have been more wrong. Louis XV decided to change ministers for two excellent reasons: first, Choiseul had foolishly promised to support Spain in a prospective war with England over the possession of the Falklands; second, in the perennial and ever graver conflict which opposed the King and the Parlement, Choiseul had been secretly encouraging the latter in its illegal resistance. That France ought not to engage in a war with Great Britain over these distant and unimportant islands which it did not even claim for itself hardly needs saying, especially since it might well have provoked a general European conflict. As for the Parlement, unlike its English namesake, it was a court of law whose members, the judges, bought their office; but because they also "registered"—i.e., recorded—the laws, they had come to feel it was their privilege to refuse registration of any edict that displeased them. Since they were rich and ultra-conservative, they automatically blocked every attempt at reform. Now, after a long drawn-out struggle, Louis XV finally decided to abolish the Parlement and replace it with a proper tribunal.* For all these reasons, Choiseul had to go.

* For a full exposition of this critical question, see this author's *Louis the Beloved, the Life of Louis XV* (Doubleday, 1984).

The Dauphine, although shocked by his dismissal, managed to hide her feelings, at least before the King; only she now hated the new ministers with that intensity usually felt only by the young and stupid: whatever Marie Antoinette's charms, and they were considerable, intelligence was not one of them. Interestingly enough, the glum, slow-witted Dauphin knew better than to espouse his wife's new cause. Everyone at Court noticed that he was polite to both the favorite and the ministers, thus showing himself rather cleverer than most people had expected him to be.

At the very top of Marie Antoinette's enemies list, right after Mme du Barry herself, came the new Foreign Minister, the duc d'Aiguillon. Although away in Vienna, Maria Theresa had regretted Choiseul's fall, she felt perfectly able to work with the duc d'Aiguillon, who was just as committed to the alliance as his predecessor. Indeed, she soon came to prefer him on the simple grounds that he was so imcompetent as to be unable to make trouble over the partition of Poland. For Marie Antoinette, however, d'Aiguillon was an easy target: when she was rude to the favorite, she upset the King; when she pretended not to see the minister, no one cared except d'Aiguillon himself—and the Austrian Ambassador.

Already before Choiseul's fall, and even more afterward, the Court was divided into two sharply opposed factions, a situation for which Marie Antoinette had not been prepared; and because all depended on the King, the intrigues on both sides consisted either of laying traps to push the unwary into displeasing the Monarch, or of little conspiracies to influence him on some specific point. That neither made any difference in the end deterred absolutely no one, least of all Mesdames: it was as good a way of passing the time as any. Even for those who had been raised at Versailles, it was difficult not to make a mistake; but when someone like Marie Antoinette came along, then obviously disaster was sure to follow; and although Maria Theresa had failed to tell her daughter about this, she was quite aware of it, so she provided her with a guide and counselor in the person of her Ambassador.

The comte de Mercy-Argenteau quickly proved to be yet another of the Empress's inspired choices. The scion of a noble Belgian family* with estates in Hungary, he was the quintessential international Austrian, at ease in any court, sophisticated, witty, well-mannered, and extremely shrewd. In no time at all, he gained the Dauphine's trust as well as that of the Foreign Minister and even, miraculously, that of the favorite. A seasoned courtier himself, he had an acute ear for the newest gossip and a quick sense of how it could either be used for his purposes or rendered harmless. His reports to the Empress are models of the genre—full of information and insight, wise suggestions, and amusing anecdotes. As for his role, it was clear enough: he was to preserve and tighten the alliance by all possible means. To that purpose all must serve, including the Dauphine, who had been instructed to heed his advice. Indeed, she could have had no better guide, since he was constantly aware of the latest shift of power at Court or within the ministry, was well liked by Louis XV, who never hesitated to speak to him frankly, and had easy access to the favorite. Just as important, in a world where etiquette was all and royalty, who lived in public, were virtually inaccessible in private, Mercy, as Austrian Ambassador, was able to visit the Dauphine almost as often as he liked.

* And therefore an Austrian subject: Belgium was at that time the Austrian Netherlands.

III

The life which Marie Antoinette found herself leading at Versailles between 1770 and 1774 was not only utterly different from that of the Austrian Court, it was also hectic, confusing, and exhausting. By virtue of her marriage to the Dauphin and of the fact that, quickly and visibly, she was able to control him, Marie Antoinette was a potential power; but as long as Louis XV lived, anything might happen: if she really displeased him, she could even be sent back to Vienna. That this remained a possibility was due in part to the heedless arrogance with which she treated Mme du Barry, in part to the nonconsummation of her marriage.

The very first duty of a Dauphine or a Queen was, obviously, to produce an heir. In Marie Antoinette's case, this necessity was particularly urgent because a child would consolidate the alliance. If, on the other hand, she proved sterile, then the marriage might even be dissolved, a very serious blow to the alliance. And although she was very young, Marie Antoinette knew quite well what was expected of her, but while she was eager to do her part, the Dauphin proved to be, at the very least, backward. Louis XV, that great connoisseur of women, had found the Dauphine very attractive if a little flat-chested, a shortcoming which had vanished by 1773. With a dazzling complexion, a charming smile, and an appealing face, she should have been enough to titillate even the uncouth Dauphin; but while he undoubtedly liked, then loved his wife, he seemed curiously unwilling to give her a more substantial proof of these feelings. It was bad enough that he did no more than sleep on his wedding night: his excessive restraint was written off to shyness and extreme youth, since he was still only fifteen. What seemed at first odd, then worrying, then catastrophic, was that as the months grew into years, Louis-Auguste still shied away from sexual conjunction with his wife. After a while Louis XV, who remembered his own youthful ardor, sent for his physician and asked him to talk with the Dauphin. Perhaps the subject was too delicate, perhaps the physician failed to ask the right sort of pointed questions: at any rate, he reported that the Dauphin did not suffer from any physical problem and that all would be well as soon as he overcame his shyness. That was only partly right. The Dauphin was indeed oddly shy in spite of Marie Antoinette's encouraging attitude; he literally did not know what he was supposed to do in bed; but he also suffered from phymosis, a condition curable only by circumcision. As a result the suspense continued year after year, and it forms one of the recurrent themes of the correspondence between the Empress and her daughter.

Even if they did not have sex, the Dauphin and the Dauphine quickly became a pair in every other respect; but instead of finding in her husband the maturity and guidance she so sorely needed, Marie Antoinette discovered that she was the superior partner. Louis-Auguste, it is true, was more prudent than his wife in his treatment of Mme du Barry, but in every other respect, he was even more childish and bewildered while wholly lacking her charm and graciousness. Thus when the Dauphin became less sullen, then positively polite, the change was rightly credited to Marie Antoinette. It was also noticed that the two young people had long private conversations and that they behaved in what was obviously a prearranged way. As Mercy told Maria Theresa, there could be no doubt that Marie Antoinette controlled her weak, slow husband; and that situation remained unchanged to the very end.

Next in importance in Marie Antoinette's personal life, but first in every other respect, came the King. Mercy never ceased urging the Dauphine to pay more attention to him, to try and please him, in a word to gain such influence over him that, as he aged, he would turn more and more to her and she would eventually be able to influence his policies. In fact and exceptionally, Mercy completely misread the King, but it can be said at least that he was not the first to do so. Not only was Louis XV kind and, to those who knew him well, charming, not only did he have the kind of manners which made his friends feel utterly at ease—although without ever forgetting, the duc de Croÿ commented, that he was one's master—but he also shrank from any sort of confrontation. Thus, for instance, instead of calling in the Dauphine and telling her to be polite to Mme du Barry, he asked Mercy to serve as his ambassador, obviously a far less effective way of handling the situation; but then again, large as it sometimes appeared, this remained a minor problem. When it came to running the government, Louis XV knew exactly what he wanted and showed it very clearly when he dismissed Choiseul, prevented the impending war between Spain and Great Britain, and abolished the Parlement.

The King, of course, always remained the central figure at Versailles, and whenever Marie Antoinette wanted any small favor for her ladies or for herself, it was the King to whom she went; but he always remained distant and somewhat intimidating. Mercy noticed that she could never quite feel at ease with him, so in her need for a family, for intimates of her own rank, she turned to Mesdames. Although hardly united themselves—Madame Adélaïde despised her stupider sisters, who resented her domineering temper—they provided the Dauphine with a little circle in which she could relax and be her age; indeed, to Mercy's great annoyance, they encouraged her more childish pastimes so that soon Marie Antoinette was visiting her aunts every day. It was also Mesdames who passed the Court gossip, suitably distorted, on to the Dauphine and generally encouraged her adolescent pride when it came to dealing with Mme du Barry. Whatever they didn't dare to do themselves could thus be carried out by the Dauphine at no risk to themselves: it was an ideal situation, since they had everything to gain and nothing to lose.

Their influence was all the greater that the one other older woman who should have been a mentor and a friend for Marie Antoinette, the comtesse de Noailles, proved to be weak, difficult, and tiresome. Oscillating between gross flattery and continual nagging, the dame d'honneur became someone whose presence the Dauphine dreaded. While it is true that she was stiff and quite unable to understand the needs of a fifteen-year-old, it must also be said for Mme de Noailles's that in continually urging the Dauphine to behave according to the etiquette, she was doing no more than her duty. She might perhaps have tried to explain to the reluctant teenager just why the etiquette was so important instead of merely demanding an endless compliance with frequently dull, tiring, and excessively complicated ceremonies; as it was, Marie Antoinette never believed that all those rules, all those hours spent standing, nodding, curtsying, greeting, eating, playing card games in public, deadly though they might be, were also an essential part of her job. Nicknaming the dame d'honneur "Madame l'Etiquette," she made fun of her and proceeded to neglect some of the most essential jobs of a Dauphine, and later a Queen.

Although Marie Antoinette's life was not always dreary or uncomfortable, there were long hours spent on just the kind of etiquette-dictated occupations she hated: public card playing, for instance, took place almost every evening. It was the occasion for the courtiers to gather around the royal family, and thus very useful to the latter; but for the Dauphine it meant playing old-fashioned, uninteresting games very, very slowly. Again, when she made her way around the *cercle*, the circle of ladies, the Dauphine made herself visible and accessible, but it is easy to see why a young woman should have found it a great chore to have to say a few words to each of some hundred ladies for whom she cared nothing: to someone brought up in the easy, relaxed atmosphere of Schönbrunn, it was almost unbearable.

At first the Dauphine just did what she was told; then, as the months passed, she realized that she could sometimes have her own way, and, safe in the knowledge that the King was unlikely to scold her, she did exactly that. In short order, however, she found out that her mother had no intention of relinquishing her control: Marie Antoinette, the Empress thought, was lazy, silly, frivolous, and quite incapable of sustained effort, aside from not being very bright. Left to her own impulses, she would endanger the alliance, a risk Maria Theresa had no intention of taking. And since she felt quite able to guide her daughter, she proceeded to do so in the correspondence which forms the main part of this book.

Clearly such correspondence would be useful only if the two women could be absolutely frank with each other; strict secrecy would therefore have to be maintained. All normal mail was subject to the attentions of the French *cabinet noir*, a body of officials who read all letters and communicated their contents to the King, so a system of couriers was set up: once a month, more often in case of special events, an envoy brought in a letter from Vienna and returned with Marie Antoinette's answers as well as Mercy's dispatches. No one except the mother and the daughter was ever supposed to see this correspondence, and Marie Antoinette believed this actually to be the case. In fact the Empress sent copies of her letters and the Dauphine's answers to Mercy, who was thus exactly informed both of Maria Theresa's demands (which he had usually suggested in the first place) and of Marie Antoinette's responses. And since the Empress could only praise, scold, or advise her daughter if she knew exactly what was happening at Versailles, Mercy transformed himself, secretly of course, into a master spy. He himself faithfully reported everything he saw or heard, not excepting his frequent conversations with the Dauphine;

but he also hired members of her Household who reported to him at frequent intervals the smallest events, the least important conversations concerning the young woman. Not a single detail of her life escaped the Ambassador's notice; moreover, he also had spies in Mesdames' entourage so as to find out all about the influence, the urgings of the aunts; even in the King's own apartments he had people reporting everything that concerned the Dauphine. All very effective. Marie Antoinette would naturally have been outraged by this had she been aware of it, but it is the measure of Mercy's efficacity that she never found out about it. Still, it was one of his primary objectives never to let her guess that the information reaching the Empress came from him.

As a result Mercy and Marie Antoinette sometimes had conversations worthy of a Beaumarchais comedy, in which the one angrily wondered who was telling her mother about her various trespasses while the other responded with a display of sympathetic bewilderment. Marie Antoinette believed Mercy to be on her side—the exact reverse of the truth—and Maria Theresa was always careful to indicate a source other than the Ambassador for her information. Time after time, as she launches herself on a new set of reproaches, she cites the accounts given to her by travelers, stories printed in the press, or even, sometimes, public rumor.

The letters in which Mercy conveyed his information were divided into two categories: the "open" reports, which were also read by Joseph II, the eldest son with whom Maria Theresa shared the tasks of government, and by Prince Kaunitz, the Chancellor; and "for your eyes only" letters, which were to be seen by the Empress alone. These latter, of course, are the richest in intimate, often unflattering detail. In publishing the correspondence between Maria Theresa and Marie Antoinette, therefore, it is essential to include extracts of Mercy's reports: while they sometimes run to endless, tiresome detail (which has been eliminated from the extracts), they can also give a lively, vivid, accurate picture of Marie Antoinette. Then, too, the process through which the Empress's advice reaches her daughter stands revealed. We read Mercy's complaints and his suggestions; we go on to Maria Theresa's letter embodying these suggestions and come finally to Marie Antoinette's reaction, both on paper, in her reply, and orally as it is revealed by Mercy.

That there was something rather shameful about all the spying, all the secrecy can hardly be denied. Far worse, however, is the fact that this was all done so as to mold Marie Antoinette into an obedient tool of Austrian policy while pretending that it was all for her own good. In some indirect ways, of course, it was: she could be more useful if she was popular and respected; but if in order to serve Austria, she had to affront the French, then that was just too bad: not for nothing did she become that hated figure, *l'Autrichienne*, the Austrian woman who cared nothing for France or her people. What we discover, therefore, as we read the correspondence which follows is not merely an account of life at Versailles and the vicissitudes of a marriage, but also the workings of a conspiracy. As a result the Empress's endless protests that she only has her daughter's happiness at heart ring singularly hollow, and her pious exhortations stand revealed as the rankest hypocrisy.

Indeed, it is particularly entertaining to watch her trample her own principles while pretending it isn't so. When, for instance, the Dauphine set off a minicrisis by her obstinate refusal to notice Mme du Barry, we see the Empress, who refused ever to see women of uncertain reputation, urge her daughter to be amiable to the "creature" whom she must look on as simply another lady at Court. All morality forgotten, Marie Antoinette is imperiously commanded to say a few words to the favorite while, in the most delicious of reversals, her doing so is presented as a highly ethical act.

The syllogism developed by the Empress runs like this: it is your duty to please your grandfather the King; it will please him if you speak to Mme du Barry; therefore, speaking to Mme du Barry is a moral imperative. After some resistance, Marie Antoinette actually swallowed this; but, switching her ground, she now claimed that, appearances to the contrary notwithstanding, Louis XV did not *really* want her to be pleasant to the comtesse.

Even this intriguing reversal of her moral standards might have failed, however, had it not been for another of Maria Theresa's talents: the ease with which she could make her children feel guilty. Using a combination of whining about her miserable life, protestations of love, and moral considerations, we watch as time and again she makes Marie Antoinette feel that she is hurting the most devoted of mothers. Of course, in playing on her daughter's emotions she had help: Mercy himself, who could both embroider on the Empress's themes and report Marie Antoinette's reactions, and the cleric who served him as an accomplice.

The abbé de Vermond had been sent to Vienna to serve as the Archduchess's French reader, and he had helped teach her the language; then he had followed her back to France, where, after some hesitation on the King's part, he had been reappointed as her reader. He, therefore, had easy access to the Dauphine and was among the very small number of people allowed into her private apartments. From the very beginning he cast his lot firmly with Mercy and Austria, a decision for which, in the course of time, he found himself amply rewarded; but he managed to convince the always gullible Marie Antoinette that he was devoted to her personally and wanted no recompense other than his small salary. As a result she confided fully in him without realizing that he passed on every word she said to Mercy; and he did his best to influence the Dauphine in whichever direction Vienna preferred. Because she was surrounded with flatterers, the young woman was particularly open to people who spoke to her (apparently) with gruff honesty, and the abbé de Vermond, realizing this, took full advantage of it.

To the French, however, the abbé had a very different look. Mme Campan, Marie Antoinette's devoted First Woman of the Bedchamber, bemoaned his influence. "He often led the Queen into actions whose consequences she did not understand," she wrote in her memoirs. "He never ceased mocking the etiquette of the House of Bourbon; the young Dauphine was constantly encouraged by his sarcasms to free herself from it and it was he who made her get rid of a great number of customs whose wisdom and political utility he could not understand. He gave us the sorrow of seeing [Marie Antoinette] blending with the qualities which charmed all who knew her wrongs which harmed her reputation and her happiness."* Mme Campan is quite right: even more than Mercy, it was Vermond who helped influence Marie Antoinette in the worst of directions, that of her enslavement by Vienna. Just as important, however, was his contempt for the Versailles etiquette. That at first glance its rules seem absurd, unbearable, even comic cannot be denied; but in a Court eaten with envy and calumny, among a cynical people prone to criticize and sometimes to see evil where there was none, the etiquette not only surrounded the sovereigns with a very necessary glamour, it also protected their reputations. This was particularly necessary in the case of a young and pretty woman married to a sexual incompetent; and while there is every reason to think that Marie Antoinette did in fact remain faithful to Louis XVI, she soon acquired a reputation worthy of Messalina.

Still, the Dauphine's greatest misfortune was perhaps her lack of reliable friends. She could never be really close to Louis XV because of Mme du Barry; Mesdames simply used her; and when she tried to find among her brothers- and

* Mme Campan, *La Cour de Marie Antoinette*, Paris, 1971, p. 38.

sisters-in-law a replica of the family circle at Schönbrunn, she soon discovered that she had blundered, instead, into a hornet's nest. Although the Dauphin's two brothers could hardly have been more different from one another, each in his own way was dangerous. The elder brother, the comte de Provence, was a fat, pedantic young man, an accomplished liar and hypocrite who nursed his resentments. Because he felt, with some justification, that he was far more intelligent than Louis-Auguste, he also thought it unbearable that his brother should be the heir to the throne, and was determined to undermine him in every possible way. In the meantime he engaged in a series of intrigues aimed at making himself more influential while, if possible, making the Dauphin look like an ass. His wife, a Piedmontese princess, was almost as treacherous as her husband, whose ambition she shared. She specialized in making Marie Antoinette look frivolous by ostentatiously refusing to attend certain balls and other entertainments. It was, at least, some comfort to the Dauphine that the comte de Provence was even more incapable of consummating his marriage than the Dauphin.

The youngest of the three brothers, the comte d'Artois, was almost the exact opposite: tall, slim, graceful, elegant, highly competent sexually, he was also frivolous, arrogant, and extravagant so that he earned a lasting unpopularity by the time he was eighteen. At first Marie Antoinette much preferred him: at least, he amused her; he danced beautifully and invented all kinds of excursions and entertainments which appealed to her; but she soon realized that too close a friendship might prove dangerous. As it was, a rumor soon went around according to which Artois and Marie Antoinette were lovers. Worse, from her point of view, Artois, who married the sister of Mme de Provence, immediately consummated his marriage, leading her to fear, with reason, that the comtesse d'Artois would be the first to produce an heir.

Although the Provences and the Artois were a slight improvement on Mesdames, they still left Marie Antoinette without a friend. She could not expect to find real companionship in her husband, for whom she felt a contempt tinged with fondness. The comtesse de Noailles constantly antagonized her, so she began to look for someone new. Early in 1774 she discovered the princesse de Lamballe. Born a Princess of Carignano, an offshoot of the House of Savoy, which ruled over Piedmont and Sardinia, she was a distant relative of the comtesses de Provence and d'Artois, but had nothing in common with them: for one thing, unlike the other princesses, who were almost grotesquely ugly, Mme de Lamballe was a great beauty: her abundant fair hair, huge blue eyes, and dazzling complexion made most people forget her extreme stupidity. When Marie Antoinette met Mme de Lamballe, she was a twenty-two-year-old widow: her husband, a distant relation of the French royal family and a great libertine, had died of syphilis at the age of twenty-nine. Now she lived with her father-in-law, the duc de Penthièvre and added to her looks all the charms of a distinguished melancholy. This immediately appealed to Marie Antoinette, as did Mme de Lamballe's extraordinary —indeed ridiculous—sensitivity, which led her to burst into tears at the slightest provocation. Here, the Dauphine felt, was someone she could trust, someone who understood her and with whom she herself could sympathize. Mercy, reporting this, breathed a sigh of relief: Mme de Lamballe, he thought, would be a desirable counterweight to Mesdames' influence.

IV

Although, during her first years at Versailles, Marie Antoinette was really little more than a child, the patterns that defined the rest of her life were set then, and the main aspects of her character are revealed. Already we hear about her charm, her graciousness, her elegance; already people are beginning to complain that she pays attention only to those who amuse her. She quickly established her domination over poor Louis-Auguste. She showed very plainly that in her view she had almost endless rights and practically no duties. As we watch her develop during this early period of her life, the figure we see emerging bears a striking resemblance to the Marie Antoinette of the late eighties.

Present, too, from the very beginning are her extraordinary powers of resistance to suggestions which would deprive her of pleasure or revenge. The great corset controversy—she wouldn't wear one—is the first example of that obstinacy which became so marked, and so disastrous, a feature of her character. Along with this it is hard to overlook a resentment of extraordinary intensity against the people who, in her view, have not treated her properly: the hapless duc d'Aiguillon is a prime example of this. Finally we watch her as ever more firmly she rejects all constraints so as to do only what amuses her. All this, coupled with an unusual lack of sensitivity to public opinion and other people's feelings did much to limit her undoubted personal kindness, her quick reaction to suffering when it was right where she could see it, and what must in the end be described as her charisma.

We can see all this so clearly because of this most private of princely correspondences. Few people have been as closely observed as Marie Antoinette, few have exchanged such candid letters over a ten-year period. As we read on, Marie Antoinette's very soul is bared to us; we understand why she was so beloved by a few, so hated by many, and how she came to her disastrous end.

SOURCES

This volume relies on three different sources:

1. The correspondence between Maria Theresa and Marie Antoinette preserved in the Staatsarchiv, Vienna. This was published in its entirety by Georges Girard, *Correspondance entre Marie Thérèse et Marie Antoinette*, Paris, 1933. The original letters were written in French, which was then considered by many to be the language of civilized society.

2. The reports of Mercy, published by Arneth et Geffroy, *Correspondance secrète entre Marie Thérèse et le comte de Mercy-Argenteau*, Paris, 1874.

3. The letters written by the Emperor Joseph II to his brother Leopold, Grand Duke of Tuscany during his visit to Versailles in 1777. These letters, which have never been published in full, are preserved at the Staatsarchiv, Vienna, under the following classification marks: 7 F.A. Sammelbände, 291 und 299.

Maria Theresa to Marie Antoinette, 21 April 1770

[Rules to be read once a month]

This twenty-first of April, day of your departure. —When you wake up, you will immediately upon arising go through your morning prayers on your knees and read some religious text, even if it is only for six or seven minutes without concerning yourself about anything else or speaking to anyone. All depends on the right beginning for the day and the intention with which you begin it, for it may change even indifferent actions into good, even praiseworthy ones. You must be very strict about this, for it depends on you alone and your temporal and spiritual happiness may depend upon it. The same is true for the evening prayers and the review of the day's actions. . . . You will always write me and tell me which book you are using. You will pray during the day as often as you can, especially during the celebration of Holy Mass. I hope you will attend it every day in the proper spirit, and twice on Sunday and holidays, if such is the custom at your Court. Much as I wish you to pray and read good books, however, you must always conform to French customs and never try to introduce anything new. You must not do anything unusual, nor cite our customs, nor ask that they be imitated; on the contrary, you must absolutely lend yourself to what the Court is accustomed to doing. Go, if you can, after dinner,* and especially every Sunday to Vespers and to the *salut.* I don't know whether the French normally have the angelus rung; but pray at that time—if not in public, then at least in your heart. The same is true for the evening, or for when you pass a church or cross, without, however, behaving in ways other than the customary ones. That won't prevent your heart from concentrating inwardly on prayer, the presence of God being

---

* Dinner, in the 1770s, was eaten around two.

the only means to achieve this no matter what the occasion; your incomparable father had that quality to perfection. As you go into church, you must feel the deepest respect; do not allow yourself the kind of curiosity which causes distractions. All eyes will be fixed upon you; you must therefore not shock anyone. In France people behave in a very edifying way in church and generally in public. . . . Stay on your knees as long as you can; that will be the best position to set an example. Do not allow yourself any grimaces which only look hypocritical: that is a reproach to be avoided above all else in that country. You will take communion every six weeks if your confessor approves, as well as on the major holidays, and especially on the feasts of the Virgin; on those days, or the day before, remember the particular devotion of your House to the Holy Virgin, from whom it has always received a special protection. Read no book, even the most indifferent, until you have received your confessor's permission: this is a particularly important point in France because books are published there which, although they are full of agreeable erudition, can nonetheless be pernicious to religion and morals. . . . Never forget the anniversary of your late dear father's death, and mine in its time: in the meantime you can use my birthday as the date on which to pray for me. As for the Jesuits, you must abstain entirely from any comments, either for or against.*

[Private instruction]

Do not take on any recommendation; listen to no one if you want to have peace. Do not be curious; that is a point about which I worry greatly. Avoid any sort of familiarity with underlings. Ask M. and Mme de Noailles what you

* The Jesuits had recently been expelled from France, a policy which caused much controversy. Mesdames in particular were known to be opposed bitterly; but it was the work of Choiseul, who had arranged Marie Antoinette's marriage, and was therefore the touchiest of subjects.

must do in every case, demand that they tell you how, as a foreigner who wants to please your new country, you must behave; let them tell you sincerely whether there is anything that needs emending in your attitudes, your speeches, or the rest. Answer everyone pleasantly, with grace and dignity: you can if you want to. You must also learn how to say no. In my states and in the Empire, you cannot refuse to accept pleas, but you will give them all to Stahremberg* and will tell everyone to speak to him, or to Shaffgotsch, if he is not available; tell everyone that you will send their requests to Vienna, since there is nothing more you can do. From Strasbourg on, you will accept nothing without first consulting M. or Mme de Noailles, and you will send them all those who talk about their business to you, telling them pleasantly that since you are a foreigner yourself, you cannot undertake to recommend anyone to the King. If you wish, you can add, to make your point more strongly, "the Empress, my mother, has forbidden me to take on any recommendation." Do not be ashamed to ask everyone for advice and do nothing on your own. You have one great advantage since Stahremberg will travel on with you from Strasbourg to Compiègne;† he is much liked in France, much attached to you. You can tell him everything and rely entirely on his advice; he will stay on for another eight or ten days at Versailles. You can write me frankly through him. At the beginning of every month, I will send a courier from here to Paris: in the meantime you can get your letters ready so as to send them off immediately as soon as he arrives. Mercy will be ordered to send him off promptly. You can also write me through the post, but on very few subjects, only on what anyone might know. I do not think you should write your family, except for special cases and the

* Former Ambassador to France and Chancellor Kaunitz's chief assistant.
† The Archduchess was to meet the King and royal family at the palace of Compiègne, some forty miles north of Paris.

Emperor,* with whom you will make arrangements about this. I think you could write your uncle and aunt as well as Prince Albert. The Queen of Naples† wants to hear from you, I see no difficulty there. She will tell you only reasonable and useful things; her example should serve you as a model and an encouragement, her situation having been in everything and being still much more difficult than yours. She used her intelligence and a respectful manner to overcome many great obstacles; she has given me much pleasure and is well thought of everywhere: you may thus write her, but let everything be such that it can be read by anyone. Tear up my letters; it will allow me to write you more freely. I will do the same with yours. Do not expect to hear about domestic affairs here: they consist of nothing but uninteresting, boring facts. About your family you will speak truthfully but tactfully: even though I am seldom wholly pleased with them, you may find that others are worse, that there is simply childishness and jealousy about trifles, but that elsewhere it is about more important matters. One more point about the Jesuits. Say nothing, either for or against them. You may quote me and say I told you to speak neither good nor evil of them, that you know I respect them, that in my lands they have done much good, that I would be sorry to lose them, but that if the Pope decides to dissolve the order, I will do nothing to stop him; that I have always spoken well of them, but that even in my private circle I have never liked to talk about this wretched business.‡

* Joseph II, Marie Antoinette's brother.
† Marie Carolina, Marie Antoinette's sister.
‡ Joseph II, unlike his mother, favored the dissolution of the order, which was finally ordered by the Pope in 1772.

Maria Theresa to Marie Antoinette, 4 May 1770

Madame my dear daughter,

So there you are—where Providence has settled you must live. If one is to consider only the greatness of your position, you are the happiest of your sisters and all princesses. You will find a loving father* who will also be your friend if you deserve it. You may trust him completely; you will risk nothing. Love him, obey him, try to guess his thoughts; you cannot do too much of this at the time when I lose you. . . . As to the Dauphin, I say nothing; you know how touchy I am on that point; the wife must be completely submissive to her husband and must have no business other than to please him and obey him.† The only true happiness in this world is a happy marriage: I can say so freely. All depends on the wife, on her being willing, sweet, and amusing.

There is but one voice about you until Gunzburg from where I have received the latest news today; you speak the first and last word to everyone, you are forthcoming and amiable, but more than anything it is the sweetness of your expression which enchants everyone. Do not be familiar, it will flatter no one because it is too ordinary; but kindness is what reassures and brings everyone closer.

I urge you, my dear daughter, to read my paper [i.e., the instructions] on the twenty-first of every month. I ask you to obey me on this point; I only fear that you will neglect your prayer and religious readings; then a tepid faith and insufficient prayer will follow . . . Love your family, be close to them, to your aunts as well as to your brothers- and sisters-in-law. Do not allow people to bother you, you are so placed as to silence them when you wish, or at least to avoid them by walking away from them . . . knowing you, I fear your curiosity may lead you astray on this point.

* That is, Louis XV.
† A classic demonstration of the Empress's hypocrisy.

You will give the enclosed letter to the King from me and will talk to him as often as you can. You can never say too much about my feelings for him. You will also give the enclosed letter to Madame Adélaïde; these Princesses are full of virtues and talents; you are lucky to have them; I hope you will deserve their friendship.

The Choiseuls must know that I have asked you to pay particular attention to them. Don't forget the Durforts and the abbé Vermond. Don't forget your mother, who, though far away, will cease to care about you only with her last breath. I give you my blessing and am always your faithful mother.

Mercy to Maria Theresa, 15 June 1770

. . . The King continues to be very pleased with Mme la Dauphine; she caresses him with grace and in a very touching way. The King finds her "spontaneous and a little childish," but, he adds, "that is right for her age." Mesdames de France are enchanted with Mme la Dauphine; the Court and the public warmly praise her affability and the graceful things she says to those who see her. They find her full of attractions . . . but . . . I must tell Your Majesty that amidst a quick and frivolous nation and in a very stormy Court, it is easier to win popularity than to retain it over time. In order to do so, Mme la Dauphine must watch herself on several small points among which that of her dignity is one of the most essential. HRH* sometimes forgets herself in the way she sits at her meals or at cavagnol.† Often her clothes are untidied by the little amusements of the day; but I must also say that in church Mme l'Archiduchesse

* Her Royal Highness.
† A card game played in public by the royal family.

behaves in the most proper, most respectable manner. HRH, because she is of a cheerful nature and without any bad intention, sometimes jokes about the people whom she deems ridiculous; this has already been noticed here and could become all the more dangerous in that this Princess knows how to use wit and sarcasm so as to make her comments very biting; but the most important need is to get HRH to overcome her extreme distaste for reading and other serious occupations.

. . . She shows so much love for Your Majesty, so much respect, such desire to please you, that I am quite sure that if Your Majesty should think it right in your private letters to insist on the three points above, it would be much more effective than the advice which might come from elsewhere.* . . .

Mercy to Maria Theresa, 15 June 1770

Madame du Barry thought it necessary to go and pay court to HRH one morning. She was received simply and easily. It was done with dignity and in such a way as to displease no one.

Marie Antoinette to Maria Theresa, 9 July 1770

Madame my very dear mother,

. . . We leave tomorrow, the tenth, for Choisy,† from

* With his first report, Mercy has thus already set up the system which was to last for the next ten years, and the Empress responded to his suggestion with enthusiasm: in her next letter to Marie Antoinette, she does exactly as Mercy had asked.

† Choisy was a small château built for Louis XV near Paris.

where we will return on the thirteenth to go to Bellevue* on the seventeenth, and on the eighteenth to Compiègne, where we will stay until August 28, and from there will go and spend a few days in Chantilly.† The King is infinitely kind to me and I love him dearly, but his weakness for Mme du Barry is really pitiful. She is the most stupid and impertinent creature imaginable. She played cards during two evenings with us at Marly;‡ twice she was placed next to me, but she didn't speak to me and I did not try to start a conversation with her; but when it has been necessary, still, I spoke to her.

As for my dear husband, he has changed much and all for the best. He shows me much friendship. He certainly doesn't like M. de la Vauguyon** but fears him. A curious incident happened the other day. I was alone with my husband when M. de la Vauguyon rushed to the door in order to eavesdrop. A valet de chambre who is either stupid or honest opened the door and there was M. le duc, stuck like a piling in a fence, unable to back away. So I pointed out to my husband the inadvisability of allowing people to eavesdrop, and he took it very well.

As I promised Your Majesty, I would tell you about my least illness; I will therefore mention that I had a little colic, but dieting stopped it. My husband, at the same time, had an upset stomach, but it did not stop him from going hunting.

. . . I forgot to tell you that I wrote the King yesterday for the first time; I have been greatly afraid to do so because

* Bellevue, designed by Lassurance for Mme de Pompadour, was built on crown land and had thus become the King's property when the marquise died in 1764.
† The country residence of the princes de Condé, who were the King's distant cousins.
‡ The pavilions and splendid gardens near Versailles.
** The duc de la Vauguyon was the Dauphin's Governor. A servile, hypocritical member of Mesdames' cabal, he left his pupil in a state of almost total ignorance and was widely disliked, not the least by the Dauphin and Dauphine.

I know that Mme du Barry reads them all; you may be sure, my very dear mother, that I will never make a mistake either for or against her.

Your Majesty will allow me to send her a letter for Naples in which I warn my sister to send me her letters through Vienna. I have the honor of being, with the most respectful affection, your most loving and obedient daughter.

Marie Antoinette to Maria Theresa
Choisy, 12 July 1770

Madame my very dear mother,

I cannot express how touched I am by the kindness Your Majesty has shown me, and I can swear to you that I have not received one of your dear letters without having the tears come to my eyes because I am separated from so kind and loving a mother; and although I am very well situated here, I still ardently wish I could see my dear and very dear family for a moment at least. . . .

As for what you ask about my spiritual exercises and the *générale*,* I will tell you that I have only taken communion once; I confessed the day before yesterday to M. l'abbé Maudoux, but since it was on the day I expected to leave for Choisy, I did not take communion, because I thought I would have too many distractions. As for the générale, it is the fourth month I have missed it, but for no good reason. Our trip to Choisy was delayed by a day because my husband had a cold and a fever, but he got over it in a day for, having slept for twelve and a half hours, he found himself quite cured and able to leave. We have thus been here since yesterday—where, from the time we dine at one to one in

* The *générale Krottendorf*, or simply the *générale*, was the code word used by both the Empress and the Dauphine to denote the menstrual cycle.

the morning, we never go back to our apartments—which I find very unpleasant because, after dinner, we play cards until six, then we see a play, which lasts until nine, then comes supper, then again, cards until one, sometimes even one-thirty, but the King, who saw yesterday that I was exhausted, was kind enough to send me back to my rooms at eleven, which pleased me greatly, and I slept very well until ten-thirty [the next morning], although I was alone; my husband was still on a diet and so he came in before supper and immediately went to bed in his room, which otherwise never happens.

Your Majesty is kind enough to take an interest in me and you even want to know how I spend my days. I will tell you, therefore, that I get up at ten, or at nine, or at nine-thirty and that, having been dressed, I say my morning prayers; then I breakfast and then go to my aunts [Mesdames], where I usually find the King. That goes on until ten-thirty; after that, at eleven, I go to have my hair dressed. At twelve they call in the chamber, and then anyone can come in as long as they belong to the Court. I put on my rouge and wash my hands in front of everyone; then the men leave and the ladies stay and I dress in front of them.* At noon we have Mass. If the King is at Versailles, I accompany him, my husband, and my aunts to the Mass; if he's away, I go alone with M. le Dauphin, but always at the same time. After Mass we have dinner together in public, but it is over by one-thirty because we both eat very quickly. From there I go to M. le Dauphin's apartment and, if he's busy, I come back to mine, I read, write, or work since I am embroidering a waistcoat for the King which hasn't progressed much, but I hope that with God's grace, it will be finished in a few years. At three I go back to my aunts', whom the King visits at that

* The first time, the Dauphine simply put on a loose, comfortable dress, now she is arrayed in the full Court costume, complete with *paniers* (side hoops), deep *décolleté* and jewels.

(40)

time; at four the abbé [de Vermond] comes to see me, at five, everyday, I have a singing or harpsichord teacher until six. At six-thirty, I almost always go to my aunts' when I do not go for a walk; you must know that my husband almost always accompanies me to my aunts'. At seven we sit down to cards until nine, but when the weather is nice, I go for a walk, and then the card playing takes place not in my apartment but in my aunts'. At nine we have supper, and when the King is away, my aunts come and have supper with us, but when the King is there, we go to their apartments after supper and wait for him; he usually comes at ten forty-five, but, while waiting for him, I lie down on a large sofa and sleep until he arrives; if he's away, we go to bed by eleven. That is our whole day. As for what we do on Sundays and holidays, I will keep it for another time.

I beg my very dear mother to forgive me if my letter is too long, but chatting with her is my great pleasure. I also beg her pardon if the letter is dirty, but I had to write it on two successive days while I was at my toilette because I had no other free time, and if I don't answer all your questions exactly, it is because I have been so prompt to burn your letter. I must finish getting dressed and go to the King's Mass. I have the honor of being the most obedient of daughters.*

I send you the list of the presents I have been given as I think it might amuse you.

* While Maria Theresa's final formulas are always the same, Marie Antoinette's change with her mood, or her feelings of guilt, and can be highly revealing.

Mercy to Maria Theresa, 14 July 1770

HRH has been quite careful about her reading; it is always followed by a serious conversation with the abbé de Vermond on the events and talk of the day; this method has the very best results because, in spite of her inborn impatience, Mme la Dauphine forgets nothing that is said to her; she listens docilely, and one is sure that she pays attention to anything reasonable. . . .

The last stay at Marly was a rather difficult time for Mme la Dauphine; she behaved with all the caution imaginable. She found herself having to play lansquenet every evening with the comtesse du Barry, and sometimes even seated next to that woman, but HRH never betrayed herself by any gesture which people might have noticed, or which could make them say that she had treated the favorite well or badly. . . .

The King is still perfectly pleased with Mme la Dauphine and shows it by many small marks of love and many small attentions.

Mercy to Maria Theresa, 14 July 1770

Every day [Mme la Dauphine] rules M. le Dauphin's mind more thoroughly. She behaves to him with such cheerfulness and such grace that the young Prince is overwhelmed; he speaks to her in confidence of things which he had never mentioned to anyone. His dour and secretive character had made him impenetrable until now, but Mme la Dauphine can make him say anything she wants.

Mercy to Maria Theresa, 14 July 1770

On Sunday the eighth, M. le Dauphin and Mme la Dauphine had a very lively discussion. . . . The result was that M. le Dauphin said to Mme l'Archiduchesse that he was unaware of nothing regarding the estate of matrimony, that at the beginning he had made a plan for himself which he had not wanted to discard, that now the time had come and that at Compiègne he would live with Mme la Dauphine with all the intimacy required by their union.*

. . . There can be no doubt that with a little caution she will be able completely to dominate him.

Mercy to Maria Theresa, 4 August 1770

[I have explained to Mme la Dauphine] the drawbacks of following Mesdames her aunts so exactly. These Princesses, although they are thoroughly respectable, have never known how to behave in any given circumstances. I can see clearly that they are instilling their principles into Mme la Dauphine, that they make her shy and draw her away from the King; besides, Mesdames often allow themselves to talk in ways which are at least indiscreet. Mme la Dauphine joins them, repeats it all, and I know positively that some people have been telling all this to the King so as to harm HRH. . . . The questions on which I have had the most effect have been those of her dignity and the mocking comments.

M. le Dauphin gave himself an indigestion because he ate too many pastries; at supper that evening, Mme la Dauphine had all dishes of this kind taken off the table and forbade

* The Dauphin was referring to the eventual consummation of his marriage.

that they be served for a while; the Dauphin smiled and was pleased with this mark of attention.

. . . The comtesse de Noailles tells me that she cannot convince Mme la Dauphine to wear a corset, that as a result her waist is growing misshapen, and that her right shoulder was out of kilter. . . .

Mercy to Maria Theresa, 20 August 1770

Mme la Dauphine went to the King's apartment, where he kissed her and greeted her most tenderly. It was noticed on this occasion that the King always receives Mme la Dauphine better when she goes alone to see him and is not accompanied by Mesdames her aunts.

. . . HRH talked to me about the Dauphin, saying that she was pleased with him, that all his little shortcomings were the result of the poor education he had received, but that at bottom he was a good man, that he was good-natured and had the best character; these are the exact words used by Mme la Dauphine, and she said them in a moved and tender way. . . . She added that [the Dauphin] showed pleasure and trust in listening to her . . . that he had nothing but contempt for the comtesse du Barry and her cabal; that when she asked him why he allowed himself to be part of those people's circle,* he answered that he had to be careful. . . .

---

* In order to be closer to the King, the Dauphin had asked to be invited to his suppers and private stays in the small châteaux near Paris; and that, of course, meant seeing Mme du Barry.

Mercy to Maria Theresa, 20 August 1770

Since M. le Dauphin's last illness, he has no longer slept, as heretofore, in Mme la Dauphine's apartment. There are, however, no reasons to worry, except that nature, which is very slow in M. le Dauphin, does not act in him,* probably because he was weakened by his sudden growth; but his physique shows nothing which would prevent him from developing a good and robust health as long as he is careful in the overly violent exercise† which could become very bad for him. The Prince finds Madame l'Archiduchesse charming; he likes being with her and shows her a kind of good will and sweetness which he was not thought to possess. Mme la Dauphine rules him for all the little things and he never contradicts her; thus with a little patience we should see the proper order thoroughly established; but since in this country they want everything done before its time, the King and Mesdames speak in a way which only troubles and worries Mme la Dauphine.

Mercy to Maria Theresa, 19 September 1770

Mme la Dauphine finds it a bore to hold her Court in the evening, and she avoids doing so a little too often; Mesdames then do so, although it goes against the etiquette and the invariable custom which, if there be no Queen, makes the Dauphine responsible for all ceremony. . . .

People are already trying to give [the comtesse de Provence]‡ an important role because the party of the duc de la

* That is to say, the sixteen-year-old Dauphin showed no desire to have sex.
† Mercy refers here to the passionate, indeed frantic, hunting in which the Dauphin indulged.
‡ The Dauphin's younger brother, the comte de Provence, was about to marry a princess of Savoy.

Vauguyon and of the comtesse du Barry are counting on that princess's protection.

. . . The refusal of a corset, the unwillingness to hold court and play cards in public, the disfavor of the comtesse de Noailles,* a little more shyness vis-à-vis the King—all these and other little circumstances result from Mme Adélaïde's advice. Mesdames were educated in such a way as to make them shy and devoid of all pleasing qualities, and they would like Mme la Dauphine to imitate them. I will give a recent proof of this. A few days ago, the Paris municipality and the Estates of Languedoc were to harangue the royal family. Mesdames, who were consulted by Mme la Dauphine, tried to convince her that no answer was required on these occasions and that they never said anything. It took repeated attempts by the abbé de Vermond to convince Mme la Dauphine that she must not behave in this way, of which all France complains. HRH allowed herself to be convinced and made . . . the most graceful answer with which the public is delighted. . . .

Mercy to Maria Theresa, 20 October 1770

HRH seems decided to treat Mme la comtesse de Provence very coldly; she expects Mesdames her aunts to behave the same way and that thus Mme de Provence will meet such difficulties that her beginnings will hardly be very brilliant. I have not yet openly fought this system, which I believe to be very dangerous, bad, and useless; one sure result would be a war within the royal family and a deluge of difficulties and intrigues among the courtiers. . . . HRH does not

* The Dauphine disliked the comtesse de Noailles because the dame d'honneur harped on the exigencies of etiquette, much to Marie Antoinette's exasperation.

need to use such rigorous means to maintain her superiority; that is guaranteed her by her rank, and even more by her wit and her attractions. . . . HRH is looking better every day.

. . . HRH has finally agreed to wear a corset quite regularly. . . .

For some time now, the King has increased his tenderness, his attentions and all the marks of a caring friendship for Mme la Dauphine. . . . HRH lives here* in the late Queen's apartment which is next to the King's; if that Monarch could once form the habit of visiting Mme la Dauphine during the day, the results might be excellent . . . but she must absolutely behave exactly in the opposite manner to Mesdames her aunts. . . .

HRH talked to me with emotion about her sensitivity to the love shown her by Your Majesty; she then showed some chagrin that Your Majesty seemed upset by some reports about her person and her position, and she cited the question of the corset. . . .

Mme Adélaïde and Mme Sophie are busy trying to make Mme l'Archiduchesse dislike Mme Victoire, who is without doubt the best of the three sisters and the one with the most character. I also know about the dangerous advice Mme Adélaïde gave her in relation to Mme de Provence. . . .

Mercy to Maria Theresa, 20 October 1770

[In the matter of the marquis de Durfort, HRH] is held back by Mesdames Adélaïde and Sophie: . . . the comtesse de Narbonne, Mme Adélaïde's dame d'atours, doesn't want Mme Victoire's dame d'atours to be a duchess and that is

* At Fontainebleau.

what has stopped the promotion of the marquise de Durfort.*

Maria Theresa to Marie Antoinette
Schönbrunn, 1 November 1770

Madame my dear daughter,

At long last that impossibly slow courier arrived here at nine last night and brought me your dear news. Thank God your health is good, according to the courier who was part of your personal staff; he finds you taller and broader. If you did not reassure me about the corsets you are wearing, I would be worrying about that, for fear of, as they say in German, *auseinandergeben, schon die Taille wie eine Frau, ohne es zu sein.* I ask you not to let yourself go: this would suit neither your age nor your place; it brings with it uncleanliness, negligence, and even a general carelessness; that is why I keep tormenting you about it, and I cannot do enough to prevent the smallest circumstances which might give you the sort of failings that have afflicted the whole French royal family for many years: they are kind, virtuous for themselves, but in no way capable of appearing to advantage in public, of setting the tone, or of having fun in a proper way, and that has been the cause of the King's straying, for he found no amusements with them and therefore felt he must look for them elsewhere. It is possible to be virtuous, cheerful, and worldly: but when one is so withdrawn as hardly to see anyone (I must tell you this to my great regret as you have seen it to be the case, these last years, in Vienna), there are always many malcontents, people who are jealous or en-

* If Mme de Durfort had become a duchess, she would also, ipso facto, have gained precedence over Mme de Narbonne, obviously an intolerable humiliation for the latter.

vious, and then unpleasantnesses; but if one sees the great world, as we used to do here some fifteen or twenty years ago, then one avoids all these problems and feels better in body and soul. . . . It is for you to set the tone at Versailles; you have succeeded perfectly; God has given you so many graces, such sweetness, and docility that everyone must love you. . . .

I am grateful to you for having told me in detail about your prayer books and your religious texts. . . .

As for the other books you read with the abbé, I would be delighted to hear about them also; this could even be useful here or in Tuscany;* in the future you would please me if you sent them to me every month, and in order to spare you the trouble of writing them, the abbé could list them on a separate sheet, which you would add to your letter or which the abbé would give to Mercy, if it suits you, as I do with this journal. If you find it too long or dull, you only have to tell me and I will end it, but knowing how attached you are to your family and native land, I will go on until you tell me to stop.

Our Marie-Anne† is entirely cured of her fever and is in better health even than before. She attends all the hunts and promenades, but not the theater. [Princess] Windischgrätz, who has arrived in a state of exhaustion, also told me how amiable and attractive you can be when you want. She told me that she hadn't been able to speak to you at length, that you have every reason to be happy, but then, because she had to tell the truth in response to my questions, she admitted that you take poor care of yourself, even when it comes to cleaning your teeth; this is a key point, as is your figure, which she found worsened. You are now at the time of life when you are developing your shape; it is the most critical;

* The Archduke Leopold, Marie Antoinette's brother, was Grand Duke of Tuscany and lived in Florence.
† One of Marie Antoinette's sisters.

she added that you were badly dressed and that she dared tell your ladies so. You write me that you sometimes wear clothes from your trousseau: which did you keep? I thought that if you sent me your measurements, I would have corsets made for you here. They say the ones they make in Paris are too stiff; I will send them by the courier. . . .

You will receive by this courier the present that our Marie-Anne is sending you and, soon, our Marie's table which has turned out well. I hope that a certain bust will have arrived; I minded doing without it, but I hope you will send back a good portrait, especially painted by Liotard,* who is going to Paris by fast mailcoach to send me one. Please give him the time he needs.

My dear daughter! Tomorrow is a great day of consolation for me, a day† which, for fifteen years, has given me nothing but satisfaction. May God keep you for many long years, for my happiness and that of your family and people. Mercy writes me that you spent the morning of the fifteenth‡ in prayers and adds that you thought it the best way of celebrating the day. You can imagine how deeply that charming thought has touched me; you are capable of these good actions, but you didn't write me about it in your last letter; I kiss you tenderly and give you my blessing, my dear daughter. I am always your faithful mother.

ALREADY by the late summer of 1770, Marie Antoinette's hostility to Mme du Barry had become so manifest that her ladies started to snub the favorite. In September, at the small theater in the château of Choisy, several of the Dauphine's ladies occupied the first row of seats. Mme du Barry, who came in after them, asked to make room; they

* Jean-Étienne Liotard, Swiss-born painter.
† November 2, Marie Antoinette's birthday.
‡ Maria Theresa's birthday.

refused, and one of them, the comtesse de Gramont, was particularly rude. After a heated exchange, Mme du Barry left the theater and went straight to Louis XV, who at her request exiled Mme de Gramont—that is, sent her to her country house.

This was a great blow to the Dauphine, since in this case the favorite had outpowered her; but she bided her time and took advantage of Mme de Gramont's illness in November to ask that the lady be allowed to return to Paris, where she could consult her physician. Although Marie Antoinette presented this as an act of mercy, it was nothing less than an attempt at proving that she could undo Mme du Barry's earlier success. All in all she had much to gain: if the King consented, it might well be a first step toward becoming more influential than the favorite; but if he refused, Marie Antoinette would sink to Mesdames' level, and be thought powerless and unimportant. Naturally she consulted Mercy, and it was he who worked out the strategy described in the next letter.

Mercy to Maria Theresa, 16 November 1770

[On the nineteenth] after the card game, Mme l'Archiduchesse, who was having supper with the King, used the occasion to tell him, in the sweetest, most graceful way, about the comtesse de Gramont's request, and the reasons why it should be granted. The King looked a little embarrassed and told Mme la Dauphine, with a friendly look, that he would think about it and would soon give her an answer. . . . [The next morning] Mme la Dauphine had the duc de la Vrillière called in, told him about her talk with the King, and asked the minister (within whose department it is) to ask the King for his orders and not let him be unaware that

he was being sent by Mme la Dauphine. The duc de la Vrillière did so, and the King answered that first it must be
checked that the comtesse de Gramont was really ill, and
that, besides, the comtesse du Barry must be warned, since
her consent was needed before a person who was exiled only
because she had offended her could be allowed to return.
. . . The duc de la Vrillière obeyed. . . . The favorite said
she was opposed to Mme la Dauphine's request.

On the twenty-first . . . there was a public supper . . .
and Mme la Dauphine spoke again to the King about the
comtesse de Gramont. His Majesty, looking serious, answered, "Madame, I thought I had told you that I would
give you an answer when the time had come." Mme la Dauphine, without looking in the least embarrassed, retorted,
"But, Papa, besides motives of humanity and justice, think
how upsetting it would be for me if a woman who is part of
my Household were to die in your disgrace." These words,
spoken charmingly, had the greatest effect on the King; he
smiled, and in a now friendly tone he assured Mme la Dauphine that she would soon be satisfied.* . . .

For a long time now Mme l'Archiduchesse has been
urging M. le Dauphin not to stay out hunting so late. . . .
M. le Dauphin came back late. . . . Mme la Dauphine
preached a very strongly worded little sermon to him. . . .
M. le Dauphin listened to it with good temper and submis-
sively; he admitted he was wrong, promised not to be late
again, and apologized in so many words. This is a most remarkable circumstance, especially since the next day it became obvious that M. le Dauphin was showing Mme la Dauphine many more friendly attentions than usual. . . .

I have bought three persons in Mme l'Archiduchesse's
service . . . who give me an exact account of all that happens in her private apartments; I am informed, day by day,

* Four days later, the permission was granted.

of the Archduchess's conversations with the abbé de Vermond, and she conceals nothing from him; I learn through the marquise de Durfort about every word that is said at Mesdames', and I have more people and better means still to find out what happens when the King and Mme la Dauphine are together. To this I add my own observations.

Maria Theresa to Marie Antoinette
Vienna, 2 December 1770

Everyone still praises you; what happy moments you are giving me, my dear child! Public approval would not satisfy me completely, but the Duke and Duchess Aremberg cannot sufficiently tell me about it, and there are especially Mercy's reports which praise you. Now I come to the point where surely you have already rushed to find me: that of horse riding. You are right to believe that I could never approve of your riding while you are still only fifteen. Your aunts, whom you cite, didn't start until they were thirty. They were Mesdames,* not the Dauphine; I am a little annoyed with them for having sustained you with their examples and their encouragement; but you tell me that the King and the Dauphin approve of it, and I have no more to say:† it is for them to order your life, it is in their hands that I have placed that sweet Antoinette; riding spoils the complexion, and your figure after a while will be affected by it, and even more noticeably so. . . . Accidents cannot be predicted; that of the Queen of Portugal, and of several others,

* Mesdames were unmarried and likely to remain so; they ran little risk, therefore, of a miscarriage.
† Having announced that she had no more to say, the Empress then goes on at length with her scolding—a typical trick.

who have not borne any children afterward, does not reassure me.

Now that I have pointed all this out . . . I take you at your word. . . . "I will never ride to hounds."* I accept your offer, and on that subject alone I will try not to worry; but I will have no excuses or subterfuges on this. What reason would I have to deprive you of something you enjoy if I did not fear its consequences? You will render me this justice, that I have always given my children all the freedom and all the pleasures possible; would I now want to deprive you of them, you who give me such consolation? But do not expect me to mention this again. . . . I have shown you the dangers; you are authorized by the King;† I have no more to say. . . .

I am impatient to receive Liotard's painting, but [want to see you] in Court dress, not in a negligee or dressed as a man because I like to see you in the place which suits you. I kiss you.

Mercy to Maria Theresa, 17 December 1770

As HRH was returning from the hunt, the postillion of her carriage fell and was unlucky enough to have four of the horses run over him. He was picked up, covered with blood and unconscious. Mme la Dauphine stopped there for over an hour; she sent everywhere for a surgeon; in the meantime an adjutant of the Guard who was following her got off his horse and bandaged the sick man with all the zeal and attention possible. They wanted to take the postillion away in a

* Riding to hounds involved galloping and jumping; it was thus more risky than a simple pleasure ride.
† Marie Antoinette had so arranged things that it looked as if the King had ordered her to hunt, whereas, in fact, she had asked for permission to do so.

(54)

post chaise, but Mme la Dauphine forbade it, saying very rightly that the jolting would be intolerable for a man covered with contusions; finally they brought a stretcher, on which the wounded man was carried to Versailles. . . . When HRH was back, she called for the surgeons in order to find out how the wounded man was and showed her joy when she was told he might not die. She ordered her First Surgeon to look after him and give her his news every day. She thanked the adjutant, who at first had looked after the sick man. When Mme l'Archiduchesse told the details of the accident before the entire court, she added, "I called everyone my friend, pages, grooms, postillions. I told them, 'My friend, go and fetch a surgeon; my friend, quick, get a stretcher, see if he speaks, if he is conscious.' " On hearing this, all were touched and admiring, and everybody at Versailles said that she was the true daughter of Maria Theresa and heir of Henri IV.* . . .

Some reading does take place, but it is not long or serious enough, and I think it necessary that Your Majesty deign to insist again. . . .

HRH is not always careful to greet the King with as much enthusiasm and obligingness as she should; besides, she still talks about the favorite and is always egged on by Mesdames.

Maria Theresa to Marie Antoinette, 6 January 1771

Madame my dear daughter,

Hardly had I received the regular post, which arrived only on New Year's Day, than yesterday another courier

* Henri IV (who reigned 1589–1610), the founder of the Bourbon dynasty, was known for his kindness to his people.

informed us about the dismissal of the Choiseuls.* I must admit that I feel it; I have always found their policy honest, human, and closely attached to the alliance; that being said, I will not discuss the [King's] reasons, and you will do so even less. I hope that the King will find them worthy successors who will also deserve our trust. Never forget that your marriage was brought about by the Choiseuls and that you have a duty to be grateful to them. You need Mercy's advice more than ever, as well as the abbé's, who, as I know him to be an honest man, will no doubt be shocked by this blow; but do not allow yourself to be linked to any faction, remain neutral in everything; take care of your religious duties, please the King, obey your husband. . . .

I advise you to show a greater reserve than ever about all the current events, to allow yourself neither confidences nor curiosity, if you want to have a peaceful life and retain, as you have perfectly until now, everyone's approval; you must admit that it is because you followed my good advice. I am sorry to have to tell you: do not confide even in your aunts, whom I greatly esteem. I know what I am saying. Mercy may not even know about this, but I am not speaking without reason. I am delighted about the balls you are giving and which will be very good for the Dauphin.†

Mercy to Maria Theresa, 23 January 1771

Of all the ideas which Mme Adélaïde manages to pass on to Mme la Dauphine, there is not one but is completely wrong and highly noxious for HRH. Mme Adélaïde has no consis-

* That is, the duc de Choiseul, Foreign Minister, and the duc de Praslin, Minister of the Navy.
† The Dauphin's stiff and awkward manners would, the Empress supposed, be improved by attending his wife's balls.

tency or system of behavior; she had openly declared herself in favor of the duc de Choiseul and the duchesse de Gramont. The day after the dismissal of that minister, she was the first to blame him and to attack his sister, which scandalized everyone. Such inconsistency in action also applies to her advice and I always fear her effect on Mme la Dauphine, who listens to her all too well. . . .

When HRH behaves according to her own feelings, she always acts in such a way as to be admired and adored. There is no day in which she does not show excellent judgment, a singular acuteness of understanding, and a good, generous, and compassionate character. As for natural attractiveness, it cannot be more markedly possessed or better used. . . . Her hold on M. le Dauphin's mind is everywhere manifest and that young Prince is visibly changing for the better. . . .

Mme l'Archiduchesse's passion for horse riding still continues.

Maria Theresa to Marie Antoinette, 10 February 1771

Madame my dear daughter,

. . . I am delighted that you anticipated my instructions in the rather delicate case of the Choiseuls' exile; you will continue in the same way and will not end your attitude of kindness. Do not let yourself be carried away by contrary examples; do not take up the frivolity of the French, remain a good German,* glory in being one, and [remain] the friend of your friends.

I owe you praise for at last talking to the King about my message regarding Durfort;† I could not understand that

* No advice could be more likely to make the Dauphine unpopular.
† French Ambassador to Vienna before Marie Antoinette's wedding.

lengthy delay! If you see him, you can tell him I remember the balcony from which we watched the little bride* racing in her sleigh and how I made him, unintentionally, suffer from the cold, since I did not feel it myself. Ingenhouse writes me he has found you very well and taller, that he saw the whole family and found them all in excellent health, that he thought he might not be able to approach you because of the etiquette, that the Ambassador allowed him to see you; I cannot believe that a man of our Court would be denied access to you; you have ignored so many other etiquettes that you will not allow this one to continue.

I am impatiently waiting for your portrait. I am afraid that carnival, and your rides, which I read in all the gazettes that you continue indoors when the cold, will have delayed it. I am afraid your complexion and even your figure will be harmed by it if you take too much of that exercise. Please tell me frankly whether you dance better than here, especially the contredanses: I hear many good things about these balls and about the Dauphin, which gives me great pleasure because you are praised for his change: how happy you are! I am beginning to worry about your not being Dauphine.† I am afraid the future comtesse de Provence may precede you: she is much praised for her sweetness and excellent character, though she is not beautiful but has an interesting face and a good figure.

I am impatiently waiting for news, by return courier, about your reading and studies. . . . I must even point out to you that your letters are everyday more badly written; in ten months you should have improved. I have been a little ashamed when I have seen the letters you have written to ladies here go through several hands. You must work with

* Marie Antoinette.
† The Empress is referring to the fact that her daughter's marriage had not been consummated.

the abbé or some other person on your handwriting so it will be more even.

I am happy to read what you tell me about the King's care and kindness for you: try to deserve their continuation and believe me always all yours.

Mercy to Maria Theresa, 17 March 1771

M. le Dauphin, who until recently had seemed unaware and indifferent to the current intrigues, suddenly showed great disdain to his Governor, the duc de la Vauguyon, and absolute contempt for the comtesse du Barry, the Chancellor, and all those who belong to their party. . . . This was of course brought to the King's notice, along with hints that this change had been provoked by Mme la Dauphine's exhortations. I am informed that the King believes this and is displeased.

[Having called in the comtesse de Noailles, the King] first praised HRH's character and graces, but he added that he feared the effects of her extreme impatience; that he thought it good that in private Mme la Dauphine should be naturally cheerful, but that in public, and when she is holding court, she should show more reserve . . . that Mme la Dauphine spoke too freely "of what she saw, or thought she saw, and that her rather exaggerated remarks might have unpleasant consequences within the family." . . . He asked the comtesse about the advice given to Mme la Dauphine and added that it was not always good advice. The dame d'honneur agreed; she said that the King must know more than she did on this, and that her respect for the source of this advice* precluded her from discussing it. The King answered, "I know the source and am very displeased." . . .

* That is, Mesdames.

Mme la Dauphine spoke to the King that evening and said she was sorry that her Papa did not like her or trust her enough to speak to her directly on what might please or displease him. HRH said this with all the grace so natural to her. The King looked extremely embarrassed, avoided all particulars, and assured Mme l'Archiduchesse that he thought her charming and loved her with all his heart; he kissed her hand, hugged her, and approved of everything HRH had just said. That behavior of the King's is the result of his character and his habit never to scold his children, bearing what he does not like rather than remedying it by a direct confrontation.

IN REPLACING the Parlement by a regular, nonpolitical court, Louis XV was saving the monarchy. Not only was justice itself better administered—the Parlement judges were open to bribery and often took years to reach a verdict —but it also became possible to reform some of the regime's most glaring abuses. By 1770 it was perfectly obvious that the tax system was inequitable and unproductive: the poor paid, the rich did not. Now the King could bring in a fairer tax law; but it was resisted by the privileged, led by the Princes of the Blood Royal, who realized with horror that they would have to pay a ten percent income tax. There can be little doubt that Louis XV's reforms would have prevented the Revolution of 1789; but the Dauphin and the Dauphine looked on them as the work of the du Barry "cabal"; and so, when Louis-Auguste became King, he immediately reversed everything his grandfather had done. The Parlement was reinstated and promptly blocked all progress.

Madame my very dear mother,

I am delighted that Lent has not damaged your health. Mine is still rather good—I have the générale quite regularly; this time it was nine days early. . . .

I would be really upset if the Germans were displeased with me; I will admit that I would have spoken more to M. de Paar and to the little Stahremberg if their reputation here was better. Still, when we were having the balls, I called for M. de Lamberg and Stahremberg, and as soon as I saw they danced, I had them dance with me.

There are many goings-on here right now; on Saturday there was another *lit de justice** to affirm the dissolution of the old Parlement and the installation of a new one; the Princes of the Blood Royal refused to come and protested against the King's decisions; they wrote a very impertinent letter which they all signed, except for the comte de la Marche,† who is behaving very well in this occasion. What is more surprising about the behavior of the Princes is that M. le prince de Condé‡ had his son, who is not yet fifteen years old and has always been brought up here,** sign as well. The King told him to leave, just like the other Princes, who are forbidden to appear before him or before us. The Dukes, although they went [to the lit de justice], have protested, and I'm told that twelve of them have been exiled. . . .

Your Majesty may feel fully reassured about my behavior to the comtesse de Provence. I will surely try to gain her friendship and her trust without, however, going too far. But I am afraid that if she is not very bright and hasn't been

* A ceremony in which the edict was registered by the Parlement at the King's express command.
† The younger brother of the prince de Condé.
‡ The King's distant cousin.
** That is, at Versailles.

warned, she will be completely on Mme du Barry's side. They are trying all they can to win her over for her dame d'atours, Mme de Valentinois,* belongs completely to that party. . . .

I keep preciously the book you sent me, for everything that comes from you will always be very dear to me; you must be sure of that if you know the lively and respectful love that your very obedient daughter will have for you her whole life.

Maria Theresa to Marie Antoinette
Schönbrunn, 8 May 1771

. . . I write now before the miniature which represents my very dear daughter but do not find it has that look of youth she had eleven months ago, and unfortunately a change in condition is not the cause; I await that news with great impatience and hope that the wedding which is to take place in a few days will bring my wishes to a speedy realization; but I cannot repeat it enough—never be bad-tempered about it; [use] caresses, cajolings, but without too much urgency, which would spoil everything. Sweetness and patience are the only means you must use. Nothing is lost, you are both so young: on the contrary, it is all the better for your healths, you are both growing stronger; but it is natural for we old parents to wish for the consummation without which we may not hope to see our grandsons and great-grandsons.†

You will please me greatly, my dear daughter, if you tell me how you find your sister-in-law; according to Ro-

* One of the favorite's closest friends.
† The Dauphin was Louis XV's grandson.

senberg's* report, she will give you no cause for jealousy; instead you can pity her and look after her: that will make you look good and be the right thing to do—not in order to run her life, [since] that would be as wrong as feeling jealousy, but to help her out, for I am told she is unattractive, very shy, very awkward, but also very well brought up; with time this can develop into the right sort of friendship. . . .

What you tell me of the two ladies assigned to the comtesse de Provence must convince you that you must be very careful; what a difference between Mme de Noailles and those two! I will grant you that she exasperates you because she is always trying to do you good, but she is nonetheless someone who has the reputation of being honest and attached to you; that is a great point, and since she comes from one of the greatest families, where will you find flawless ladies who neither indulge in intrigues nor seem dull to you? I am delighted, after what you tell me of Saint-Mégrin, to be spared him; but it is high time an ambassador were sent to us, and a minister† appointed, for it is very difficult to communicate without one. . . .

My dear daughter, people say—and are even surprised—that you see our Ambassador so seldom, that you speak to him only in passing, and that you even seem more embarrassed than trusting with him. They even cite the examples of the Queen, your grandmother,‡ and that of your mother-in-law,** who saw their family ministers twice a week in their apartments, talked to them, and treated them everywhere with distinction. If people suggest otherwise and ad-

* Austrian diplomat and friend of the Imperial family.
† After Praslin's dismissal, the duc de la Vrillière, Minister of the King's Household, took on the interim of the Foreign Ministry; a new Minister, the duc d'Aiguillon, was appointed at the end of May 1771.
‡ That is, the late Marie Leczinska, Louis XV's defunct wife.
** Maria-Josepha of Saxony, the Dauphin's mother, who had died some four years earlier.

vise you not to do the same, I fear it is not for your good.
. . . I am now all the more convinced that people are right
to be surprised by the little care and protection you show
the Germans. Believe me: the French will respect you more
and trust you more if they find that you have the solidity
and frankness of the Germans. . . . When one is young and
sees these sorts of things every day [i.e., the Germans being
criticized], it is very difficult not to follow suit; therefore,
you must have a lady or a minister who can warn you in
time. Greet important Germans with distinction; treat all
the others well, especially those who are my subjects or belong to one of the great [noble] Houses; and to the less important ones—that is, those who are not allowed at Court
here—show them kindness, affection, protection. . . . Making people like us is the only amusement and happiness of
our [royal] condition. It is a talent which you have mastered
so perfectly! Do not lose it by neglecting that which gave it
to you: you owe it neither to your beauty (which in fact is
not so great), nor to your talents or culture (you know very
well you have neither); it is your kind heart, your frankness,
your amiability, all exerted with your good judgment.*
They say that you don't bother speaking to the great nobles
or distinguishing them; that when you sit down to play
cards, you only chat with your young ladies, whispering
into their ears, laughing with them. . . . Giving people the
distinction they are entitled to is an essential matter which
you must not neglect, especially since you did so well in the
beginning.

They also speak of the games you indulged in last winter.
Do not let yourself go to your propensity of making fun of
others; you have a tendency to do so; if people realize you
have that weakness, they will indulge you only too well, and
you will lose the respect and confidence of the public, which

* This up-and-down sentence is typical: praise is carefully mixed with criticism so as to instill a feeling of guilt.

are so necessary, so pleasant, and which you still possess so completely. My love for you would make me go on and on; please forgive me all these repetitions, but I look on them as the basis of your happiness, so you can see how much I care. Don't think that it is Mercy who wrote me about all this, but I must repeat that it is astonishing how much we know here; I correspond with no one, but many others do and know the smallest details.*

Mercy to Maria Theresa, 22 May 1771

The letter which Your Majesty wrote Mme la Dauphine at the beginning of April has had such a good result that ever since then I have noted a very remarkable diminution of most of the little problems which were outlined in my very humble reports. This positive change is particularly visible in two essential areas: that of the talk about the critical situation here, and that of the proper greetings to those who pay court to Mme la Dauphine. . . .

I told her that the people who belong to the comtesse du Barry's party were boasting about being treated badly by HRH and that they should not be given the impertinent satisfaction of thinking that Mme l'Archiduchesse was concerned with them, that the best way to punish them was to speak to them now and again with an easy and indifferent look, and that if Mme la Dauphine had spoken even once to Mme du Barry herself, I was very sure that this would have upset all the wicked plans of a cabal whose greatest illustration comes from the way they withstand the important efforts the royal family makes against them.

Mme la Dauphine, without disagreeing with my idea, stopped me on the question of the comtesse du Barry and

* As usual, the Empress is lying so as to shield Mercy.

said naively that the fear of displeasing Mesdames her aunts would always prevent her from saying a word to the favorite.

Maria Theresa to Mercy, 6 June 1771

Van Swieten* feels that if a young woman as attractive as the Dauphine cannot wake up the Dauphin, all remedy would be useless; that, therefore, it is better not to try any and allow time to change so strange a way of behaving.

Maria Theresa to Marie Antoinette
Laxenburg, 9 June 1771

I am writing to you from Laxenburg; we arrived here last night; there is an encampment of four regiments of infantry and three squadrons of cavalry; every evening at six we will have some maneuver or exercise, if the weather permits, since this whole month has been very rainy. There have been very severe inundations, which will prevent many movements. All this week will be filled thus, the next with theatricals, and the one after with an encampment of all the troops who are going to Hungary to form the army. I must admit it upsets me to see no hope of peace when I wish for it so ardently.

   . . . Thank God your health is still good; I do not disapprove of your outings, but you must do nothing to excess, especially riding horses. I am sorry to hear that you have broken your promise to me and that you gallop at the hunt. I only agreed to your taking that exercise on the condition

* The Empress's doctor.

that you wouldn't hunt; your silence on this point upsets me doubly; as you can imagine, what a thousand people* see can hardly remain a secret. . . . All the letters from Paris and Versailles speak about you at length, and about your wise and friendly behavior to your sister-in-law, but what I like above all is what Mercy writes me, and the encomium he gives you. People don't speak much of that Princess, but they dare to make comparisons. Go on behaving this way, my dear daughter, and you will see that we are giving you good advice. See Mercy oftener and don't worry about what people will say. The King surely has nothing against this, since he approved of it for the Queen and the Dauphine; and as for the others, you don't need their approbation: it is up to you to set the tone, not up to them. Display no ill temper or jealousy, and the others will at last tire of trying to make you feel [these emotions] when they see you firm and peaceful. I agree with you that the consummation of the comtesse de Provence's marriage is probably more boast than reality. . . .

Marie Antoinette to Maria Theresa, 21 June 1771

Madame my dear mother,

It is with much pleasure that I received your dear letter the day before yesterday and learned that Your Majesty is in good health. As for me, I feel perfectly well; my dear husband took medicine today because he had an indigestion two nights ago. He threw up a lot and, as he went upstairs to his apartment in the morning, he felt faint twice, but he is in very good health now and has promised me very firmly that it won't be long before he sleeps here again.

* Again the Empress is shielding Mercy.

We are still on the best of terms, my sister, my brother,* and we; I hope it may always continue. My sister is very sweet, obliging, and cheerful. She is very fond of me and trusts me completely; she told me herself that her marriage was not at all consummated. She is not at all prejudiced, as we feared, in favor of Mme du Barry or M. de la Vauguyon; she talked to me about them very reasonably and behaved very well when one day at Marly she was sitting next to her.

I am desperately sorry that Your Majesty thinks I broke my promise regarding the hunt; I only went once, to a deer hunt, and did not even follow it closely. . . .

I do not mention, my dear Mama, the nomination of M. d'Aiguillon [to the foreign ministry], since I stay away from politics. I hear that it is the Coadjutor of Strasbourg† who is being sent to Vienna. He comes from a very great family, but the life he has led is more that of a soldier than that of a coadjuteur.

Adieu, my dear Mama, I kiss you with all my heart and love you dearly.

Mercy to Maria Theresa, 22 June 1771

The need for small amusements, the ease with which they can be found at Mesdames', often preclude any further thought so that, fearing boredom, Mme l'Archiduchesse behaves in ways which otherwise her own wisdom would prevent.

* The comte and comtesse de Provence.
† A Coadjutor was a bishop's designated successor; in this case, Marie Antoinette is referring to Prince Louis de Rohan, who later became Bishop of Strasbourg, a cardinal, and the great dupe in the Affair of the Queen's Necklace.

Maria Theresa to Marie Antoinette
Schönbrunn, 9 July 1771

The courier . . . will find you in the greatest amusements and pleasures at Compiègne and I flatter myself that, once there, you will love me enough not to break your promises to me by riding in a hunt. . . .

I await in vain the list of the books you read every month; is the abbé Vermond no longer with you? I would be sorry if he weren't but sorrier still if he is without your using him. At your age the world forgives many frivolities and childish acts; but as time passes they will bore everyone and you yourself will suffer from them; for someone in your situation, reading is a necessity. . . . I will not conceal from you that people are already talking about you and that you will lose the esteem people had for you. . . . A continually dissipated life without any serious occupation would even trouble your conscience.

I am delighted that you are on such good terms with your sister-in-law; it is fitting for both that you remain close friends. God prevent jealousies and intrigues from disturbing you. You pleased me greatly by writing me about the appointment of M. d'Aiguillon and Rohan's destination; if this last is not respectable, especially as a cleric, he will not do here and anyone else would be better; but as you very well say, you have nothing to do with politics and I can only urge you to stay away from it altogether: it is too complicated even to dare make a judgment, but I must warn you that they are not pleased about the manner in which you received this new minister, and you generally show too much dislike to all that party:* you needn't lower yourself, look for them, or cajole them, but you belong like them to

* That is, Mme du Barry's friends. This letter marks the beginning of the great du Barry crisis: as months passed, the Dauphine went on snubbing the favorite, to the King's growing anger.

the King's Court, and as his children you owe even more respect and obedience to him than the others. . . . Until now, it has all been explained by the fact that Mesdames were influencing you, but with time the King may get annoyed and you must know that these Princesses, with all their virtues and real merit, have never won the esteem, either of their father or of the public. . . .

I am not sorry to hear that the comtesse de Provence is no farther into the estate of marriage than the Dauphine; these Princes are really too young; you need patience and sweetness. Too much ardor would put him off.

Mercy to Maria Theresa, 24 July 1771

[After I had spoken to her at length] Mme la Dauphine, who was playing lansquenet* with the King and the royal family, found herself sitting next to the comtesse du Barry; HRH put on an easy expression which showed neither disgust nor annoyance; she spoke to the favorite when the game made it necessary, all with a good grace, doing neither too much nor too little. . . . The cabal since then has changed its language and is about to make an effort to win Mme la Dauphine's good graces.

. . . The progress made by HRH on the soul of M. le Dauphin becomes more remarkable every day. Monday, before M. le comte de Provence and Mme la comtesse de Provence, Mme la Dauphine reproached M. le Dauphin because of his immoderate taste for the hunt, which was destroying his health, and because of the rough and neglected look that exercise was giving him. M. le Dauphin thought to shorten the scolding by retiring to his apartment, but Mme la Dau-

* A slow and exceedingly dull card game played at Court as a matter of etiquette.

phine followed him there and went on discussing in strong terms the drawbacks of his way of life. That language so upset M. le Dauphin that he started to cry. Mme la Dauphine also started to shed tears and the reconciliation was very tender. Mme l'Archiduchesse did not forget that the dispute had begun at Mme la comtesse de Provence's; she brought M. le Dauphin back there. M. and Mme de Provence asked whether they were reconciled; M. le Dauphin answered with a very good grace that lovers' quarrels never last long.

It would no doubt be contrary to decency, even to Mme la Dauphine's dignity, if she were too amiable to the members of the ruling party; but given the present state of this Court, it also seems indispensable to me that HRH seem unaware of what the real situation is, and that she show neither hatred nor dislike to anyone. . . . When the comtesse du Barry is in the circle of the ladies who pay court to HRH, Mme la Dauphine, who speaks to all the ladies, should also speak once only to the favorite, either about her dress or her fan or some other topic of the kind. It is certain that such a move would at least stop many annoyances. . . . Besides, I have noticed that Mesdames, who urge Mme la Dauphine to remain severe and silent, do not forget discreetly to do little favors for the comtesse du Barry. . . . It seems that Mme la Dauphine is always put forward and used as an instrument of a hatred they dare not avow.

Maria Theresa to Marie Antoinette
Schönbrunn, 17 August 1771

. . . I was waiting with impatience to hear what you would say on what Mercy told you from me, but I saw you had delayed that conversation until after the departure of the courier; however, what has reassured me is that Mercy writes me that on his advice you have already begun to be polite to the dominant party* and even said a few vague words which had a wonderful effect. . . . I am delighted that you should have followed his advice so quickly. I am always sure of your success once you start something because God has given you such an appearance and so many charms, together with your kindness, that all hearts belong to you . . . [but] I hear from everyone, and far too often, that you have greatly abated the efforts you made to be amiable and polite, to tell everyone something pleasant and suitable, and to make distinctions [of rank] . . . it is all blamed on Mesdames, who have never won anyone's respect or confidence; but what is even worse than the rest, they say you are beginning to ridicule people, that you laugh at people to their face. That would cause you the greatest prejudice, and rightly, and would even make people doubt that you were kind-hearted. To please five or six young ladies or young men, you would lose all the rest. . . . All the courtiers who want to please you will behave the same way, because they are usually idle, and the least useful people in a state, and worthwhile people, who will not want to be ridiculed or angered, will stay away so that you will be left with the kind of bad company which encourages every vice.† . . .

I can imagine how embarrassing it must have been to refuse Broglie‡ because of his wife: I cannot deny that I feel esteem for him because he showed me so much zeal in the critical situation which was mine after the battle of Prague. You can, whenever convenient, tell him that I still remember it. I am delighted that Durfort has the entrées** in your apartment; he deserves them because of his real qualities

* That is, Mme du Barry and the duc d'Aiguillon.
† An accurate prediction: that is exactly what happened.
‡ The maréchal de Broglie, whose wife was not received at Court.
** The right to enter the rooms of any member of the royal family was ardently coveted.

and because he was happy enough to witness the solidity of the union through your marriage.

Everything I hear about the way you four people* are together gives me great pleasure; your sister-in-law cannot compare with you as far as appearances go, but her character is more solid and she knows more; you can only gain, therefore, in being always friends, and naturally you will be spending many years together. It is all the more important to be close and use the friendship for you personally as well as the good of the state. As long as you are on good terms, no one will dare to intrigue; but the least coolness would open the field and you would feel many an inconvenience, both for the peace of your life and in its pleasures.

I will admit my weakness: when you wrote that it would take a miracle for your sister-in-law, as for you, to become pregnant, I was pleased. . . .

Mercy writes me that you were very pleased with the little writing desk I sent you; that you immediately looked for my windows† and said the most charming and touching things. Imagine how I felt; do not spoil those qualities of kindness and tenderness you have, and do not copy originals which, no matter how great their true merit, have never succeeded with the public.‡ . . .

Marie Antoinette to Maria Theresa, 2 September 1771

Madame my very dear mother,

I was delighted by the arrival of the courier as his lateness had begun to worry me. M. de Mercy talked to me about the subject concerned by Your Majesty's instructions; I think he

* That is, the Dauphin and Dauphine, the comte and comtesse de Provence.
† It had an inlaid view of Schönbrunn.
‡ The Empress is, as usual, referring to Mesdames.

will be pleased with my answers and hope you are fully convinced that my greatest happiness consists in pleasing You. I will also try to treat Broglie well, although he was rude to me personally. I am desperately sorry that you believe what people tell you, that I no longer speak to anyone. You must trust me very little to believe that I am so unreasonable as to amuse myself with five or six young people and neglect those I must honor.*

I am very far from having the ideas Your Majesty thinks about the Germans: I will always be proud to be one. . . . So long as good subjects come, they will be pleased with the way I will receive them. I feel sorry for my brother Ferdinand as his departure is coming close, since my own experience has taught me how painful it is to live away from one's family. I expect there will soon be an outcome to his marriage: as for me, I still live in hope, and the love which M. le Dauphin shows me more and more every day will not allow me to doubt it, although I would prefer to have it over.† We four live well together. The comtesse de Provence is very sweet and cheerful in private, but does not appear so in public. . . . I will not mention all the annoyances of *ce pays-ci*;‡ M. de Mercy will surely tell you what is worth telling; as for me, I will always have as little as possible to do with it all. . . .

Mercy to Maria Theresa, 2 September 1771

[The King sent for Mercy to meet him at Mme du Barry's. There,] the King came close to me and said, "Until now you

---

* This was an out and out lie.
† The marriage, in other words, has still not been consummated.
‡ *Ce pays-ci* (this country) refers to the Court, where manners and customs were so different from those prevailing in the rest of France as to make it seem a separate country.

have been the Empress's Ambassador, but I would like you now to be mine, at least for a little time." After that introduction, the King looked more embarrassed; he told me that he had wanted to talk to me in private about Mme la Dauphine, that he loved her with all his heart, that he thought her charming, but that being young and impatient and "having a husband who was not able to lead her," it was impossible for Mme l'Archiduchesse to avoid all the traps set for her by intriguers. . . . He then told me that he noticed with annoyance that Mme la Dauphine was giving in to preventions, to hatreds, which were not really hers and which "were suggested to her"; that she treated badly, in the most overt way, the persons whom the King allowed into his private circle; that without wanting to restrain Mme l'Archiduchesse's preferences for this or that person, she was only being asked to treat all people presented at Court in the way they had a right to expect.

. . . On the tenth, I found out that the comtesse du Barry was to join the circle of ladies the next day. . . . I warned Mme la Dauphine. . . . HRH promised me that she would address a few words to the favorite but said that she wanted me to be there; that at the end of the card game I must find the favorite and speak to her; that Mme l'Archiduchesse as she went around would stop near me and, as if by accident, speak to the comtesse du Barry. . . . I begged her not to tell Mesdames her aunts about this little arrangement; she promised, but unfortunately the secret was not kept.

On the eleventh in the evening I joined the circle; the comtesse du Barry was there; Mme la Dauphine called me over to say that she was frightened, but that the arrangement still held. The card playing was ending, HRH sent me to the favorite with whom I started a conversation. Immediately all eyes turned toward me. Mme la Dauphine started to speak to the ladies, she was coming close and was only two steps away when Mme Adélaïde, who was watching her carefully, raised her voice and said, "It is time to leave; let us go: we will await the King's return at my sister Victoire's." With this, Mme la Dauphine left and the arrangement failed. That little scene was followed by much talk at Mesdames'; they criticized my advice severely; Mme la Dauphine, however, was good enough to defend me, especially after M. le Dauphin said very calmly, "As for me, I think that M. de Mercy was quite right and that you are wrong." . . .

I very much doubt that the King will take it upon himself to speak about all this to Mme la Dauphine, the subject would be too embarrassing . . . and the royal family, safe in the knowledge that the King won't speak, thinks it can abandon all caution. . . . In these circumstances Mme Adélaïde retains all her influence over Mme la Dauphine.

Maria Theresa to Marie Antoinette
Schönbrunn, 30 September 1771

Madame my dear daughter,

I saw Vicquemont and Mercy: both have given me much consolation by assuring me that you are in good health, very cheerful, content, and popular. Mercy told me he had seen you in private twice and for a rather long time. I am pleased that you changed [your habits] according to my wishes that you see those who come from here more familiarly; but he confirmed what everything I read tells me—that you act only on your aunts' advice. If you will read my instructions, you will see what I wrote you on that subject.* I respect them, I like them, but they have never known how to win the respect or affection of their family or the public, and you

* In fact, the Empress had said the very reverse of all this. See her letter of May 4, 1770.

want to go the same way. That fear and embarrassment about talking to the King, the best of fathers, or to people to whom you are advised to speak! Admit this embarrassment [to Louis XV], that fear of saying merely good day; a word on a dress, on a bagatelle, costs you so much, this is self-indulgence, or worse. . . . You made such a good start. Your appearance, your judgment, when it is not directed by others, are always true and for the best. Let yourself be guided by Mercy; what interest do we, he and I, have other than your particular happiness and the good of the state? Give up those contrary examples: it is for you to set the tone after the King, and you must not be ruled like a child when you want to speak. . . . I demand that you convince him by your every action of your respect and your love. . . . Should you even fall out with all the others, I cannot excuse you [from obeying]: you have one goal only—it is to please the King and obey him. . . .

You write me that, for my sake, you are treating the Broglies well, even though they were disrespectful to you. Here is again a failing, and of the same kind: can a little Broglie ever be disrespectful to you? I cannot understand it. No one has ever been disrespectful to me, or to any of your ten brothers and sisters; if he displeased someone in your suite, you must not know about it, even less take it on to yourself; it should be enough for you that the Broglies have the King's esteem; you must not listen, act, or even think otherwise. If you care about living in peace, about your future, act thus and in no other way.

. . . Do not take what I am telling you here as a scolding, or as reflecting bad temper on my part; take it for the greatest proof of my love and of the interest I take in you; that is why I write you all this so strongly. . . . I do not demand of you that you give up the people you usually see—God preserve me from it!—but I want you to ask Mercy's advice rather than theirs, to see him more often, to speak to him about everything, and to repeat nothing of what he says to anyone else: you must begin to act on your own. . . . You must know how to play your role if you want to be respected; if you give in, I can foresee great troubles ahead: nothing but vexations and little cabals which will make you unhappy. I want to prevent that and beg you to believe in the advice of a mother who knows the world, loves her children passionately, and wants to spend her dreary life in being useful to them. . . .

Mercy to Maria Theresa, 15 October 1771

Although Your Majesty deigned to authorize me to suppress your letter [of September 30] to Mme la Dauphine, I did not think I should hesitate to give it to her because there was no time to be lost in remedying a problem so deeply rooted that I very much fear Your Majesty may have to keep up a tone of authority for some time: that alone can free Mme la Dauphine of the noxious prejudices instilled in her by Mme Adélaïde. . . .

Mme l'Archiduchesse, who was at her toilette, opened Your Majesty's letter immediately. She read it quickly, and I saw that she was struck by it. Since I have come to know just what these first reactions mean, I was not much satisfied with those I noticed on this occasion. HRH said very little to me, and in a tone imbued more with impatience than docility or the willingness to be convinced: I needed no more to foretell what her answer will be. She will no doubt be reticent to Your Majesty on the question of the favorite: Mme l'Archiduchesse will surely say that the King showed her no displeasure in this matter; that what the Monarch asked me to tell her was only under the influence of the cabal; but that at bottom the King is rather indifferent about the way his favorite is treated. That is what Mme Adélaïde never tires of repeating to Mme la Dauphine. HRH will perhaps say that she has on occasion spoken to the King; in fact that is true, but it has only been in very rare instances, always with awkwardness and constraint, and never on essential questions. . . . I feel quite sure in advance that Mesdames will not be mentioned.* . . .

Marie Antoinette to Maria Theresa, 13 October 1771

Madame my very dear mother,

. . . You will allow me to justify myself on all the points you write me about. First, I am desperately sorry that you believe all the lies people write you from here instead of what you may hear from Mercy and myself. You must believe that we want to fool you. I have good reason to believe that the King of himself doesn't wish me to speak to du Barry;† not only has he never mentioned the subject to me, but he is even friendlier to me since he knows I have refused —and if you could see, as I do, everything that happens here, you would realize that that woman and her clique would never be satisfied with just a word, and that I would have to do it again and again. You may be sure that I need to be led by no one when it comes to politeness. As for the Broglie, if you were better informed, my dear Mama, you would know that a little Broglie can be disrespectful in ce pays-ci as he would not be in Vienna. I wrote with all the politeness imaginable to Mme de Boufflers that the King would not grant her request; the Broglies thought it a good

* Mercy was perfectly right. See Marie Antoinette's letter of October 13, 1771.
† That was Mesdames' line—and altogether false.

idea to ridicule my letter and gave out copies of it: that is hardly a dislike felt on behalf of someone in my suite. . . .

The death of Mme de Villars caused me many vexations. M. de la Vauguyon kept bothering me, and went so far that he asked M. le Dauphin to write (even though he didn't want to) M. d'Aiguillon so that he would speak to me in favor of Mme de Saint-Mégrin. Even though people tell you that I don't dare speak to the King, I did speak to him with M. le Dauphin's agreement, and he allowed me to refuse the request. I asked him at the same time to let one of my ladies be appointed as the dame d'atours,* but he refused at Mme du Barry's suggestion. I have been given the duchesse de Cossé, daughter of M. de Nivernais† and daughter-in-law of the maréchal de Brissac. She has a very good reputation; the King told me to announce her appointment to her and told me he was not telling anyone else; and yet, already the day before, M. d'Aiguillon had gone to warn Mme de Cossé and fifty people knew the secret. I complained to the King that the indiscretion of his friends was making me look ridiculous; he received me well and told me he was sorry. . . .

You will surely have heard, my dear Mama, about the accident of Mme la duchesse de Chartres, who was just delivered of a dead child; even though it is terrible, I still wish it had happened to me, but there is still not hope of it, even though M. le Dauphin always sleeps with me and treats me in the most friendly way. . . .

So as to show you the unfairness of the Barry's friends, I must tell you that I spoke to her at Marly; I do not say that I will never speak to her anymore, but cannot consent to do so at an agreed day and time so that she can talk about it in advance and act triumphant. I beg your pardon for what I have written you so strongly on this subject; if you could have seen the sorrow that your dear letter caused me, you

* The dame d'atours was the Mistress of the Wardrobe.
† A popular diplomat and man of letters.

would quickly excuse the confusion of my language and believe that, now as for the rest of my life, I feel the deepest love and the most respectful submission to my dear Mama.

Maria Theresa to Marie Antoinette
Vienna, 31 October 1771

This letter will arrive too late for your birthday, but you may be very sure that I have not forgotten it, that I thank God daily, praying that He will keep you such that you may save your soul and do good in the country where you are while making your family happy and furthering, inasmuch as may be in you, the glory of God and the welfare of man. . . .

I did not think it a bad thing to see you defending yourself on the subject of my last letter. Everything that shows me your sensitivity and your candor endears you to me; but try and see whether you were not feeling impatience rather than hurt feelings as the result of my remonstrances; and what upset me, and convinced me that you have little desire to amend yourself, is your absolute silence when it comes to your aunts, although they were the most important subject in my letter and the cause of all your mistakes. . . . Do my love and my advice deserve less reciprocation than theirs? I must admit that this thought wounds my heart. . . . I am not comparing myself to these respectable princesses in any way; I respect their private life and their solid qualities, but I must always repeat that they have earned neither the public's esteem nor their intimates' love. . . . They have become odious, unpleasant, and boring, even for themselves, and the object of intrigues and unpleasantness. . . .

Good news is filling me with joy—news from your sister

the Queen of Naples as well as news of Ferdinand,* who is delighted with his wife; I . . . confide in you, under pain of secrecy, the fact that on the very first night after she became his wife, they were very visibly in love and that the visit of the générale, which came unfortunately on the seventeenth, caused much impatience.

All this news, which should have overcome me with pleasure, was shadowed by my thoughts on the danger of your situation. . . . I have heard nothing of your reading or your studies for months now; I have received nothing on this from the abbé, who was supposed to send me an account of your necessary and reasonable amusements every month; all that frightens me: I see you striding with a nonchalant calm toward ruin, or at least to very serious mistakes. What pain, what efforts you will have to endure before you can make up for all this! . . . You tell me that you have spoken to the King; that should be a daily occupation, and [you should] not wait until the time when you have something to ask him. . . . You will waste all your efforts if you write him instead; neither character nor language will speak for you, while, on the other hand, there is something so touching about you in person that it is very difficult to refuse you what you ask. . . .

You will have seen our occupations in the paper; here we are in town at the best season of the year. The Emperor won't come for another ten days; he took a terrible trip all through the mountains—luckily the weather was perfect— to observe the situation in this fair kingdom† which, for the last three years, has been deep in misery because the crop has failed completely. We, and especially the Emperor himself, are trying to devise means of helping, but since the failure is everywhere, there are many unfortunates who per-

* Ferdinand IV, King of the Two Sicilies, had married Maria Carolina of Habsburg.
† Bohemia.

ish. You can imagine how affected I am by all this, especially since the crop has been very mediocre in Hungary, so the means are slow and difficult.

Marie Antoinette to Maria Theresa, 15 November 1771

Madame my very dear mother,

I am deeply touched by what you so kindly wrote me about my birthday. I especially want to follow the good advice you give me, my dear Mama. . . . I do not think I did wrong when I gave in to my impulse and told the little secret to M. le Dauphin! I did not sound reproachful, but he was still a little embarrassed. I still hope for the best; he really loves me and does everything I want, and will conclude everything when he feels less awkward. . . .

When I wrote you, my dear Mama, that I needed no advice when it came to behaving properly, I meant that I had not consulted my aunts. However friendly my feelings for them, they can never compare to those I have for my loving and respectable mother; I do not think I am blind to their failings, but I think that they have been greatly exaggerated.

Although the condition of the Queen [of Naples] often makes me think about mine, I still share my dear sister's joy.

Ever since the summer, the trips and the hunt have stopped me from reading regularly; I have still read something almost every day.

The comtesse de Provence's smallpox went very well; she will hardly bear any marks. I saw her before she left for La Muette, with the consent of the King and M. le Dauphin. . . .

Mercy to Maria Theresa, 16 November 1771

She spoke to me at last about the letter she had received from Your Majesty, and Mme l'Archiduchesse seemed very worried about the way Your Majesty would interpret her answer, which she admitted she had written too precipitately. That admission allowed me to speak about many of my thoughts, and Mme la Dauphine was so moved that tears came into her eyes. "After all," she told me, "the Empress knows that I will always do what she wants me to do." . . . We then talked about the favorite, and HRH assured me she would treat her well when the occasion presented itself.

Marie Antoinette to Maria Theresa, 18 December 1771

Madame my very dear mother,

Please accept my respects and wishes for the New Year; your children only wish to please you, and I want to do so as much as the others. . . .

I send you my measurements and those of M. le Dauphin; mine were taken without shoes or coiffure; as for him, he was wearing very flat shoes, and his coiffure does not matter as it is very low; even though I have grown much taller, I am no thinner; as for M. le Dauphin, although very much tanned by the outdoors, his complexion is improving and his health grows stronger; he becomes more pleasing every day, and the only thing lacking to make me completely happy is to be in the same condition as the Queen; I hope it may happen soon, and I believe that the wicked rumors people whisper about his impotence are just so much nonsense.

When I write you, my dear Mama, about the du Barry, it is with the utmost frankness, and you may be sure that I am too cautious to talk about her in the same way with the people here.

The comtesse de Provence came back to us a week ago; she is hardly marked and almost not flushed at all. They say that her husband tells all kinds of horrors against the duc de Choiseul, but I don't believe a word of it and we continue to be great friends.

Even though the Carnival is very lengthy, it already began in October and we have a dance once a week in my apartments.

I went today to watch M. le Dauphin's shooting; he shoots admirably, and very cautiously; he killed some forty birds; that is the best proof that he is not as nearsighted as one would think when one meets him. . . .

Marie Antoinette to Maria Theresa, 21 January 1772

Madame my very dear Mother,

No doubt Mercy will have written you about my behavior* on New Year's Day, and I hope you are pleased. You may be sure that I will always sacrifice all my opinions and distastes as long as it is nothing spectacular or dishonorable. My life would be miserable if there were to be discords between my two families; my heart will always belong to mine and my duties here would be hard indeed to fulfill. . . .

I was very wrong in what I wrote you about the comte de Provence; he has really dishonored himself in the business of Mme de Brancas; his wife does exactly as he does, but that is due only to timidity and stupidity, for she is, I believe, very unhappy. Still, I am on very good terms with them, even though I don't trust their character, which is not as

* The Dauphine had at last spoken to Mme du Barry.

sincere as mine. As for the comte d'Artois,* although still being schooled, he shows he likes honesty, a feeling he certainly has not learned from his Governor.† He [Artois] resisted when he [la Vauguyon] tried to have an honest man whom M. de Choiseul had made Secretary to the Swiss Guard dismissed; and so he has the approval of his eldest brother, who has also shown in the Brancas business that he felt more friendship and trust for his wife than for the comte de Provence.

Mercy to Maria Theresa, 23 January 1772

In relation to Mesdames, Your Majesty's advice is proving effective, and I see with great satisfaction that Mme l'Archiduchesse (at least in certain cases) frees herself from the domination Mme Adélaïde tries to maintain over her. What happened on New Year's Day gave me a recent proof of this. It is customary for all women presented at Court to attend the royal family on that day. I was informed that the comtesse du Barry was expecting to do her duty, and on the last day of the old year, I obtained an audience from Mme la Dauphine, during which I used every imaginable means to convince HRH not to treat the favorite badly. It was not without difficulty that I was able to get a promise on that subject. The essential point was that Mesdames should not be consulted; luckily, that is what happened. In the morning the next day, the comtesse du Barry appeared at Mme l'Archiduchesse's; she came with the duchesse d'Aiguillon and the maréchale de Mirepoix. Mme la Dauphine started by speaking to the first of these ladies; then, pressing on to the favorite and looking at her with neither awkwardness

* The Dauphin's youngest brother.
† M. de la Vauguyon.

nor affectation, she said, "There are many people today at Versailles," after which HRH immediately spoke to the maréchale de Mirepoix.

I went to Mme l'Archiduchesse's dinner, and when she left the table, she had me come in and told me, "I followed your advice; M. le Dauphin here is my witness." The Prince smiled but said nothing; then Mme l'Archiduchesse told me herself what had happened and ended by saying, "I spoke to her once, but I am determined to go no farther, and that woman will never again hear the sound of my voice." . . . That very evening the King greeted Mme la Dauphine more tenderly than usual.

Mme la Dauphine is becoming better spoken every day; she answers quickly, properly, and has a way of expressing herself which is free of any borrowed routine; she has, in particular, a talent for speaking to a whole circle [of courtiers] in such a way that each can think the words addressed to him. In spite of this talent, which gives Mme l'Archiduchesse great charm, it is still true that she does not speak enough to important people and never says a word to strangers. Finally, HRH rarely speaks at the times when it would be most flattering for her to do so—during her meals, for instance, when there is always a crowd to watch her. . . .

M. le Dauphin persists in his affection, his eagerness, and his kindness to Mme la Dauphine. He is even more occupied and enchanted with her, but the circumstance most essential to their marriage remains suspended. M. le comte de Provence is in the same situation, and there is reason to believe that he will remain thus longer than M. le Dauphin.

Maria Theresa to Marie Antoinette
Vienna, 13 February 1772

I am sending you through Mercy on this separate sheet my answer to yours of January 21, where you tell me that you followed my advice on New Year's Day. The effect of my advice showed that it was good, and it really made me laugh to see that you fancied that ever I or my minister could give you advice *against your honor:* not even against the strictest decency. . . . Your agitation after those few words,* the announcement that you won't do it again make me tremble for you. . . . Who can give you better advice, be more deserving of your trust than my minister, who knows the State thoroughly and all those who work in it? . . . But it is not enough merely to speak with him: *you must follow all the advice he will give you without fail: you must, through a consequent and wise behavior, position yourself so as to be wholly self-sustaining.* The King is old,† the indigestions from which he suffers are not unimportant: there can be changes for the best or the worse with the du Barry, with the ministers. The comte de Provence's behavior must be watched with great attention and circumspection. You will find many people who will tell you stories against them, who will try to antagonize you; but be very careful: these same people may be doing the same thing with them. Carefully avoid all schisms within the family; hide your feelings, don't react, and remain kind: that is the only way to preserve peace at home. . . .

* "There are many people today at Versailles, Madame," the sentence Marie Antoinette finally said to Mme du Barry.
† He was sixty-two years old.

Mercy to Maria Theresa, 29 February 1772

I found Mme l'Archiduchesse very concerned with Your Majesty's last letter; she was very struck by the possibility of a cooling off between the two courts and the reasons which might provoke this. "This is all more serious than I would have thought," she told me. "You were right to tell me about this; I am writing the Empress that I would never forgive myself if my behavior were to provoke such a catastrophe; and, rather than risking it, I am resolved to overcome my dislike of the favorite. In all cases my heart would be with my family, and if there were quarrels, I know that doing my duty here would be very difficult."

. . . Since Mme la Dauphine has begun to open her eyes on Mesdames' rule and on its drawbacks, HRH has decided to free herself from them. She is now on good terms with her aunts, is easy and friendly with them; but she no longer blindly adopts other people's opinions; she thinks and decides for herself.

Mercy to Maria Theresa, 15 April 1772

HRH is still admirably well treated by the King; the favorite has not appeared at the circle since New Year's Day, but she is quiet and makes no complaint. I explained to her that after having been well received by Mme la Dauphine, it was wise and proper to let things be unchanged for some time, that little by little the party spirit within the royal family would fade. . . . The favorite, who still shows me the same trust, agreed with this thought. . . .

Mercy to Maria Theresa, 15 May 1772

For some time now, and always on Mesdames' advice, Mme la Dauphine has allowed herself to be convinced that she should grant protections, make recommendations that are neither fitting nor just. . . .

The friendship between Mme la Dauphine and M. le comte and Mme la comtesse de Provence is growing stronger; it seems that these last have really deserted the party of the favorite and the duc d'Aiguillon; at least they behave as if they have. The comte de Provence tried to have a conversation on this subject with Mme l'Archiduchesse; he told her that she must agree that she had long mistrusted him, that, on his side, he admitted that she was not altogether wrong, but that now, he had really backtracked; that he knew the duc d'Aiguillon, what a wicked intriguer he was, and that he would no longer be the minister's dupe. Mme la Dauphine listened to these overtures without saying anything compromising. I had begged her to beware, and in fact time will still have to pass before one can be sure of the comte de Provence's sincerity. His character is not noted for its truthfulness.

Marie Antoinette to Maria Theresa
Versailles, 13 June 1772

Madame my very dear Mother,

I am awaiting with the greatest impatience the news of the Queen's delivery.* I do blame the people who prejudiced her against male doctors. I would happily put myself into the hands of anyone they might want if it made sure that I could be in the same situation. The good weather has

* Maria Carolina of Naples was about to give birth.

come to this country also. I hope the crops will be good; we need them badly. . . .

I cannot tell you, my dear Mama, how sorry I am about the Infanta;* it is very surprising that she made no better use of all your good advice and of all you said to her through Rosenberg. In spite of that, I will seize eagerly any occasion I may have to lessen the bad impression it may cause here. . . .

I have just had a letter from the Bohme.† The Queen is indeed happy, and so am I at this moment, to know that she has given birth so easily; even though the baby is only a daughter, I imagine that she must still be pleased because of the hope it gives her of having sons.

The comte d'Angivilliers, a clever man who was attached to the education of M. le Dauphin and who is in charge of the royal garden, would like to have a few samples of Austrian and Bohemian mining. I thought that my dear Mama would like to give me a way of obliging a man of merit; I take the liberty of sending her the list of what he would like. . . .

Mercy to Maria Theresa, 15 June 1772

All Your Majesty's letters have been received with respect and much fear. The frivolity of HRH's entourage, her habit of never being reprimanded or contradicted or even advised, by the King or M. le Dauphin, added to the three-hundred-league distance [from Vienna] are no doubt the reasons why the sterner letters have not always produced the desired ef-

* Maria Amalia of Habsburg, another of the Dauphine's sisters, was married to the Infante Don Philip, Duke of Parma, who was Louis XV's grandson. At her instigation, Don Philip had just dismissed his Prime Minister, Dutillot, whom both Louis XV and Maria Theresa wanted him to keep.
† The Queen of Naples's *femme de chambre.*

fect. Never has a mother had more right to speak with authority: I expounded this great truth to Mme la Dauphine whenever the letters upset her, and she agreed but thought that she was not loved and that she would always be treated with rigor. The last letters have finally destroyed that thought, and Your Majesty can be ever more certain of being able to lead Mme la Dauphine in all that pertains to her position or her duty.

. . . M. le Dauphin and Mme la Dauphine now see [the Provences] more often; they sometimes spend evenings together instead of visiting Mesdames. This small amusement is most useful . . . in making it rarer that they take part in the idle gossip at Mesdames'. . . . Since Mme la Dauphine now likes music again, she now and again holds small concerts for the young royal family. . . . I cannot sufficiently express how charming Mme l'Archiduchesse proves to be on those occasions, she pays attention to everyone, behaving with judgment and kindness to all.

IN 1772, RUSSIA, PRUSSIA, and Austria, after long negotiations, came to an agreement and proceeded to seize about half of Poland's territory. It was greatly feared, in Vienna, that France, traditionally the ally of Poland, would react strongly. In the event, and sensibly, Louis XV did nothing: he could hardly fight the three other major European powers for the sake of a faraway country which had always been a liability. When in her next letter Marie Antoinette worries about a break between her two families, she is referring to the possible consequences of the partition.

Marie Antoinette to Maria Theresa
Versailles, 17 July 1772

. . . I saw Mercy and, after having read your dear letter, talked to him about what you had said. He showed me his, which touched me greatly and gave me food for thought. I will do my best to contribute to the conservation of the alliance and close union; where would I be if there were to be a break between my two families? . . .

I will not wait until after Compiègne to tell you about my reading. I have been reading for some time with the abbé the *Mémoires de l'Estoile;* it is a diary of the reigns of Charles IX, Henri III, and Henri IV.* One can see day by day what happened during that period—the good and bad actions, the laws and customs. I find there the names, the offices, and sometimes the origins of the people who are at Court. I am also reading the letters of a mother to her daughter and of a daughter to her mother. Even though they are entertaining, they have good principles and very good morals.

. . . The comtesse de Noailles has just had a great fright. The chevalier d'Arpajon, her youngest son, has just had smallpox; he had been inoculated by Gatti; that is not the first such case among those who have been inoculated by that particular doctor, so those who were are now very frightened.

A bishop near Gunzbourg sent me eight medals that he had struck in gratitude of the wheat Your Majesty sent to the poor people who had none; this monument pleased me greatly. No one in my place has ever heard her mother talked about with as sincere admiration as is the case with you. I wrote the bishop to thank him. . . .

My dear Mama is very kind to take charge of my list for M. d'Angivilliers. I am sure I am giving him great pleasure.

* Charles IX, reigned 1560–75; Henri III, 1575–89; Henri IV, 1589–1610.

Mercy to Maria Theresa, 18 July 1772

For the last few weeks, Mme l'Archiduchesse has had moments of sadness which do not last long but announce nonetheless the beginning of a few unpleasant thoughts about M. le Dauphin's incomprehensible behavior [in not consummating the marriage] and about the uncertainty to which it gives rise.

Mercy to Maria Theresa, 14 August 1772

M. le Dauphin only suffers from the consequences of a deplorable education; he shows, however, that he has some essential qualities—he is honest, he is well able to listen to the truth; one need not even be careful in telling it to him: that is what Mme l'Archiduchesse does every day, not without success.

. . . On the twenty-sixth . . . I warned HRH that the comtesse du Barry would soon be coming, and I begged her to receive this woman properly. . . . The favorite came with the duchesse d'Aiguillon after the King's Mass. Mme la Dauphine first spoke to the latter; then, turning toward the favorite, she said a few words about the weather, about the hunt, so that without addressing the comtesse du Barry directly, the favorite could still think the words were aimed at her as well as at the duchesse d'Aiguillon. It was quite enough to please her.

Marie Antoinette to Maria Theresa, 14 October 1772

Madame my very dear Mother,

Please accept my wishes and respects for the feast of Saint Theresa; I will ask tomorrow that this patron saint be the intercessor to preserve your precious health. . . .

My sister Marianne is good enough to tell me that there is a new portrait of Your Majesty. It would be a great favor if you could let me have a copy of it. . . .

Milk continues to be very good for me. I sleep for an hour or two every morning after I drink it. People who hadn't seen me in a while say I have put on weight.

Even though our time is fully occupied here, I read at least a little every day. I have started to read the *Anecdotes of the Court of Philip-Augustus* by Mlle de Lussan. . . .

The plan of Schönbrunn and Vienna gave me great pleasure. I have been fully repaid for the efforts I made to find the places which have been changed by the pleasure I felt in paying attention to this. My apartment at Schönbrunn is indeed honored to shelter Your Majesty. I am pleased if it sometimes spares you from having to go upstairs; nothing is more tiring for the breathing. . . .

Marie Antoinette to Maria Theresa
Versailles, 15 December 1772

Madame my very dear Mother,

The gazettes aren't yet right: I do not despair of its happening soon.* I think he isn't yet strong enough: certainly, the moment it happens, I will not waste a second in writing you about it. Mercy will surely second my eagerness.

I suspect that people have told you more about my caval-

* The consummation of her marriage.

cades than the reality. I will, my dear Mama, tell you the whole truth. The King and M. le Dauphin enjoy seeing me on a horse. I say it only because everybody noticed it; especially during the stay at Compiègne, they were delighted to see me wearing the hunt uniform. . . . I would not believe that people could take as an accident what happened to me in the forest of Fontainebleau; there are here and there in the forest large stones; in one of these places, as I was going up at a very slow pace, my horse, who did not see one of these stones which was covered with sand, slipped; I made a movement which held him back and went right on. . . .

All the letters you receive will surely tell you about the new dispositions of the princes. M. le prince de Condé wrote the King in his own name and that of his son to show his submission. The letter was very good, although he didn't mention the Parlement in it, but that was as agreed. The King allowed him to come the next day, and both he and his son visited us all, with all going very well on both sides. A few days afterward, with the King's permission, I invited the duc, the duchesse, and Mlle de Bourbon to my ball. As for M. le duc d'Orléans, his son, and M. le prince de Conti, they haven't come back yet, but we hope it won't be long.

I neglect nothing in paying court to the King and acting on his wishes whenever I can guess what they are. I hope he is pleased with me; it is my duty to please him, my duty and my glory if I can help to preserve the union of our two houses.

Mercy must be pleased with the silence I have kept for a long time about everything which makes people criticize the favorite. The King had a slight fall yesterday; we worried for a moment but were reassured when we were told that he was continuing the hunt. We were waiting for him when he came back; he was in a very good mood and was not hurt at all. . . .

Maria Theresa to Marie Antoinette
Vienna, 31 December 1772

What you say as an excuse for breaking your promise to me, about riding to hounds, would have been permissible if a year ago or more, the first time you did it, you had told me about it. . . . But now that I have learned about it in the gazettes, I must admit I feel it, and it throws a shadow on the future, on your trust for me. . . . I have nothing more to say since the King and the Dauphin approve of this: you will never again hear a word from me on this subject; but it is your silence that hurts me. . . .

I will end my preaching with the old year. . . . I expect to hear about the New Year and the effect of my advice as regards your behavior toward the favorite. On that point I cannot allow you merely to stay out of the intrigues against her; you must follow my advice, treat her politely, and speak to her as you would to any other lady received at Court. You owe it to the King and to me; no other person has a right to your compliance. . . .

Mercy to Maria Theresa, 16 January 1773

Mme la Dauphine called for me and talked about the last letter she has received from Your Majesty. HRH seemed rather upset about her lack of openness in the matter of riding to hounds, and she said she was surprised to see that Your Majesty was aware of these details. I told Mme l'Archiduchesse that it was perfectly simple, that everybody is always watching her, and that, therefore, not even the least of her actions can escape the public's attention. . . . I pointed out to her how little Your Majesty wants to deprive her of her amusements and that according to what she herself had been kind enough . . . to let me read, I had never seen a tone of authority in Your Majesty's letters, but on the contrary that of a loving mother who wants her daughter to realize she is her very best friend; that the only answer Mme la Dauphine could offer to so precious a feeling was to show Your Majesty absolute trust, that it would be very painful to Your Majesty not to feel this even in the smallest occasions. Upon these words I saw her shed a few tears. She said to me with the most charming naivete, "I have not a single thought in my mind which I would not tell my mother; writing is the difficulty and I am afraid of worrying her by getting things wrong. I wrote her that it was in order to please the King and the Dauphin that I sometimes have hunted; you know that is true." I said it was, but I added that in cases like these it seemed necessary that Mme la Dauphine write about it all to Your Majesty.

. . . HRH told me what she thinks of M. le Dauphin. He has, she feels, a marked preference for justice, order, and truth, good common sense and perception in his appreciation of things; but Mme la Dauphine fears the Prince's laziness, his lack of vigor without which he can neither think nor feel strongly enough to act effectively.

. . . Then HRH said to me, without prompting, "I love the Empress, but I fear her, though from afar; even when I write her, I never feel at my ease." I answered that this shyness did not seem proper and that it had many drawbacks, that I had not noticed the same fear in HRH when in my presence the Emperor had reprimanded her. "Oh, that is very different," she answered, "the Emperor is my brother; I answered him when he annoyed me and was used to joking with him."

Marie Antoinette to Maria Theresa
Versailles, 13 January 1773

How you punish me for my forgetfulness! Above all, quickly tell me that you still trust me or I will feel wretched. I did tell you the truth about the approval of the King and M. le Dauphin; it is true that I have no great merit in complying [to their wish]. I would not dare tell you that I ride slowly and carefully if I didn't have as witnesses my two equerries, who never leave me and who are very grave and reasonable men.

The King found out about my sister's* pregnancy through a letter from the Infante, which he didn't answer. According to custom, the Infante has written M. le Dauphin and my brothers;† but the King did not allow them to answer. As for me, I keep silent like my two families. We must hope that when the Infanta has several children, she will understand her duty better and work at pleasing her parents.

I have also heard about the Queen's‡ pregnancy and what pleased me most is that they say that this pregnancy is quite different from the other, which makes me hope for a boy. If only I could say as much for myself! I am convinced that when this terrible spell is at last broken, all will go very well; and, in fact, the spell is only youth and clumsiness. . . .

New Year's Day here is a day of crowds and ceremony. I can claim no merit and deserve no blame respecting my dear Mama's advice: the favorite came to my apartments at a time when there were many people; I couldn't have spoken to everyone and so spoke in general. I have reason to believe

* The Duchess of Parma; she and her husband were still shunned by both families.
† The comtes de Provence and d'Artois.
‡ That is, the Queen of Naples.

that the favorite and her sister,* who is her main adviser, were pleased; still, I think that two days later M. d'Aiguillon tried to convince them that they had been badly treated. As for the minister, he has never complained of me in relationship to him, and in truth I have always been careful to treat him as well as the other ministers.

You will have learned, my dear Mama, that the duc d'Orléans and the duc de Chartres† have returned. I am delighted for the peace and tranquillity of the King; but I do not think that my dear Mama, in the King's place, would have accepted the letter they dared to write and are having printed in the foreign gazettes.

We are having the first of my Monday balls today at the comtesse de Noailles's; they will continue until Ash Tuesday; they will begin an hour or two later so as not to be as tiring as last year at the beginning of Carnival. In spite of the pleasures of carnival, I am still faithful to my dear harp, and people say I have been making progress. I also sing every week at the concert given by my sister Madame; even though the attendance is small, we have great fun and besides it pleases my two sisters. I still find time to read a little; I have started the *History of England*, by Mr. Hume; it seems quite interesting to me, although one has to remember that it was composed by a Protestant.

All the gazettes will be talking about the cruel fire at the Hôtel-Dieu;‡ they have had to move the sick into the cathedral [Notre Dame] and the Archbishop's palace. There are usually five or six thousand sick in the hospital; in spite of the care that was taken, it was impossible to prevent a part of the building from burning, and even though this accident happened two weeks ago, there is still some fire in the cel-

* Actually, her sister-in-law, Chon du Barry.
† The duc de Chartres was the duc d'Orléans's son; both were Princes of the Blood.
‡ Paris's only charity hospital, it was next to Notre Dame.

lars. The Archbishop published a letter ordering a charity drive; I sent a thousand *écus*.* I never mentioned it; I am being given embarrassing compliments, but they say it must be so as it gives a good example. . . .

Maria Theresa to Marie Antoinette
Vienna, 31 January 1773

Madame my dear daughter,

I am delighted that your carnival should be so pleasant, and all I hear about is your figure and the way you dance this year. . . . I was also delighted with the thousand *écus* which you sent to the Hôtel-Dieu. You are very right to say that you are sorry it became public; these actions should be known only by God, and I am quite sure that it was what you meant; but the others also have good reasons for making it known, as an example, indeed you say so yourself. My dear little one! We òwe it to give this kind of example; it is an essential and delicate part of our estate. The oftener you can be kind and generous without overspending, the better, and what in others would be ostentatious prodigality is proper and necessary with us. . . .

I am not pleased with what happened on New Year's Day; you were overly prepared; you must repair this as soon as possible; the month of February is as good for this as the month of January. I do not ask too much when I demand that you speak four or five times a year to the favorite in a natural way, and you cannot better confound M. d'Aiguillon than by giving him no hold on this point. I will even say more; your behavior to the King will be easier, more trusting when you feel you deserve no reproach on this point for,

* An *écu* was worth three *livres*. One *livre* is worth approximately $4.50.

according to all I hear, the King is more loving to you than you are to him. . . .

My dear daughter, these are four points that I recommend to you with all the love you know I bear you. Don't say that I scold, that I preach; say instead: Mama loves me and is always concerned with me and my welfare; I must believe her and console her by following her good advice. . . .

Marie Antoinette to Maria Theresa
Versailles, 15 February 1773

I wrote you a week ago through the Palffy;* I hear that she has only left today. I was telling you about a cold, now completely cured, and of a charming fête that my sister, Madame, had given me, followed by a little ball which lasted until three in the morning. We went—M. le Dauphin, the comte, and comtesse de Provence and I—last Thursday to the Opera Ball† in Paris; we kept the utmost secret. We were all masked; still, we were recognized after half an hour. The duc de Chartres and the duc de Bourbon, who were dancing at the Palais-Royal‡ right next door came to meet us and asked us pressingly to go and dance at Mme la duchesse de Chartres's; but I excused myself from it as I had the King's permission for the Opera only. We returned here at seven and heard Mass before going to bed. Everybody is delighted with M. le Dauphin's willingness to have this outing since he was believed to be averse to it.

The garden of Schönbrunn seems to me vastly improved; I can hardly believe that everything I see on the plan can

* Countess Palffy, one of the Empress's ladies, was coming to Versailles.
† A costumed ball open to everyone, which was given during the Carnival in the Opera.
‡ The Paris residence of the duc d'Orléans and his family.

already have been carried out; the transformation of the mountain especially must be a very pleasant change.

If people saw me with the King in private, they would agree that I don't look embarrassed; in public it is something else, but then I would be blamed if I behaved the way I do in private. We think that the marriage of the comte d'Artois with the sister of the comtesse de Provence has been decided, although not officially declared. We are still on very good terms. On Thursday I will attend a morality play in which my little sister* will perform; I send it to you, my dear Mama, so that you can see what our amusements are like. This proverb was written by someone called de Drombold, a friend of Mme de Graffigny. When the courier arrives, Lent will already have begun; I dread it for the health of my dear Mama.† I beg her to remember all her children need her, and I more than the others.

Mercy to Maria Theresa, 17 February 1773

Mme l'Archiduchesse is on very good terms with the King; she is sometimes a little more at her ease with him; but this happy manner is not sustained often enough. . . . It must be noticed that every time the King is treated by Mme la Dauphine in a friendly manner, even a familiar one, he always comes to tell me what Mme la Dauphine has just said. This happened again just recently at the comtesse du Barry's, and the favorite then said several very pleasant things to me about the graces of Mme la Dauphine.

---

* Madame Elisabeth, the Dauphin's youngest sister, was nine years old.
† This is because no meat could be eaten and meatless diets were considered weakening.

Maria Theresa to Marie Antoinette, 3 March 1773

The Palffy hasn't arrived yet; I await her impatiently so I can talk with her about you, and find out whether she thinks you have changed since the first time she saw you. The cold you had, and which Mercy told me about, of which I am grateful, was beginning to worry me. Thank God it is all over and you had fun during the Carnival. I find the script of the morality play you sent me very pretty. I am sending you some music for the harp; you will tell me whether you have been able to play it. You are quite right to say you cannot picture the changes of the mountain at Schönbrunn: they exist on the plan only and will never be carried out; you know that the Emperor doesn't like Schönbrunn, and it would be ridiculous to begin such an undertaking at my age. . . . Your excursion to Paris was well greeted by the public. What you write me about the marriage of the comte d'Artois surprises me: two sisters of the same house; there were rumors about a princess of Saxony. I must admit that this great rush to marry off the third [brother] gives one to think, not at all pleasantly, that this is becoming a heavy game; you must watch yourself all the more carefully and neglect nothing so as to protect yourself from attack. What you say about the way you are with the King reassures and pleases me; it is an essential point for you. My health is good; I was bled, five days ago, as a precaution. I am not eating any meat, but that is always good for me and it doesn't upset me at all. . . .

Your rides will be a substitute for dancing if you have the same amount of free time. Please be moderate. I rush this courier off to you to stay on schedule. Since February is three days short, it will only be sent tomorrow very early. I kiss you tenderly.

Marie Antoinette to Maria Theresa
Versailles, 15 March 1773

The assurance you give me about your health is a great good for me, especially at the beginning of Lent. It is very good luck that meatless meals don't upset you; I am observing Lent. I admit that I find meatless meals disgusting, but they do not make me ill. . . .

The marriage of the comte d'Artois with the comtesse de Provence's sister will be declared tomorrow. Ever since this marriage has been talked about, I have thought a great deal about the union which must exist between the two sisters; with prudence, and the help of M. le Dauphin, I hope not to be embarrassed by them. I realize that this rush to marry the comte d'Artois does not provoke very pleasant thoughts about my sister and myself;* but I must admit there are many other reasons: it is hoped to marry my sister† to the Prince of Piedmont. About this, M. le Dauphin and I were exposed to a dangerous strategem three weeks ago. M. de Boynes, the Minister of the Navy and a friend of M. d'Aiguillon's, had a message conveyed to us in the deepest secrecy, according to which he was the master of making the comte d'Artois marry either Mlle de Condé or the Princess of Savoy, adding that he would act only according to our preference. We neither of us hesitated to answer him that we were obliged to him, that we would always be happy with the King's decision, and that it was none of our business.

The King has told Lassone, my physician, that he thought M. le Dauphin and I were awkward and ignorant; he conversed very seriously about what ought to be done; finally

* Marie Antoinette means that since neither the comtesse de Provence nor she herself had been able to provide an heir, the comte d'Artois's marriage had become urgent.
† Mme Clotilde, one of the Dauphin's sisters, did in fact marry the heir to the Kingdom of Sardinia, which was ruled over by the House of Savoy.

he ordered him to instruct us both. M. le Dauphin came to my study so his attendants wouldn't know; he spoke without shyness and much sense. Lassone is very pleased and hopes for the best. . . .

I thank you, my dear Mama, for the music you sent me; it did not seem difficult to me and I played it immediately with one hand while waiting to learn it with the other.

They thought in Paris that we would return to the Opera Ball and ever since then it has been crowded, and the people of the Opera have earned a lot of money. I hope that next year we won't disappoint the public and go more than once. . . .

Mercy to Maria Theresa, 17 March 1773

HRH added that one of the ideas which affected her the most was the fear that the good relations between this Court and Your Majesty should be altered, that it would be for Mme la Dauphine the greatest of miseries, that she would have no such fear if M. le Dauphin had some authority or voice in the government, that she was quite sure of this Prince's feelings about the union of the two Courts, that she would have no difficulty in making him think the right way, and that she could flatter herself she had the kind of domination over her husband which he would never resist. . . .

This progress in Mme la Dauphine's reflections and ideas showed me that the time is nearing when it will become possible to speak to her usefully of the most important and serious topics.*

* The Empress promptly replied that Mercy was mistaken about this: Marie Antoinette, she said, was too empty-headed and silly.

Marie Antoinette to Maria Theresa
Versailles, 18 April 1773

It was high time that the courier arrived: I have been worried to death for the last four days. I have been amply repaid by seeing that my dear Mama is pleased with me; it is not altogether my fault as regards the King; I do try and please him and am happy enough to succeed sometimes, but it is not always possible to guess what he is thinking because, truth to tell, the people who surround him often make him change; still, if I am not mistaken, it seems to me the King is pleased with me.

It has been a month since I have had letters from the Brandis.* . . . Since the letters that come by post are given to me by my dame d'honneur, people noticed I was no longer receiving them, and it looked bad. I would be greatly obliged to you, my dear Mama, if you asked her to write more regularly.

M. le Dauphin gave excellent answers to Lassone when he spoke to him several times. He has a good constitution, he loves me and has good will, but he is of a nonchalance and laziness which he overcomes only at the hunt; I still have good hopes.

Eating no meat made me disgusted with Lent, but I have grown accustomed to it; my health has not been affected; I have even put weight on; I do not wish to put on any more. The wedding day of the comte d'Artois will be November 16; part of his Household was appointed yesterday; it will be just as numerous and composed of great names as that of the comte de Provence; still, there should be clever and reasonable people around my brother: although very amiable, he is awfully high-spirited. . . .

I am delighted that the Queen feels better; I hope that she will be clever enough to give us a boy. If I were happy

* Countess Brandis had been Marie Antoinette's governess.

enough to follow her example, I would hope that my dear Mama would help me with her advice in his education and would have the consolation of seeing him married; perhaps they will be all the healthier for coming late. . . .

Maria Theresa to Marie Antoinette
Vienna, 4 May 1773

I am sorry the delay in last month's courier had you worried; bad news always comes fast, and you may be sure that if something happened to the family or to me, we would send estafettes;* so in the future let your charming and tender heart be at peace about delays, which can easily happen . . . as for the correspondence with the Brandis, you will please leave it to the arrangement with the courier. The Emperor leaves the day after tomorrow and I go to Schönbrunn; but the improvements will be limited to small, inexpensive things—conveniences, really. The Emperor's trip will last much longer than three months; he will be gone for six, if he does everything he intends, especially that trip to Poland in October.

I am very pleased with the way you behaved about the comte d'Artois's Household; we are often gratuitously accused of actions we had not even imagined, since all we want, both for the good of our State and the public peace, is to maintain and tie even closer the alliance which continues so happily between us; and I admit that the recent rumor that we were allied to Russia shows how much the others want to end this good understanding. . . . The tale about the accident in the Toulon fleet, which all the ministers save

* Mounted couriers.

ours have been repeating so eagerly, upsets me because it will make France look bad.

Enough politics; Mercy is very pleased with the way you understand affairs of state; but you must also pay attention to them and use whatever means are necessary. When you follow Mercy's advice, you are really following mine since he has my trust and is greatly attached to your person and the alliance; he thinks in a French way as a good German. . . . The Queen worries me; she says she is so large and heavy at five months. That shouldn't be; she had a few signs of a miscarriage, but after she was bled, they stopped; even so, I am not reassured. I am not given the consolation, my dear daughter, of seeing you in this state. I admit it is the only thing which could make me want to prolong my more than sad days. . . .

Marie Antoinette to Maria Theresa
Versailles, 17 May 1773

We have been having sickness, but thank God all is well. M. le Dauphin had a sore throat and a light fever which only lasted three or four days; it is over and he is being purged today. There is a rumor here that M. le Dauphin is truly my husband, but that is not the case; I think his illness really hurt us because he was a little more forward than usual. It might all have been done earlier, but now it will be again greatly delayed. You may believe, my dear Mama, that I would take great pleasure in writing you, with the utmost eagerness, about so essential a point, since every day makes me aware of your love for me.

My aunt Victoire* had the measles and got through it

* One of Louis XV's daughters.

well; now she is only on a diet but must stay away from us for two weeks, which I regret.

I hope and wish the good understanding [between France and Austria] to continue; there is a good thing about ce pays-ci: it is that while rumors spread quickly, they vanish just as fast; but I think that M. d'Aiguillon is a little ashamed not to have taken better measures about the fleet in Toulon. . . .

My brothers are going to Paris next week for the [funeral] service of the King of Sardinia;* I hope that M. le Dauphin and I will make our official entry there next week—it would give me great pleasure. I daren't talk about it yet, although I have the King's promise; it wouldn't be the first time they made him change. The Emperor's departure frightens me, especially since he will be gone for such a long time.

The [military] parade which was to take place on Monday has been postponed to Thursday; I was sorry that M. le Dauphin was unable to go. It was a handsome sight; there was a huge crowd, since it took place just outside Paris. The King was very pleased with it.

I promise, if I am happy enough to have children, that I will pay more attention to their health and not follow my own opinion. We must hope that if my dear Mama is kind enough to start writing to the Infanta again, she will settle down and admit she was wrong.

You are at Schönbrunn, my dear Mama; how I wish I could take myself there! I would follow your steps during the evening walks; I would be better able to enjoy your good advice and to show you how my soul is full of respect and love for the best of mothers.

---

* The King of Sardinia was the father of the comtesses de Provence and d'Artois.

Madame my very dear Mother,

I am shamed by your many kindnesses. The day before yesterday, Mercy gave me your precious letter, and yesterday I received the second one; what a wonderful way to celebrate one's name day. Last Tuesday I had a fête which I will remember as long as I live; we made our official entry into Paris. As far as honors go, we were given every possible one; all that, although important, is not what touched me the most; it was the love and enthusiasm of the poor people who, in spite of taxes which weigh so heavily, were beside themselves with joy because they could see us. When we went for a walk in the Tuileries, there was such a crowd that for three quarters of an hour, we could move neither forward nor back. M. le Dauphin and I several times told the guards not to strike anyone, and that made a very good effect. Such good order obtained throughout the day that in spite of the huge number of people who followed us everywhere, no one was hurt. When we came back from our walk, we went on to an open terrace and stayed there for a half hour. I cannot describe to you, my dear Mama, the intensity of the joy and the love which were shown us at that moment. Before we left, we waved to the people, which greatly pleased them. How happy we are, in our condition, to earn the love of a people so easily! Nothing can be more precious: I felt it deeply and will never forget it.

Something else which pleased me greatly during that fine day was the behavior of M. le Dauphin. He answered all the speeches admirably, noticed everything that was being done for him, and especially the people's joy and enthusiasm, and he showed them much kindness. . . . We go tomorrow to the Opera in Paris; this is much desired, and I even think that we will go on two other days to the Comédies Française and Italienne.* I feel more strongly every day how much my dear Mama did to place me. I was the youngest of all and she treated me as if I were the eldest, so my soul is filled with the most loving gratitude.

The King has been kind enough to free 320 debtors from prison; they owed to the nurses who breast-fed their children; they were freed two days after our entry. . . .

I am very happy about Your Majesty's hope for the maintenance of the peace; while the intriguers of ce pays-ci devour one another, they will bother neither their neighbors nor their allies. I begin to be less worried about the Emperor's trip, since he has left the Banat in good health. I was pleased to see General Stein; I will be even happier to see Neny† because he can better give me news of my dear Mama. I wish Mme de Schwarzenberg could lend me a little of her fecundity. Thank God M. le Dauphin is still in good health, so I have hopes. The Queen's throwing up is upsetting; I hope that will stop as her pregnancy progresses; I very much hope she will give me a nephew. . . .

THE FACT that the Dauphine, who lived at Versailles, was only making her official entrance into Paris at the end of three years' residence in France is an eloquent comment on the distance which separated the Court from the people. Her very success with the Parisians only added to their mutual incomprehension. In 1773 Louis XV was unpopular and Mme du Barry was hated. When the people cheered Marie Antoinette, therefore, they were showing their hope for the future and underlining the contrast between the Dauphin's virtuous young wife and the former

* The Comédie Française performed French plays—by Corneille, Racine, Molière, Marivaux, Voltaire. The Comédie Italienne's specialty was *commedia dell'arte* and light farces.
† Maria Theresa's secretary.

prostitute. Unfortunately, as a result of her visit, Marie Antoinette believed that all she had to do in order to retain her popularity was to smile and be gracious. As she later found out, this was not the case, but she never understood that her day-to-day behavior, the money she spent so heedlessly, and her influence on government policy counted as well. It was thus with real surprise and indignation that upon being hissed in the mid-1780s, she asked, "But what have I done to them?" She was in Paris, she was smiling: what more could the people want?

Mercy to Maria Theresa, 16 June 1773

Nothing could be added to HRH's success on her entry into Paris; the public was seized with enthusiasm for Mme l'Archiduchesse . . . Wherever she went, she looked at the people with a smile; she greeted people of distinction; when, after her dinner, she went for a walk in the garden of the Tuileries, where, without exaggerating, there were more than fifty thousand souls, and where people had even climbed onto the trees, HRH gave the guards the order not to push the people away but to let them come as near as they wanted. . . . All one heard was applause and endlessly repeated exclamations: "How beautiful she is! How charming she is!"

Mercy to Maria Theresa, 17 July 1773

M. le Dauphin and Mme la Dauphine have been coming to Paris every week to see, one after the other, the shows at the Opera, the Comédie Française and the Comédie Italienne.

The King decided that on these first visits TRH* would appear with all the ceremony that would be used if the Monarch himself were there. In consequence, at each trip, the guns of the Bastille and the Invalides saluted. Two companies—one of the Gardes françaises, the other of the Swiss Guards—were on parade with their flags outside the theaters when TRH arrived. Two men of the Royal Bodyguard were on duty in front of the stage and a group of the Cent-Suisses was massed in a square under TRH's box. All this deployment which, by the awe it could have caused, might have dampened the public's joy, failed to have that effect, and it would be impossible to add to the demonstrations of pleasure, good will, and enthusiasm which the public displayed with all the vivacity customary to this nation. It was always to Mme la Dauphine that it was addressed, and I could fill volumes with the touching remarks made about the looks, the grace, the kind and open expression of Mme l'Archiduchesse. It is true that HRH let no occasion pass in which she could give proof of her qualities, and the people were immensely touched by her reiterated orders not to push away those who came close to her. . . . In a word, all throughout, Mme la Dauphine was so successful that there is practically no example or remembrance of another similar occasion. . . . This universal homage . . . has produced the double effect of pleasing the King and embarrassing the cabal.

Mercy to Maria Theresa, 17 July 1773

All the influence that HRH has on M. le Dauphin has still not altered his extraordinary taste for all building work, such as masonry, carpentry, and others of the kind . . . he

* Their Royal Highnesses.

works himself with the laborers, moves the materials, beams, and paving stones, and, spending hours at a time at this unpleasant occupation, he returns from it a hundred times more tired than the men he works with. I noticed recently that Mme la Dauphine was extremely annoyed and upset over this behavior.

Marie Antoinette to Maria Theresa, 17 July 1773

Madame my very dear Mother,

Only your satisfaction could add to the joy and the feelings I will have all my life for the way I was received in Paris. I will admit to my dear Mama that as we left for Compiègne, I felt a little sorry to go farther from that good city; it is true that I was moved to tears, especially at the Comédie-Italienne when the public and the actors shouted together, "Long live the King!"; Clerval, one of the actors, then added, "And his dear children!" and was very much applauded. I can compare that great day only to the one when my dear Mama came to the theater after the birth of my nephew in Florence.* Although I was still very young, I was fully aware that all hearts were moved by my beloved mother's presence. M. le Dauphin behaved beautifully every time he went to Paris and, if I say so myself, he made himself popular by the look of union between us; perhaps that is why people say he kissed me in public, although it is not true; but my dear Mama is very wrong to think he has never done so except when I arrived here; on the contrary, for a long time now, everybody has noticed the attentions he pays me. . . .

* The Empress had leaned over the front of her box and shouted, "Our Leopold has a son," an announcement which was greeted by cheers and rapturous applause.

One of the leading officers of the musketeers is back from Naples and keeps praising the Queen. You cannot imagine, my dear Mama, how much that pleases me; I hope that you are wrong about the time of her delivery, considering her size. . . .

I am impatient for the Emperor's return; I would rather he didn't see the King of Prussia. The abbé is at your feet; he was equally thrilled, for me and for his compatriots.* You are kind indeed, my dear Mama, to send me the list of Laxenburg; since I have no hopes of ever seeing my fatherland again, it is a great consolation for me to know what happens there.

Some people have tried, lately, to annoy us; thank God, the worst is over and we are no longer worried. M. le Dauphin's party and mine are such that they will never misbehave to the King or to us. . . .

Marie Antoinette to Maria Theresa, 13 August 1773

Madame my very dear Mother,

The presentation of the young Mme du Barry† went off very well. A minute before they came to me, I was told that the King had spoken neither to the aunt nor to the niece: I did the same. But still I can assure my dear Mama that I received them with great politeness: everybody who was there agreed that I looked neither embarrassed nor eager to see them leave; the King can surely not be displeased, for he was in a very good mood during the rest of the evening which he spent with us. The trip [to Compiègne] will end

* Marie Antoinette is referring to her reception in Paris. It is worth noticing that she considers the French are the abbé's compatriots, but not hers: she is still Austrian.
† The comtesse's niece by marriage.

much better than it might first have seemed; we hear nothing more about movements or intrigues; the union between us is perfect.

We have had three little fêtes at the marquise de Durfort's; we will have another next week; I very much hope it will not be so hot, especially for the dance, for it is today excessively hot.

I am delighted the Emperor is not having his meeting [with Frederick II], but I will only be completely reassured once he is back from his travels. I am sending him a word with this courier.

Mercy has already told me about Prince Louis [de Rohan]; his bad behavior causes me every kind of chagrin. It is even worse for this country, which he dishonors, than for Vienna, which he scandalizes; whenever Mercy thinks that the time has come, I will do what he asks, but I imagine that he will want to be careful, both because of Mme de Marsan and of M. de Soubises's favor.*

I am awaiting Neny with impatience. I am being painted, right now; it is true that no painter has yet caught the way I look: I would happily give all I own to anyone who could express in a portrait all the joy I would feel in seeing my dear Mama; how hard it is to be able to kiss her only by letter.

My husband is moved by your kindness; I hope that he will deserve it more.

---

* Although a churchman, Rohan behaved like the most pleasure-loving of aristocrats, drinking, gambling, and womanizing in public; he especially scandalized the Viennese by going hunting on Sundays when he should have been saying Mass. Mme de Marsan and M. de Soubise were close relatives high in Louis XV's favor.

Mercy to Maria Theresa, 14 August 1773

Mme la Dauphine understands politics with the greatest of ease, but she fears it excessively; she will not allow herself to think that she may one day have authority and power; as a result she is inclined to be passive and dependent on others. . . . HRH is afraid of speaking to the King; she fears the ministers; her attendants dominate her. And yet it is of the highest importance that Mme l'Archiduchesse better understand and evaluate her strengths. . . . Besides, M. le Dauphin, although he has common sense and some good qualities, will probably never have the strength or the will to reign by himself. If Mme l'Archiduchesse does not rule him, someone else will.

Maria Theresa to Marie Antoinette
Schönbrunn, 29 August 1773

Madame my dear daughter,

. . . I have never seen a happier delivery than that of the Queen; she is delighted with her little Louise; she thinks her pretty and more like our family than the eldest; she is much more reasonable than we about this,* but what upsets me still most is that she's bound to have a third daughter. As for you, my dear children, nothing is lost yet; you are just beginning, so you can wait; but I am coming to the end of my life, that is the difference, and that "nothing new" in your situation does not please me either.

You are quite right to have told the King about it;† if he had found out from others, he would rightly have been an-

* The Empress means she didn't mind having another daughter instead of a son.
† The Dauphine's reception in Paris.

noyed. The joy everywhere is incredible; it shows how loved you are, what happiness! Keep this as the most precious thing possible.

I cannot agree with you about your reception of the young du Barry. What you tell me of the King's good temper neither convinces nor reassures me, and, I must admit it, the difference between you and the comtesse de Provence on that occasion upset me, and I would not want the King to see this difference as I do. . . .

The courier* told me that he saw you riding at the gallop during the hunt. I don't hope it was only when you had your period; now that I must believe that you are a woman, I cannot be indifferent about it; and if I were the King, I would order you to be very moderate in taking this exercise. The Queen of Portugal stopped having children early, and it is thought for that reason only.

Maria Theresa to Mercy, 31 August 1773

I must tell you frankly that I do not wish my daughter to have a decided political influence. . . . I know how immature and frivolous she is, that she cannot apply herself and knows nothing. . . . I therefore cannot make myself write her about politics and the business of the State unless . . . you tell me *precisely* what I should tell her.

Marie Antoinette to Maria Theresa, 14 September 1773

Madame my very dear Mother,

I am quite delighted about your decision to go to Ester-

* Actually, it was Mercy, not the courier.

hazy; you should indeed indulge more often in these little amusements.

I followed Mercy's advice and talked to Mme de Marsan about the Coadjutor;* she is very upset about her relative's behavior; she has since then had a conversation with Mercy, who will write you about it; in any event Mme de Marsan seems pleased about the way I spoke to her, although I did not go into detail.

Although it is very reasonable on the Queen's part, I consider it very lucky that she should be so enchanted with her little Louise.

It is true that the courier saw me riding; but it was not at the hunt, where I rode only once, and even then it was a *chasse à vue*, which makes one go shorter distances than the other kind.

As for the young du Barry, I am sorry that my dear Mama should not be pleased with me; if she could see everything that happens here, she would realize that the King's good mood was sincere, and that the only times he wants one to be polite to them is when that cabal is tormenting him. As for my sister de Provence, I have never criticized her behavior; but my dear Mama will allow me to tell her confidently about some little differences between she and I: (1.) Her Italian character gives her resources† I lack; (2.) when she arrived here, the comte de Provence was deep in intrigue and wanted his wife to behave as she has; but, as for myself, on the contrary, M. le Dauphin would not have thought it right. . . .

When we returned from Compiègne, I longed to go back to Paris; I was right, we have been admirably received; I expect to go there again to see the paintings;‡ I lent that of my dear Mama which people are very eager to see.

* Prince Louis de Rohan.
† Italians were supposed to be good at intrigues and less than truthful.
‡ The yearly Salon at which the best paintings were shown.

The reconciliation with Parma is complete; it will be a great happiness if it lasts; I am sorry that my sister is not sufficiently aware of it to have written you about it right away; it can only be due to the shame and embarrassment she feels. . . .

Mercy to Maria Theresa, 16 September 1773

After having carefully thought about the best way [of having the prince de Rohan recalled from Vienna], I suggested a method which seemed the best for avoiding all drawbacks, and Mme la Dauphine has just applied it with all the success I expected. HRH, upon her return to Versailles, called for the comtesse de Marsan and told her she thought she was doing her a kindness by confiding in her that Your Majesty had reasons to be highly displeased with the prince de Rohan's behavior, particularly in the way he seems to forget the restraint implied in his position as a bishop; that because she was concerned for her, the comtesse de Marsan, and for the prince de Soubise,* Your Majesty had been good enough to conceal until now her annoyance at the Coadjutor's lack of decency, but that it might soon become impossible for Your Majesty to restrain yourself any longer on a question which involves your conscience and that then Your Majesty, although with regret, would have to confide in the King; that Mme la Dauphine, seeing the irreparable damage that might come to the prince de Rohan, had no hesitation in warning the comtesse de Marsan so that she could take the only measures still possible in order to save the Coadjutor, and which consist in speeding his recall as much as possible. The comtesse de Marsan seemed much alarmed by this; she begged Mme la Dauphine to tell her about the complaints

* The prince de Soubise was Mme de Marsan's brother and Rohan's uncle.

against the Coadjutor, but I had warned HRH to give no details and to tell her to speak to me about this. The very next day the prince de Soubise wrote to ask me for a rendezvous in Paris; having agreed on a time the following day, we had a conversation in which I pointed out to the prince that it was best for him not to allow his relative to remain in an embassy which might lose him his fortune and his reputation, while endangering his family. . . . We finally agreed that he will immediately ask for a holiday on which the prince de Rohan will return here and that once back a pretext will be found not to send him to Vienna again. . . . I have begged Mme la Dauphine to keep all this an absolute secret; HRH risked nothing and was not compromised in this undertaking which the Rohans consider as a mark of interest and kindness.

Marie Antoinette to Maria Theresa, 21 September 1773

Madame my very dear Mother,

I cannot possibly express how deeply I feel about your kindness;* at the moment Neny arrived, I was giving audience to the Ambassadress of Sardinia and to the whole diplomatic corps. What a joy, what glory for me to show so charming a mark of maternal love! Another great joy for me is that M. le Dauphin has shown Neny how much he respects my beloved mother. Neny will tell you what he saw here and in Paris; I do not want to delay his courier; never have respect and love filled a soul as they do mine. . . .

* The Empress had sent a jeweled flower.

Maria Theresa to Marie Antoinette
Schönbrunn, 3 October 1773

Your letters of the fifteenth and the twenty-first came only twelve hours apart. I am delighted that you are pleased with my flower and hope that you will recognize yourself on the pot; it arrived just in time to serve you before the diplomatic corps. I want the whole of Europe to know how much I love you and that my happiness is linked to my children's. I must admit that the Parma business gives me great pleasure; I only hope it will continue. I don't know whether you will dare to speak to the King and tell him how grateful I am to him, from me, knowing that he rendered us important services in Spain* through his kindness. What a good father he is! That is why I demand all the attentions, all the submission from you. . . .

My other complaint is not cleared up either . . . you are riding a great deal, especially at the hunt. . . .

I kept silent as long as there was no real marriage, but now that you tell me that everything is all right,† I must speak, and you must do what you promised. A married woman can never be sure she is not pregnant, and there is never more danger than during the first four weeks. You can't even know whether you are or not. I stress this, not to frighten you, but to jolt you into thinking seriously that this sport, if you go on living together as husband and wife, is highly unsuitable.

The example of the Queen of Naples must touch you and serve you as an example, and God has blessed her sacrifice, which, for her, is much greater than it can be for you, since she has few amusements in that country and you are always in the midst of fine people and entertainments. I am still

* Louis XV had helped reconcile the Infante with his uncle, the King of Spain.
† The Empress had misunderstood.

pleased to see that you are so pleased with your visits to Paris; the Queen,* the late Dauphine,† and your aunts never went, and the King is willing to condescend to it all because it pleases his little Dauphine; how much gratitude you owe him! He grants you your wishes; do the same for him.

. . . I am very pleased with the care and attentions you had for your sick aunt;‡ that is the right behavior and shows you have a good heart. Since you spoke to Mme de Marsan, that is excellent, and I am obliged to you; I hope that the effect [of the conversation] will answer. . . .

Mercy to Maria Theresa, 12 November 1773

On October 16, Mme la Dauphine was following the King at the hunt in an open carriage when there occurred a very untoward event. The stag, closely pursued by the dogs, jumped into an enclosed garden which its owner was then working. The animal, who could see no exit, became enraged, ran to the peasant, and gored him twice, once in the thigh, the other in the body, leaving him mortally wounded. . . . The wretched man's wife, . . . seized with despair, ran toward a group of hunters she could see in the distance; it was the King and his suite. She shouted for help, announcing her husband's accident and, at that moment, fell down in a faint. The King ordered that she be taken care of and, having given marks of compassion and kindness, rode on; then Mme la Dauphine, who had returned, got out of her carriage, ran toward the woman, and held some perfume to her nose, which made her come out of her faint. Mme la Dauphine gave her all the money she had with her,

* Marie Leczinska, Louis XV's wife, had died in 1767.
† The Dauphin's mother, Marie-Josèphe of Saxony.
‡ Mme Victoire, who had just had measles.

but what was even more admirable was the kind and consoling way in which HRH talked to the poor creature. Finally, Mme l'Archiduchesse, who was touched, moved, shed tears and, at that moment, caused more than a hundred spectators to do the same. . . . Then, having called for her carriage, Mme la Dauphine gave orders that the peasant woman be taken in it back to her cottage which was in a neighboring hamlet.* HRH waited right there for her carriage to return; she asked about the care taken of the wounded man. . . . I cannot describe to Your Majesty the greatness or intensity of the sensation caused by this event, not only among the courtiers, but even more among the people of Fontainebleau. . . . The public in Paris . . . seems very moved; whenever Mme l'Archiduchesse's name comes up, it evokes a universal cry of joy and admiration.

. . . At my last audience with Mme la Dauphine, she told me about a very interesting conversation she had had with M. le Dauphin. They were talking about the arrival, within a short time, of the comtesse d'Artois, and of the sensation at Court and in the public if that princess were to become pregnant before Mme l'Archiduchesse. M. le Dauphin was the first to broach the subject; then, kissing Mme la Dauphine, he said to her, "But do you love me?" HRH answered, "Yes, you cannot doubt it, I love you sincerely and respect you even more." The young Prince seemed very moved by these words; he caressed Mme la Dauphine most tenderly and told her that upon returning to Versailles he would go back to his regimen and that he hoped "that all would go well."

* Normally only a few, well-defined categories of courtiers could ride in the royal carriages.

Mercy to Maria Theresa, 9 January 1774

The [newly married] comte d'Artois is visibly fiery, haughty, and inconsiderate. He has already earned several strong reprimands from M. le Dauphin for having forgotten on several occasions the respect he owes his eldest brother. In such cases Mme la Dauphine always intervenes to make peace between them, and toward M. le comte d'Artois she has been using the best possible method: she makes fun of the young Prince whenever he does or says something unreasonable. This mortifies him . . . so Mme la Dauphine is the only one he fears . . . as for the comtesse d'Artois, she does not speak, seems interested in nothing, and her look of shyness and indifference is highly unpopular here. Mme la Dauphine is very kind to her . . . but the comtesse d'Artois can never have any importance here.

Maria Theresa to Marie Antoinette
Vienna, 3 April 1774

You should now have Lacy* paying court to you if his health allows; he is coming to Paris only to see you, since he doesn't like being a courtier, and even less the vivacity of the French. He deserves to be well treated; he is very attached to me, and I feel only too much the void that his absence causes in every way. I wish he were better; I am very much afraid he has lost his health because of his overwork and his many wounds.

M. d'Esterhazy has behaved very badly in every way. I don't mean only because he fought [a duel] against the orders of his Sovereign and of God, but the cause is even more horrible: he is married but keeping another man's wife and

* Marshal Lacy was one of Austria's best generals.

has spent a hundred thousand florins on her, which cannot be excused. It has already been two weeks since the Chancellor, his uncle, has sent him orders to come right back; in the [Austrian] Netherlands similar occasions would constantly recur; it is time he came to do his duty. I know that you have been kind to him, it is typical of your kind heart; but unfortunately a Sovereign cannot follow her inclinations; most of the time you must act against them. That is my painful and unpleasant situation, and over time it makes our job unbearable and even dangerous.

Your situation is so brilliant that people must envy you, and they will waste no opportunity to harm you; you must therefore behave very cautiously. Since, my dear daughter, I think of nothing but your happiness, I wish I could ensure it even at the cost of my life.

Mercy to Maria Theresa, 8 May 1774

In so critical and delicate a moment as this,* Mme la Dauphine has behaved like an angel, and I cannot sufficiently express my admiration for her piety, her prudence, and her reason; the public is delighted with her. . . .

She must, in order to ensure her happiness, start taking over the authority that M. le Dauphin will only wield in the most precarious manner.

Mercy to Maria Theresa, 10 May 1774

The King was already near death yesterday; he received the Last Rites in the evening and has breathed his last this after-

* Louis XV was suffering from smallpox and was thought not likely to live.

noon between three and four. He remained conscious and gave to the last every sign of a truly Christian penitence and piety.

All here is in the greatest confusion. The royal family will go to Choisy, Mesdames will stay there in a separate house. . . . We must see first whether and how far the King will consult the Queen. It would be dangerous for her to look as if she wanted to interfere in the government before she is asked to do so.

O N MAY 10, 1774, around four in the afternoon, the Dauphin and Dauphine stood alone in a room overlooking one of the Versailles courtyards; then, suddenly, a candle burning in a window opposite was snuffed out, and outside the door a thunderous roar was heard to come rapidly closer: the Court, en masse, was rushing to pay homage to their new King and Queen, but when the doors were opened, they saw Louis XVI and Marie Antoinette, sobbing, on their knees, and heard them saying, "Protect us, Lord, we are too young to reign!"

They were perfectly right. The twenty-year-old King knew nothing about government; the nineteen-year-old Queen was both unwilling and unable to perform the ceremonial duties which devolved upon her; and within a matter of days they both demonstrated their incompetence. At first, aware that he was too raw to select new ministers, Louis XVI had intended to retain his grandfather's ministry until he was more familiar with affairs, but Marie Antoinette convinced him they must go immediately: after all, they were the "creature's" friends. In a quandary the King decided to send for M. de Machault, who had been living in the country for some fifteen years after once having been Louis XV's minister, on the sole grounds that the late Dauphin, the new King's father, had approved of him. At that point, Madame Adélaïde, who was not yet in quarantine, intervened and convinced her nephew to send for the comte de Maurepas instead.

It would be difficult to imagine a more grotesque choice. In his heyday Maurepas had never been more than a mediocre minister whose one talent was for writing the nastiest kind of scurrilous verse. Mesdames had liked him because he had been one of the linchpins of the anti-Pompadour party. Now, after some twenty years of exile, he reappeared at Court, somewhat quieter—he was seventy-three—but just as frivolous. And when eventually Louis XVI started to make better choices—Turgot, the great administrator and reformer became Finance Minister and Vergennes, Foreign Minister—Maurepas helped see to it that Turgot was fired.

On her own, too, Marie Antoinette showed she was not prepared to behave like a queen. When, for instance, the old ladies of the Court came to pay their visit of condolence, they noticed that their new Sovereign was laughing at them. Not unnaturally, the dowagers thought they were being ridiculed. In fact Marie Antoinette, very ill-advisedly, was laughing at the antics of one of her ladies who was sitting on the floor hidden by the wide-hooped skirts of her colleagues. The Queen had not meant to offend; she had merely been careless—but the results were immediate. Within days a song was circulating in Paris: "Petite reine de vingt ans,/ Vous qui traitez si mal les gens/Vous repasserez la barrière" ("Little twenty-year-old Queen,/You who treat people so badly,/You will recross the border").

Far more serious, Marie Antoinette soon started to spend money as if the treasury were a bottomless well. Already at Choisy she asked Louis XVI for a country house of her own, something no Queen of France had ever had before; and he gave her the Petit Trianon. She then enclosed its park, which had been open to the public, and proceeded to remodel it at great expense. She was seen to buy quantities of diamonds when she already had the crown jewels at her disposal. She saw to it that her friends, and her friends' friends, were given offices, grants, and pensions—all this at a time when the government ran a steady and alarming deficit. And as if to make it all more visible, she developed a passion for clothes. Soon coiffures, topped with plumes and other adornments, soared to unparalleled heights—some two to three feet—while the hooped skirts worn by the fashionable grew enormously wide. With the help of Mlle Bertin, her favorite designer, the Queen was soon spending more than twice her yearly clothes allowance of 150,000 livres ($675,000).

Even that might have been forgiven if she had proved herself the kind of ruler for which people yearned. Because of two earlier incidents—the run-over coachman and the gored peasant—in which she had reacted quickly and charitably, she was widely thought to be compassionate, and in truth she was, if the sufferer was right under her eyes; but she took absolutely no interest in the charities a Queen was expected to protect and was quickly seen to care for nothing but her own amusement. That a spirited young woman of nineteen who ruled over the most glamorous Court in Europe should want to have fun was perhaps not very surprising; what did startle people was that she thought of nothing else and, while remaining strictly chaste, seemed mad for amusements of all kinds while only paying attention to serious matters when she had a grudge to satisfy or a friend to push. Normally the King would have been expected to set limits on his wife's almost hysterical need for entertainment; but, as everyone quickly realized, Louis XVI was far too weak, far too dependent on her ever to do so.

In this case, however, there was a good hidden reason for the Queen's behavior; her frenzy was the direct consequence of her husband's sexual incompetence. An exact description of Louis XVI's problem will be found in Joseph

II's letter to his brother Leopold (see page 218); there can be no doubt that Louis's halfhearted but repeated attempts must have been extremely frustrating for Marie Antoinette. This marital problem also helps explain Louis XVI's compliance with her every wish as a compensation for his failure in bed.

As Queen, Marie Antoinette found herself caught in an even more complex set of rules than when she was still the Dauphine. "When I speak of etiquette," Mme Campan wrote, "I do not refer to that majestic order which obtains in every Court on days of ceremony. I speak of the detailed rules which pursued our monarchs in their most private moments, in their times of suffering and pleasure, and even in their most repulsive infirmities.

"These servile rules had become a kind of code; they caused a Richelieu, a La Rochefoucauld, a Duras to find, in the discharge of their servantlike functions, occasions which furthered their fortunes; and they liked . . . the custom which made the right of giving a glass of water, putting on a chemise, or taking away a chamber pot into an honorable prerogative." In fact, as Marie Antoinette soon discovered, she was always on duty; but far from adapting to this, she changed the rules instead, thus infuriating all the people who considered they had a right to serve her and be close to her. Noble ladies who had intrigued long and hard to be part of her Household suddenly found themselves frozen out; courtiers who had the entrées and could therefore expect to see the Queen often discovered that she spent most of her time in her private apartments and was unavailable to all except her particular friends. Of course they resented it and let it be known that Marie Antoinette was lazy and self-indulgent. They were believed all the more easily because the public, too, was rapidly losing its chance of seeing the Queen. It had long been the custom, for instance, that members of the royal family dined in public where any decently dressed person could come and watch them; Louis XV, in particular, was famous for the elegance with which he ate his soft-boiled eggs. As Dauphine, Marie Antoinette had been forced to observe this custom; as Queen, she promptly put a stop to it so that, more and more, she lived the life of a private person. Worse, as she grew fonder of Trianon, she began spending more and more time there, away from the Court, the Ambassadors (whom she was supposed to receive every Tuesday), and the public.

All this was seen, quite rightly, as a dereliction of duty: Marie Antoinette obviously wanted all the fun of being Queen, but would do none of the work that went with the position.

When Louis XV died, he was extremely unpopular. The accession of young, well-meaning monarchs was therefore greeted with an explosion of joy. All the popularity Marie Antoinette had enjoyed as Dauphine was suddenly multiplied tenfold. Very quickly, however, people realized that their Queen simply meant to indulge herself, and that early popularity declined—slowly at first; then, by 1778, very rapidly indeed. By 1780 she was already widely hated for her selfishness, her spendthrift habits, her favorites—Mmes de Lamballe and de Polignac—and her interference in government policy; a perfect example of the latter appears at the time of the War of the Bavarian Succession.* Not only did Marie Antoinette force the King to modify his position very substantially, she also called in the ministers repeatedly and treated them like disobedient servants. They did not like it, the public didn't either: the popular young Queen, in six short years, had become *l'Autrichienne, Madame Déficit*, the most hated woman in France.

* See page 250 ff.

Marie Antoinette to Maria Theresa
Choisy, 14 May 1774*

Madame my very dear Mother,

Mercy has written you the details of our loss; happily that cruel disease left the King with a clear head until the last moment, and his end has been very edifying. The new King [Louis XVI] seems to have his people's welfare at heart; two days before the death of the grandfather, he had 200,000 francs distributed to the poor, and this was much admired. Since the death, he is always working and answering the ministers in his own hand, since he cannot yet see them,† and he also attends to many other letters. What is sure is that he has a taste for economy and the greatest desire to make his people happy. In all he has as much desire as need to learn; I hope that God will bless his good will.

The public expected great changes immediately; the King has merely sent the creature‡ to a convent and all who bear that scandalous name away from the Court. The King himself owed this to the people of Versailles which, at the very time of the accident [i.e., the death] jeered at Mme de Mazarin, one of the favorite's humblest servants.

I am much asked to advise the King to be merciful to a great number of corrupt souls who have done much harm in the last few years. I am much inclined to do so; but, as I think of all this, I cannot help remembering Esterhazy's fate. I think Your Majesty has been angered by reports which are false on some points and exaggerated on others. It is true he was very wrong; but, still, everyone agrees that he is a man of honor and probity and that there is every reason to hope that once he is away from the temptations of that

---

* The new King and Queen had moved to the little castle of Choisy, just outside Paris, to avoid contagion.

† The ministers, having seen the late King during his illness, were contagious.

‡ Mme du Barry.

dangerous country and living in the midst of his family, he will behave well. On the contrary I fear that if he is treated with all the severity he deserves, his head will not yet be so in place that he will avoid some new mistake. I realize that carrying the weight of government, you must be just; I only wish you not to turn completely against Esterhazy.*

I am just this moment forbidden to visit my aunt Adélaïde, who has a high fever and back pains: we fear it may be smallpox. I tremble and dare not think of what may happen; how dreadful it is merely to be paying the price, and so soon, of her sacrifice.† I am delighted that Marshal Lacy was pleased with me. I will admit to my dear Mama that I was deeply affected when he came to take his leave because it made me think of how seldom I see my compatriots, especially those who are happy to be close to you. . . .

The King is leaving me free to choose for the new offices in my Household as Queen. I had the pleasure of giving the Lorraine family‡ a mark of attention by taking the abbé de Sabran as my First Almoner; he is a man of high birth, good behavior, and has just been appointed to the See they're creating at Nancy. Although God caused me to be born in the rank I now occupy, I cannot resist admiring the arrangements of Providence who chose me, the youngest of your children, for the greatest kingdom in Europe. I feel more than ever how much I owe to the love of my august mother, who took such care and worked so hard to put me in this superb place. I have never wanted more to put myself at her feet, kiss her, show her my whole soul so that she may see how full it is of respect, love, and gratitude.

* That Marie Antoinette should have defended Esterhazy, who amused her, with such fervor, is perhaps not surprising; but that she should do so at this particular time reveals how deeply she cared about the least of her pleasures.
† Madame Adélaïde, who had never had smallpox and was, therefore, not immune, nursed her father with exemplary devotion.
‡ Marie Antoinette's father, Francis I, was a member of the elder branch of the Lorraine family.

P.S. The abbé is at your feet; his respect and gratitude for your kindness are equalled only by his attachment for me.

[In Louis XVI's own hand.]

I am very glad to seize this occasion, my dear Mama, to prove my love and attachment to you. I would much like to have your advice at this very difficult time. I would be very glad to please you and thus show you my great attachment and my gratitude for your granting me your daughter with whom I couldn't be more pleased.

[In Marie Antoinette's hand, again.]

The King would not let my letter go without adding a word of his own.* I realize he would not have done too much by writing you a separate letter; I beg my dear Mama to forgive him, because of the press of business, of which he takes great care, and also his natural shyness and awkwardness. You see, my dear Mama, by the end of his note that although he loves me very much, he does not spoil me with compliments.

Mercy to Maria Theresa, 17 May 1774

This is a decisive moment for the Queen's happiness. She has never nor will ever need her august mother's advice so badly; but Your Majesty will know the best way to express this advice. Some may only require a kind and friendly tone; some may need to bear the stamp of a mother's authority. Until now the Queen has feared being scolded (that is her

---

* In fact, Marie Antoinette dictated every word of the King's message—he had not thought of writing anything.

expression) about the minor matters of her occupations or amusements. Your Majesty will deign to decide whether now an easy, indulgent tone would not be preferable for these topics. . . .

The Queen knows Mesdames her aunts, their incapacity, the power and danger of their followers; she knows exactly how to appraise them; yet because of her sweet, sensitive, and slightly lazy nature, the Queen, when she is touched, can easily give Mesdames undertakings which will be abused in the most pernicious manner. Thus it is that to my great sorrow Mesdames managed to convince the Queen that they should be allowed to move to Choisy after the late King's death, when it had first been decided, on my advice, that Mesdames would go to Trianon and would remain away from the King and Queen for some time.* Now the results are just what I expected: Mesdames immediately interfered in matters of government, gave advice, suggested sending for the comte de Maurepas, and the Queen, because she is so easy, brought to the King the ideas expressed by Mesdames, or more accurately, by the intriguers who lead them. If in these early moments the King allows himself to be dominated, and the public realizes that it is Mesdames who are really in charge, the Queen's reputation will suffer a deadly blow.

. . . The King, who has, I think, some solid qualities, has no amiability. He is rough; politics may even cause him moments of bad temper. The Queen must learn to bear with this; her happiness depends on it. She is loved by her husband; with moderation, kindness, and caresses she will gain absolute control of the King; but she must rule him without seeming to do so.

It is most important that the Queen never sleep separately

* Mesdames, who had helped care for their father, had been exposed to smallpox, which neither Louis XVI nor Marie Antoinette had ever had; they were thus contagious.

from the King. . . . It is essential that Your Majesty mention this in your letters.

Maria Theresa to Marie Antoinette
Saxenburg, 18 May 1774

Yesterday at eight o'clock at night came the sad courier
which we had been awaiting since the tenth. I will miss this
Prince, my friend, and your good and loving father-in-law
all my life. I also admire the grace of God, who gave the
King time to have recourse to His divine mercy, and the
words of the Grand Almoner, spoken for the King,* cannot
be read without tears and the hope of his salvation. . . . You
are both very young, the burden is heavy; I worry, really
worry, about it. If in a similar case, your adorable father had
not sustained me, I could never have managed, and I was
older than either of you. All I can say and wish is that you
rush nothing: see with your own eyes, change nothing, allow everything to continue as it is; [otherwise] there would
be insurmountable chaos and intrigues, and you, my dear
children, would be so confused that you could never manage. I speak from experience; what other reason do I have to
tell you especially to listen to Mercy's advice? . . . Right
now you must consider him as much your minister as mine;
in fact the two go very well together.† . . .

P.S. I hope never to hear again about the poor Barry,
whom I defended only as much as your respect for your
father and her sovereign demanded. I hope only to hear her

* "Gentlemen, the King has asked me to tell you that he begs God's forgive-
ness for having offended him, and for the scandal he caused his people [a
reference to Mme du Barry]; if God gives him health, he will look to penitence, to sustaining our religion, and to relieving his people."
† What Maria Theresa is saying here, quite simply, is that Louis XVI had
better let her govern France as well as Austria. . . .

name to learn that the King has treated her kindly, by sending her with her husband far from the Court and helping her as much as it suits him and humanity requires.*

FOR MARIA THERESA, Louis XV's death was a great opportunity. With her daughter on the throne, she could hope to control French policy: Mercy had left her in no doubt of the new King's subjugation to his wife. Against this happy prospect, however, she set her poor opinion of Marie Antoinette; she therefore began a series of admonitions concerning the solidity of the alliance and the state of Europe (always menacing, according to the Empress). All this was usually couched in language more appropriate to a love letter ("Any diminution would kill me") than to politics, and it worked. Although Mercy frequently complains about the Queen's frivolity and her lack of follow-through, her passionate devotion to Austria was never in doubt.

Maria Theresa to Marie Antoinette
Schönbrunn, 30 May 1774

You will have seen our worry by the courier sent on the twenty-sixth because we had no news since the terrible day of the tenth. The King's Ambassador having given us his notification, we rushed to send the courier off the next day with our answers, and we will go on sending one off on the first and the sixteenth; I am very anxious to have your real news, and alarming rumors cause unbearable worries. They said that the King was ill, that Mesdames Sophie and Adé-

---

* After a few months, Mme du Barry was allowed to leave the convent in which she had been confined; she settled in her house at Rueil, outside Paris, and lived there happily.

laïde were seized with the same illness. Nothing would be more natural for these two Princesses since they looked after the King;* but nothing could be more frightening than to know that the King, too, was suffering from it.† God preserve us from this! In him lies the consolation and hope of his people, his allies, his family. I cannot tell you how touched I was when I read the lines which the King wrote at the end of your letter; I prefer that cordiality to everything; and his attention in telling me that he is pleased with my dear daughter and that he thought about me in the very first moments of his difficult situation—all that moved me to tears. He even says he would like some advice; how respectable that is for someone his age! He will find it if he doesn't rush anything. Let him make it clear that he only wishes for the public good to be the father of his people, and that those who suggest means of achieving it will be heeded and rewarded, that he wants to learn by himself; if he doesn't trust those who are now at the head of the ministries, after due consideration, let him take those he thinks the cleverest as long as they are good Christians and even have moral virtues. . . . We are luckily at peace, so there is no urgency. France has enormous resources. There are terrible abuses, but they give the King more resources, for by suppressing them, he can earn for himself his people's blessing. That is a fair and grand prospect. . . .

I speak now to the King's trusted friend, who must think only of his success, and of fully deserving his trust. I hope that those who were exiled from Court will, at this glorious moment, be forgiven and that Choiseul and his sister will be among them; but I cannot help recommending to you one particular person: that is Durfort, who represented the King

* Maria Theresa is being confusing: the King whom Mesdames attended is Louis XV; the King for whose health she fears is Louis XVI.
† If Louis XVI had died of smallpox, he would have been succeeded by his brother, the comte de Provence, and Marie Antoinette would have been sent home.

here at that great moment of your marriage. . . . he has received no favor; he is honest, virtuous, and attached, as he should be, to his master; and he did very well here. I think you owe him some gratitude and should ask the King to confer some distinction or favor on him. . . .

Our two monarchies only need quiet to arrange their business. If we remain tightly linked, no one will trouble us and Europe will enjoy all the happiness of its tranquillity. . . . Mercy can tell you about everything that relates to general policies: I will keep him abreast of everything. Since my style and my writing are not the best, since my arms and my eyes often refuse to serve, I will have to use another hand in the future. You will excuse the spots and the corrections in this; I had to write it three separate times, and the wind threw it twice to the ground. You know the winds I have in my rooms. All the letters, all the gazettes even that I have read to me right now, when it comes to France, are full of praise for the King's wonderful actions; that of the 200,000 francs will always redound to his honor.

The choice the King allowed you in your Household is just as successful; I congratulate you; especially what you say about the Lorraine family is touching and right. *Only the choice of Maurepas surprises, but it is explained by Mesdames' influence.* * I cannot tell you how surprised I am that they were allowed into Choisy without the least precaution; if they catch smallpox, I certainly hope you won't stay there another day. Great God! How horrible that would be! I beg you (if, God forbid, it should happen) to use all your love and even all your authority to make the King leave right away: the others may follow, *but no aunts.*

You ask me again about Esterhazy: the longer he delays obeying my orders, the worse his case. First he must submit; then the punishment will not be so terrible; but he must

* Madame Adélaïde, actually. The Empress was right to show her surprise: Maurepas was a disastrous choice. The italics are hers.

behave properly. I cannot help contrasting your great protection for this young man who misbehaved gravely three times, and your rigor to the family and friends of that poor woman.* . . .

Mercy to Maria Theresa, 7 June 1774

HM† often sees in her *cabinets*‡ the princesse de Lamballe, née princesse de Carignan;** she is sweet, pleasant, no intriguer, and quite without drawbacks. For some time already, the Queen has felt real friendship for this young Princess and her choice is an excellent one because Mme de Lamballe, though a Piedmontese, is not at all close to Madame†† or the comtesse d'Artois. I have still taken the liberty of pointing out to the Queen that her inclination and her kindness to Mme de Lamballe demanded some moderation so as to prevent any abuses.

. . . There are always a great many people at the gates of the château [of Choisy] as well as in the Bois de Boulogne at the hours when it is thought the Queen might walk there. On those occasions HM never fails to give the public marks of the most touching kindness, and all are delighted.

* Mme du Barry.
† Her Majesty (Marie Antoinette).
‡ The *cabinets* were the Queen's private apartments.
** The princesse de Lamballe, born in the House of Savoy, was widowed, her husband, a distant relation of the royal family, having died of syphilis. She was famous for her complexion, her fair hair, her sweetness, and her extraordinary stupidity.
†† When the Dauphin became King, the comte de Provence, as the next oldest brother, took the appellation of Monsieur, with no name. His wife was Madame.

I cannot tell you how heartened and pleased I am about everything I hear about you; the whole world is ecstatic. They are right, too: a King of twenty and a Queen of nineteen, all their actions are full of humanity, generosity, prudence, and wisdom. Religion, decent living, which are so necessary to draw God's blessing and contain the people, are not forgotten; in a word my heart is overjoyed, and I pray God to preserve you for the good of your people, for the world, for your family, and for your old Mama to whom you give a new life. I say nothing about the choice of ministers, which everyone finds proper. I am very pleased about the dismissal of d'Aiguillon and la Vrillière without a *lettre de cachet*, * that hard method which had until now been the custom in France, and I like, my dear children, to see you always popular, respected, and full of kindness. . . . The King's generosity about Trianon,† which I hear is the pleasantest of houses, pleases me greatly, and what you tell me about the [late] King's will seems fine to me. Much hope rests on the millions which should be found in the King's strongbox; all that will ease the King's generous intentions. The refusals of the *don gratuit* and of the Queen's Belt‡ are worthy of you, and the Queen's quip that belts are no longer worn pleased me. Your three aunts' cure, after their admirable behavior in not leaving their father and thus risking smallpox, which they actually caught, has moved the whole world; but where I cannot remain silent and must beg you,

* The duc d'Aiguillon, Minister of War, and the duc de la Vrillière, Minister of the King's Household, had been dismissed but not exiled as was the custom. The *lettre de cachet* was a written order exiling or imprisoning its recipient.
† As an accession present, Louis XVI gave Marie Antoinette the Petit Trianon and the section of the Versailles park surrounding it.
‡ Two taxes usually offered new monarchs, which Louis XVI and Marie Antoinette had remitted.

it is not to let them come close to the King for ten weeks. . . . The strain of smallpox in France seems even more dangerous than the one we have here, and the House of Bourbon has too many bad memories;* thus no precaution can be excessive. . . .

This is the first courier I send you; it will be no inconvenience to me. I am too happy to receive your news, but if it tires you, just let me know, and I will put it off by a month. Treat me not just as your loving mother but as your intimate friend. I missed sending you wishes for your name day by the last courier; but it is every day, almost every hour that I wish you well, and on that day in particular I prayed for you. I will not answer the King so that he doesn't have to be bothered replying to my answer. If he wants to write me more often, and if it doesn't bother him, try to arrange it so that it will be like you, quite informally. I will do the same. Remember what I said in my last letter, try to be the King's trusted friend; all depends on that, your happiness and his. You have known how to make him loved by the public, how to make him amiable; you must continue the same way. The reason I told you often not to meddle in recommending appointments was that I thought your kindness was a danger, and that by nonchalance or laziness, as you say yourself, you might be fooled by others. Now that the choices are made, now that the King has a ministry, I am no longer worried, and you would make a great mistake and disappoint us if you were to withdraw altogether. You made such good choices in your Household, with the King's permission, that you will do well to go on the same way. In France it is quite different from the way we are here, and you would be as mistaken in not interfering as you would be here if you did.† . . .

* Louis XV's grandfather, mother, father, and brother had died of smallpox.
† Maria Theresa could hardly be more blunt!

Mercy to Maria Theresa, 20 June 1774

. . . As for the King's trust in the Queen, the ease with which she can learn everything, suggest her ideas and have the King act on them, there is nothing to be desired in this important matter. The Queen is moving surely toward the greatest influence which she can use successfully whenever she wants. The ministers are beginning to realize that this is the case. They are all, especially the comte de Maurepas, eager to be in the Queen's good graces.

Marie Antoinette to Maria Theresa
Marly, 27 June 1774

We have been here since Friday week; the King, my brothers, and the comtesse d'Artois were inoculated [against smallpox] on Saturday; since then they have missed taking a walk at least two or three times a day. The King had a rather high fever for three days; on the day before yesterday the eruption started and the fever went down so that it is now quite gone. He will not have many pustules, but he has some very remarkable ones on his nose, on the wrists, and chest; they are already beginning to turn white. They [the doctors] have made four small incisions; these little openings are suppurating properly, which showed the doctors that the inoculation was completely successful. The other three are a little less advanced, but the eruption has started and they feel very well.

My dear Mama's letter has rejoiced my soul; I can only be happy if she is pleased with me. All goes on very well here: my aunts came last night; since the eruption is well out, the doctors are not worried. The late King's strongbox contained much less than people thought; it only had some

50,000 francs, which makes 20,000 florins. I told the King about my dear Mama's affection for him; he is deeply moved and very grateful. . . .

Maria Theresa to Marie Antoinette
Schönbrunn, 1 July 1774

Madame my dear daughter,

You can imagine how worried I have been about the King. Much as I am in favor of inoculation, which has saved three sons and six grandsons to me, so I worry to see it undertaken at the hottest time of the year and on the three brothers at once. Thank God you had nothing to do with deciding this, although most of the letters say you did; that you should have been delighted is suitable; but I fear you must have been terribly worried. Much as this decision honors the King's personal character, it also makes one tremble for this precious life of a Prince from whom France and Europe expect universal happiness. . . . Choiseul's pardon* pleased me for the King and even the alliance. I am flattered that even those who don't think like you have found this return to Court suitable and right. I still await a few favors for Durfort, although I agree with those who say that his was a purely formal role;† but even that requires some reward. You will receive a letter through Rohan, who made his farewell visit to us yesterday. I must in fairness say that he has much improved over the last few months, but I must admit I am not sorry about the change and hope that the King will not leave Georgel here as charge d'affaires much longer.

* Choiseul had been exiled to his castle of Chanteloup ever since December, 1770. Louis XVI allowed him to return to Court but greeted him coldly.
† Durfort, an Ambassador Extraordinary, had done nothing more than ceremonial work after the Franco-Austrian marriage had been arranged.

I give you no news from here; my head and heart are full of nothing but inoculation. I count on the poor, who pray to God ardently at the Capuchin convent and at the Queen's convent, where I intend to have a *Te Deum* if God grants us the cure of *unseres werthen Königs:* a little German so you won't forget it. I kiss you.

Marie Antoinette to Maria Theresa
Marly, 1 July 1774

Madame my very dear Mother,

The inoculation is completely over; the King only suffered while he had a fever which tired him and made him feel low for two days. He will be purged tomorrow; I expect the doctors to write a report on everything that's happened. . . .

For some time now I have been thinking much about my brother Maximilian. They told me he had come to Dunkirk. I could not know that he was so close without wanting to see him. I would never have dared here, being too close to Paris, but if we had been at Compiègne, I don't know whether I could have stopped myself from inviting him to visit us for a few days. Would it be possible for him to go there from Brussels without also going to Paris? We will be at Compiègne from the first days of August to the beginning of September.

You see, my dear Mama, how freely I use your permission to treat you as a friend, in thus speaking freely to you of my dreams. . . .

[In Louis XVI's hand.]

Like my wife, I assure you, my dear Mama, that I am completely over the inoculation and that I suffered very little. I would ask for your permission to kiss you if my face were cleaner.

Mercy to Maria Theresa, 2 July 1774

Mesdames' return to Court has not made any great difference so far. They are behaving very quietly and Madame Adélaïde seems much less inclined to interfere in everything. The Queen has received Mesdames her aunts with good grace and a friendly tone, but in such a way as to show that the time of their domination is over.

Mercy to Maria Theresa, 15 July 1774

The Queen's friendship for the princesse de Lamballe gave rise to the rumor that the latter would be appointed Superintendent of HM's Household. This possibility alarmed the comtesse de Noailles.* She mentioned this to me, and I reassured her after ascertaining that the Queen had no thought of doing this.

The Queen alone is responsible for the duc d'Aiguillon's dismissal [from the foreign ministry]. . . . The King had intended to keep this minister for a long time still; it is only because of the Queen's daily and pressing requests that he

---

* The comtesse de Noailles, as dame d'honneur, had first place in the Queen's Household. There had been no superintendent for well-nigh fifty years; the appointment of one would have been in effect a demotion for Mme de Noailles.

has been dismissed. It is a great proof of the Queen's influence, but I regret the way she uses it because first she is indulging in a personal vengeance and, second, because her resentment overcame reasons in which Your Majesty's interests were involved. . . . Whenever the Queen desires something firmly, she will obtain it; but if, in the long run, she only uses her influence to satisfy her momentary whims . . . nothing will remain of the brilliant perspective now open before her.

Maria Theresa to Marie Antoinette
Schönbrunn, 16 July 1774

I promised I would tell you or warn you of what I hear about the happy reign people expect from Louis XVI and his little Queen. . . . The 500,000-livre gratification to d'Aiguillon, Monteynard's pension, and others have created a great sensation among the public, which doesn't admire the King's generosity, but wonders who influenced the King and immediately concludes: he will not stand firm and will be led by favorites.

They also speak of millions to be spent on palaces; at this time, when the number of horses [in the royal stables] is being cut back, one does not expect such expenditures, which are ten times higher. They say you cannot tell the Queen from the other Princes, that they are extremely familiar with you. God prevent me from wanting you to make them feel how superior you are to them—God made you so —but you have already been caught out a hundred times by the aunts and the comte and comtesse de Provence as well. The comte d'Artois, they say, is bold to excess; you must not tolerate that—in time it could do you real harm. You must stay in your place and play your own role: that will put you and everyone else at their ease. Be kind and attentive to all but [show] no familiarity; do not play at being their friend; thus you will avoid annoyances and recommendations. . . . This charming first gift of the King [Trianon] must not give rise to great expenses, and even less to dissipation. . . . A firm character in which justice is blended with kindness and the right sort of economizing, will make both friends and enemies respect the Monarch. . . . The King, by gathering worthy people and sending away those who like intrigue, must have friends who can tell him the plain truth. I don't know whether the King's answer printed in the *Gazette de Cologne* is true, but it is admirable and brought tears to my eyes, "that he wanted to hear all the complaints about him so as to improve himself." With God's help and that admirable desire, there is nothing we cannot hope for; all will go well; I only fear your laziness and dissipation. . . .

Marie Antoinette to Maria Theresa
Marly, 30 July 1774

Your last two letters gave me great pleasure because of the kindness with which my dear Mama thinks of everything that concerns me. . . . I may not take full advantage of this but will at least answer my beloved mother with openness and sincerity. It is indeed true that praise and admiration for the King are heard everywhere. He deserves all this by the integrity of his soul and his desire to do well; but I worry about this French enthusiasm when it comes to the future. The little I hear about business has shown me that some of it is very difficult and puzzling. . . . opinion is divided, and it will be impossible to please everyone in a country where people are so impatient that they want everything done immediately. How right my dear Mama is: principles, once fixed, must be followed. The King will not be as weak as his grandfather. I also hope that he will have no favorite, but he is too kind and easygoing, as when M. de Maurepas made him give the 500,000 francs to M. d'Aiguillon. M. de Monteynard's pension is different. He has only been given what former ministers receive; he had behaved like an honest man, and all he did wrong was to displease the dreadful set. My dear Mama can be sure that I will not encourage the King to spend great sums; on the contrary I refuse of myself the requests I am asked to make to him for money. The King is not about to spend millions on palaces—that is an exaggeration, like many other rumors, and the one on my being familiar, since my behavior is seen by very few people. It is not for me to appraise myself, but it seems to me that between us there is only the gay and friendly manner which is right at our age. It is true that the comte d'Artois is very lively and very thoughtless, but I know how to make him feel that he is wrong. As for my aunts, they no longer rule me, and I am very far from confiding in Monsieur and Madame.

I must admit I am lazy and dissipated when it comes to serious things. I want and hope to improve little by little and, without being party to any intrigue, make myself such as to justify the King's trust, for he still treats me as his friend. What the *Gazette de Cologne* says is surely in his heart, but I don't think that he actually said it. . . .

The King has dismissed M. de Boynes, Minister of the Navy;* it is not because of his abasing himself before the du Barry but because of his notorious incapacity; his successor† is supposed to be a very good man. . . .

I am beside myself with my dear Mama's kindness in allowing my brother to come to Compiègne; if he comes, I

---

* Bourgeois de Boynes was, in fact, highly competent, but Louis XVI was now anxious to get rid of his grandfather's entire ministry.
† Turgot, one of the great ministers of the century.

will do my best to cure his shyness, but Rosenberg's health makes me fear he will be unable to come. . . .

Mercy to Maria Theresa, 15 August 1774

The Queen rises between nine and ten; she has her breakfast and receives visits from the royal family. The toilette is at eleven, Mass at noon. I often have an opportunity to speak to the Queen before her dinner, which takes place at one-fifteen. HM plays music and often gives me an audience until the time for her walk, which is after five and lasts until her supper. Every night the King has supper at the Queen's and the only courtiers with the *entrées de la chambre** are allowed in at that moment. Until now there have been no hunter's suppers.

. . . On Sunday, the King and Queen attend a High Mass at nine-thirty in the parish church; after noon Their Majesties attend evensong; in the evening there is cardplaying at the Queen's . . . and the King takes supper in public.

Marie Antoinette to Maria Theresa
Versailles, 7 September 1774

Madame my very dear Mother,

I am really sorry not to have seen my brother; I was greatly looking forward to it, and the King, I think, felt as I did. . . .

I hope that my dear Mama is now reassured about the coadjuteur and that she will be pleased about the baron de

* A privilege granted a few courtiers which enabled them to see the King and Queen at special moments when the rest of the Court was excluded.

Breteuil.* He is very intelligent, and age has stilled his vivacity. The coadjuteur has been given a small consolation with which he is not too pleased, although he boasts a lot about it. He receives a 50,000-franc pension to pay his debts until he succeeds to the See of Strasbourg; I congratulate his creditors.

The people are wild with joy at the dismissal of the Chancellor and the Controller-General [of Finances]. I am not involved in any of this business but wish it were over, for I fear it may give the King much trouble and worry. I have already told my dear Mama that M. Turgot is competent and honest;† that is a great necessity for the [state's] finances. They have put M. de Sartines at the Navy; he was adored by the people when he was Lieutenant of Police;‡ still, I don't know whether he understands the Navy; perhaps he will be given another place later. . . .

When we came back from Compiègne, I felt a little unwell, which is always unpleasant when one is travelling; the extreme heat and the movement of the carriage in which I rode upset my stomach, which made me throw up a lot, and that made me very popular with the people, but my dear Mama knows very well that I am far from being pregnant. Fourteen hours of rest allowed me to recover completely, and there are no traces of it at all.

Marie Antoinette to Maria Theresa
Fontainebleau, 18 October 1774

Madame my very dear Mother,
We have been in Fontainebleau for eight days; my health

* The new Ambassador to Austria.
† Turgot had just been made Controller-General of Finances.
‡ The Lieutenant of Police was, in fact, the Governor of Paris. And Sartines, though competent, was not liked.

is completely good again. I cannot say as much for my aunt Adélaïde, who stayed in Versailles because of a double tertiary* fever she caught the day before we left. She thinks she is free from it now and expects to come next week. Before coming here, we spent five days at Choisy; the King behaved beautifully, was very pleasant to everyone and especially to the ladies, to whom he paid much more attention than one might have expected from the way he was brought up. We had supper every night, both with those who were in Choisy and with those who came from Paris; this was very popular at Court; and I think that nothing could better give the King polish or make him more loved. I would like to convince him he must do the same here. As for the hunt, it is true that it is sometimes very wild; I am very sorry about it, but I must still admit that he is more moderate now that he is the King and hunts much less. As for me, I have decided not to ride anymore for ten days before my period, which is always very heavy. There is half a suspicion and much rumor about the supposed pregnancy of the comtesse d'Artois. She was six days late, which happens quite often to her as she is irregular; still, it is true that in this case her husband behaved in such a way that she might well have been [pregnant].

I am indeed sorry I have not yet been able to find a painter who can make a portrait look like me. . . .

Marie Antoinette to Maria Theresa, 16 November 1774

Madame my very dear Mother,

I am delighted at having been able to carry out your wishes. The King has granted me the presentation of Mme

* A fever which crested after six days.

de Vergennes;* the husband, to whom I announced it, seemed touched and moved to tears.

The great business of the Parlements is at last ended; everybody says that the King was perfect; Mercy was there and will tell you about it. Although I did not want to interfere or even question him on this business, I was happy that the King confided in me. My dear Mama will appreciate it in the paper I am sending her; it is in the King's hand; he gave it to me the day before the lit de justice.† Everything went as he wished, and the Princes of the Blood came to see us the very next day. I am very happy that no one is exiled or unhappy any longer; when the Parlements were abolished, half the princes and peers were opposed; today all is successful, and yet it seems to me that if the King maintains what he has done, his authority will be greater and more firm than in the past.

I am very pleased about having convinced the King to invite gentlemen and ladies to supper with us once a week; I think it the best way of preventing his getting into bad company as his grandfather did. It will also serve to diminish the familiarity he might have had with his servants. Until now the suppers have gone perfectly; I consider it my duty to talk and pay attention to everyone.

The King has just done something charming for me. My income was only 96,000 livres, like the late Queen whose debts had to be paid three times [by the King]; I have never owed anything, but I would have had to pinch pennies: the King, without ever mentioning it to me, had more than doubled my allowance: I will have 200,000 francs a year, which makes 80,000 florins. . . .

It is true that the comte d'Artois is rowdy and does not

* Mme de Vergennes was of low birth and had had a checkered past; Louis XV had always refused permission to have her presented at Court.
† The royal session in which Louis XVI reestablished the Parlements which had been suppressed by his grandfather.

always behave as he should; but my dear Mama may be sure that I know how to stop him as soon as he begins his mischief and, far from allowing him to be too familiar, more than once I have taught him humiliating lessons before his brothers and sisters. . . .

The painters kill me and make me despair. I delayed the courier so as to allow my portrait to be finished; it has just been brought to me; it looks so little like me that I cannot send it. I hope to have a good one next month.

Maria Theresa to Marie Antoinette, 30 November 1774

Madame my dear daughter,

. . . Those two porcelain pictures gave me great pleasure; they are charming, except for my dear Queen's pretty little face, which is all wrong. No matter how bad your portrait may be, send it anyway; Lacy was scandalized to see here only one portrait of you other than that painted by the Bertrand before you left as he was when he saw the terrible portrait you have of the Emperor. I am having another one made, but it won't be finished until Easter.

I return the King's precious paper to you; that was a great day, and I hope that the future will confirm that this was a good policy. I approve infinitely, my dear prudent daughter, your refusal to have anything to do with this more than delicate business, and that you didn't even ask questions. This is all to your honor and your nineteen-year-old discretion; but the King's trust in you, the fact that he told you everything before doing it, is very flattering and consoling to me. Be sure to retain this advantage through your discretion and by making yourself able to advise him on occasions of this kind; otherwise all this won't last. . . .

I am astonished and flattered by the answer of the President of the Parlement to the King because of everything he said about you; you can imagine how my heart is moved by all this; you must keep and deserve it all. The suppers are, I think, admirable; I would rather have them three times a week than once, especially if the nights are not filled any better than now.*

Thank you for the success of Mme de Vergennes; I am really obliged to you; he rendered us real services in Constantinople,† and is an honest man and a good minister. . . . but here is something you have forgotten: I always come back to it; will the poor Durfort always be forgotten?

The business about your allowance is very touching, but especially what you wrote, that you won't ever go into debt; now you would be even more wrong than before. I am delighted that you won't have to be embarrassed by pinching pennies and that you can be generous. . . .

Marie Antoinette to Maria Theresa, 17 December 1774

Madame my very dear Mother,

I am delighted to have been able to give you a few moments of satisfaction. You will not be so happy when you hear that the comtesse d'Artois may be pregnant; she has passed the fourteenth for the second time; she does not feel unwell at all. I must admit to my dear Mama that I am sorry about her becoming a mother before I do, but I still feel obligated to pay more attention to her than anyone. Eight days ago the King had a long conversation with my physician; I am very pleased with his mood, and I have every hope of soon following my sister's example. . . .

* The Empress refers, of course, to the nonconsummation of her daughter's marriage.
† Vergennes had been French Ambassador to Turkey.

The business of the Parlement continues to go well, but there has already been an assembly of the peers;* my brothers went to it, nothing was decided, all agreed with M. le prince de Condé, who wanted to postpone the deliberation to the thirtieth of this month; that seems good to me because it leaves time to act. . . .

P.S. My dear Mama must already know that M. de Durfort was created duc de Civrac. The abbé has the honor of putting himself at your feet.

I am finally brought two portraits; they are not yet such as I would like them for my dear Mama, but I hope that she won't be displeased with them, especially the small one.

The King has just given the office of First Equerry to the duc de Coigny;† that choice is widely approved; M. de Durfort had asked for it some time ago, but he is not active enough for this office; besides, the King was kind enough to make him a duke before filling it.

Mercy to Maria Theresa, 15 January 1775

The Queen reaches daily a new degree of perfection in the way she holds Court. . . . All are enchanted with the way they are treated.

. . . The Queen came to the Opera in Paris on Friday the thirteenth. The people, crowding on her route, cheered her so as to give the most visible and extraordinary proofs of their love for the Queen. The same happened when HM entered the theater. . . . They were performing Gluck's *Iphigénie.* In the second act there is a chorus, of which Achil-

* No sooner did it sit again than the Parlement began once again to make trouble, in this case by refusing to register the very edict which revived it—hence the peers' assembly.
† One of Marie Antoinette's friends.

les sings the first line as he turns to his followers, saying, "Praise, celebrate your Queen!" Instead of that, the actor, moving to the front of the stage, said: "Let us praise, celebrate our Queen/Hymen chains her under his laws/and will make all happy." This was greeted by the public with the most incredible enthusiasm; there were shouts and applause and, for the first time at the Opera, the audience demanded that these lines be repeated and added to it shouts of "Long Live the Queen!" which interrupted the show for almost ten minutes. The Queen was so moved that she shed a few tears.

Mercy to Maria Theresa, 20 February 1775

I await the end of this Carnival with impatience, along with that of the excessive dissipation in which the Queen has indulged. . . . For the last three weeks the abbé de Vermond and I have only had a few brief moments in which to talk about serious things to the Queen; she says herself that she is too deep in her amusements to think of anything else.

Maria Theresa to Marie Antoinette
Vienna, 5 March 1775

Madame my dear daughter,

Your letter of the eighteenth, in the midst of your continual amusements of Carnival and the joy brought you by your brother's arrival,* all that is very consoling for me.

* The Archduke Maximilian, travelling incognito as the Count of Torgau, had just visited his sister.

. . . Now he is already gone; it will all seem like a dream to him. . . .

Thank God that endless Carnival is over! That exclamation will make me look very old, but I must admit that all those late evenings were too tiring; I feared for the Court's health and for the order of its usual habits, which is an essential point. All reading, all the other occupations will have been interrupted for two months. . . . When one is young, one doesn't think about it; as one ages, one realizes it, but other weaknesses put us at fault. In the same way I can't prevent myself raising a point which many gazettes repeat all too often: it is the coiffure you use; they say that from the forehead up it is thirty-six inches high, and with so many feathers and ribbons to adorn it! You know that I always have thought that fashion should be followed moderately, without ever exaggerating them. A young and pretty Queen, who is full of attractions, doesn't need all these follies;* on the contrary, the simplicity of your adornment will show you off better and is more suitable to the rank of a Queen. . . .

T HE VISIT to Versailles of Marie Antoinette's brother, the Archduke Maximilian, proved a source of embarrassment. Not only was the young man uneducated and rather ill-mannered, he also insisted that Princes of the Royal Blood pay him the first visit, a courtesy to which his rank would have entitled him only if he had not been traveling incognito as the Count of Torgau. The Princes indignantly rejected his demand, and the Archduke, therefore, never met them. Not unnaturally the public sided with the Princes; Marie Antoinette stood by her brother; and people began to notice that she was more Austrian than French.

* Maria Theresa was right, of course, and the Queen was already being criticized for her addiction to the latest and most extreme fashions.

Marie Antoinette to Maria Theresa
Versailles, 17 March 1775

Madame my very dear Mother,

My brother's departure was a real affliction; it is a cruel thing not to know whether I will ever see him again. He earned here the reputation of having been well brought up because he was polite, pleasant, and attentive to everyone. He did not succeed as well for the things he was shown because he remained indifferent. I think that in some little time he will be better able to take advantage of this kind of trip.

I hope that soon the bickering with the princes will have been forgotten; it was much worsened by some wicked people who would have liked to see an eternal rift. After my brother's departure, the King sent a message to the princes, except for M. le duc de Chartres, that for ten or twelve days they were not to come and have supper with him. Last Tuesday M. le prince de Condé and his son came back to our supper; I treated them as I always do, without mentioning anything. M. le duc d'Orléans and M. le prince de Conti have not returned yet, but that is because they have gout.

Although Carnival did amuse me a great deal, I agree that it was time it ended. We are now back to our usual routine, and I will take advantage of it to talk more with the King, who is still on very close terms with me.

It is true that I take some care of the way I dress; and, as for feathers, everyone wears them, and it would seem extraordinary not to wear them. Their height has been much curtailed since the end of the balls. . . .

Mercy to Maria Theresa, 18 March 1775

M. le comte d'Artois, who cares for nothing but frivolities, and whose behavior is that of a libertine, has imagined a kind of tourney this spring . . . at the Bois de Boulogne. The young Prince would like the ladies to be present and distribute the prizes. The Queen immediately thought this an excellent idea, and I am very busy trying to find a way to stop her. All through Carnival the rehearsals for the quadrille gave the young people only too much access to the Queen, and although the purity of her soul protects her from any danger, there always remains an excessive familiarity. . . . That is why I dread the tourney. . . . It can only displease the King and feed the pernicious dissipation to which the Queen is addicted. Recently HM has wanted to see a horse race which was run near Paris; a few young people had started this novelty as an imitation of the races they have in England. The Queen came with Monsieur, Madame, and the comte d'Artois. Although there was nothing wrong with this excursion, it is considered to be the result of an insatiable desire for amusement. . . . The Queen was not greeted with the usual applause. . . . The public sees with some displeasure that the Queen cares for amusements only and neglects to play the role to which she was called by her popularity.

Away in vienna, Maria Theresa, well informed as usual, grew increasingly alarmed at her daughter's behavior. Always a pessimist, the Empress watched with more than her usual forebodings Marie Antoinette's frivolity, her spendthrift habits, her passion for the kind of amusement the King most disliked—gambling, dancing, staying up late. This last was the most alarming of all. The marriage was still not consummated, and the Queen's habit of staying up until two or three in the morning prevented Louis XVI, who liked to go to bed early, from sleeping with his wife. This not only made the consummation of the marriage even more unlikely, it also meant that the King and Queen had almost no private moments together in which Marie Antoinette could influence French policy.

Although Mercy had recommended the use of a kindly tone, the Empress exploded periodically in a series of very sharp letters predicting a grim future for her daughter. With the benefit of hindsight, we see all too clearly how right Maria Theresa turned out to be.

Maria Theresa to Marie Antoinette
Schönbrunn, 2 June 1775

I am delighted by what you tell me about the King's behavior and the orders to the Parlement during that wretched riot.* Like you, I think there is something behind it. Our people in Bohemia used just the same language as that you report to me, except that yours used it about the high price of bread, and ours about their forced labor.† . . . In general this spirit of rebellion is becoming familiar everywhere; this is the consequence of our enlightened century. . . . I must admit that I have been very upset to read in some public prints that you are more given than ever to your excursions in the Bois de Boulogne at the gates of Paris with the comte d'Artois, all without the King. You must know better than I that this Prince [Artois] is not at all respected and that you thus share his errors. He is so young, so giddy: that may still

* As the result of an insufficient crop, the price of bread had risen sharply, but the people rioted because they thought the rise was due to Turgot's policies.
† Bohemian peasants were still, legally, serfs; as such, they owed the state free labor.

pass in a Prince; but these are very grave failings in an older Queen, of whom people thought better. Do not lose that inestimable possession which you had so perfectly.* . . .

I am sadder still about another point: all the letters from Paris say that you sleep apart from the King and that he trusts you very little. I must admit that I am all the more struck by this because you are so dissipated during the day, and if the King no longer comes to sleep with you, you will have to give up having heirs; your friendship, your habit of being always together will also end, and I foresee only misfortunes and sorrow for you in this most brilliant of positions. . . . Your only endeavor must be to spend more often the entire day with him, to keep him company, to be his best friend in whom he can confide, and to try to be up on things so as to discuss them with him and help him; he should find pleasures and security nowhere but in your company. . . . Forgive this preaching, but I will admit that these separate beds, these excursions with the comte d'Artois have afflicted my soul all the more that I can foresee their consequences; I cannot show them to you too vividly so as to save you from the abyss into which you are plunging.

Marie Antoinette to Maria Theresa
Versailles, 22 June 1775

Madame my dear Mother,

. . . The Emperor gave me great pleasure by writing me from Vienna at the time of my three brothers' arrival. The coronation [of Louis XVI] has been perfect in every way; I am told that everybody was very pleased with the King; he must be so with all his subjects; great or humble, all showed

* The Empress is referring to the Queen's popularity, and responding to Mercy's letter of March 18 (see page 161).

him the greatest interest; the ceremonies in the church were interrupted at the moment of the coronation by the most touching acclamations. I couldn't hold myself back; my tears ran down my face in spite of myself, and people liked it. I did my best during the whole time of the trip* to answer to the people's enthusiasm, and although there was much heat and many crowds, I do not regret my efforts, which, anyway, did not upset my health. It is at the same time amazing and wonderful to be so well received two months after the riots and in spite of the high price of bread which unfortunately continues. It is a prodigious thing about the French character that it lets itself be carried away by evil suggestions but then it comes right back to the good. It is certain that when people who are suffering treat us so well, we are even more obligated to work for their happiness. The King seems very convinced of this; as for me, I know that I will never forget, even if I live to be a hundred, the day of the coronation. . . .

The cold I had for a long time was entirely cured by my milk treatment. It is true that while it lasted, the King slept in his own apartment; but my dear Mama can be reassured on this point: he came back a long time ago. Besides, our apartments were very inconvenient; we could not visit each other without being seen by everyone. I had a passage made so that he can visit me, and I him, without being noticed. I am sorry that my dear Mama should judge of my rides in the Bois de Boulogne by the information in the public sheets; they often lie and always exaggerate. The days when I went there with the comte d'Artois, the King was on hunts where I couldn't possibly join him. Besides, it was with the King's knowledge, and during those rides there were always many gentlemen and ladies of the Court; Esterhazy, who was there, could say whether there was anything wrong.

* To Rheims, where the coronation took place.

I am making a great loss right now because Mme de Cossé, my dame d'atours, is retiring; I had feared she might for a long time, but I could not refuse her due to the sad state of her child, which is ravaging this poor mother. . . . In her sorrow Mme de Cossé has no other resource than to take her son to some waters in Savoy and to spend the winter in the south. I will greatly regret her because she is a woman of merit and integrity, and I will not easily find her like. I am thinking of replacing her by Mme de Chimay, one of my ladies who is generally liked. . . .

We have already improved things by the advice the King sent to M. d'Aiguillon not to come to the coronation and to retire to Aiguillon:* we avoided a formal exile, which is a barbaric thing, although he himself had used it.

Mme la comtesse d'Artois progresses in her pregnancy; she is happy enough not to fear her delivery. It is true that she is such a child that she is overjoyed because she has been told she would not be given any black medicine.

My aunts Victoire and Sophie, who shared a Household, are now separate. We had to give my aunt Sophie her own Household; that will cost more money, which I regret. . . .

I come back to these miserable gazettes whose lies afflict me so,† since I want nothing more than to keep and deserve my dear Mama's love and kindness.

P.S. I dare to send my dear Mama two coronation medals —one for her, the other for the Emperor.

T HE FOLLOWING letter, written by Marie Antoinette to Count Rosenberg, an old friend of the Imperial family, is essential for the comprehension of what follows. It

* A typical piece of vengefulness on the part of the Queen.
† It is amusing to note that complaints about the press are not a twentieth-century innovation.

also gives a vivid example of the kind of behavior which horrified Maria Theresa.

There is, first of all, her intense and long-lasting resentment of the duc d'Aiguillon. It was not enough to have him dismissed from the ministry a year earlier; now she had him exiled as well; and as a corollary there is the blind obstinacy with which she defended her friends, even when they were guilty of serious failings. The case of the comte de Guines is a perfect example of this.

Guines, the French Ambassador to the Court of St. James's, had used his official position to bring in contraband merchandise. The British Government found out and complained, so the duc d'Aiguillon, then Foreign Minister, recalled Guines for consultations and demanded an explanation. Guines failed to provide one, and as a result a prosecution was started. Luckily for the Ambassador, it only came to trial early in 1775, by which time d'Aiguillon was out of office and Marie Antoinette in a position of power. To no one's surprise, the judges, who were well aware of the royal wishes, found Guines not guilty; but, not content with this miscarriage of justice, the Queen went on to seek revenge against those she considered Guines's enemies. D'Aiguillon was the first victim, swiftly followed by Turgot. It didn't matter much, perhaps, if d'Aiguillon was sent off to his country house, but Turgot was an exceptionally competent, farseeing, and honest minister, who was just then trying to improve the deplorable state of the royal finances, and who furthermore enjoyed a well-deserved popularity. Naturally people deplored his dismissal and blamed the Queen.

The little tale in the letter, relating just how Marie Antoinette had manipulated Louis XVI into letting her see the duc de Choiseul, cannot have surprised Maria Theresa; what horrified her, however, was her daughter's indiscretion in letting the world know just how things really stood; and calling her husband "the poor man" was inexcusable, even if that is how she thought of him. In fact, as the Empress was beginning to realize, Marie Antoinette was quite incapable of hiding her feelings or pretending a respect she did not feel for her husband. There was, for instance, the well-known episode of the clocks. Marie Antoinette, who thought her husband a great bore, was always trying to be rid of his company. One night, when she was anxious to be left alone with her friends, she had all the clocks in her apartment advanced by one hour so that the King would leave that much sooner. He did of course, but when he reached his bedroom, he found it empty of his usual attendants. When the attendants finally came, they were told what had happened. Since at the same time all of the Queen's friends thought the story deliciously amusing, it spread quickly and did no good to either Louis or Marie Antoinette.

Finally the Queen's attempt at concealing the planned nomination of Mme de Lamballe as Superintendent of her Household was typical of the way she now ran her life: her friends must be gratified in every way possible, even if it meant antagonizing people and spending money unnecessarily. When, shortly afterward, the comtesse de Polignac replaced Mme de Lamballe as Marie Antoinette's favorite, these friendships became an open scandal—not, rumors notwithstanding, because they were sexual, but because places and pensions were monopolized by the Polignac set. Maria Theresa was right to worry: after only a year on the throne, Marie Antoinette was already displaying all the faults that were to make her the most hated of Queens.

I was not at my ease, Monsieur, when I wrote you my last letter because it was to go by post. I must go all the way back to M. d'Aiguillon's departure to give you a full account of my behavior. That departure is altogether my work. I had had enough; that nasty man kept up all sorts of spying and unpleasant talk. He tried to brave me more than once in the business of M. de Guines; immediately after the judgment, I asked the King for his removal. It is true that I didn't want to use a lettre de cachet, but he gained nothing by this because instead of staying in Touraine, as he wanted to do, he was asked to keep going all the way to Aiguillon, which is in Gascony.

You may have heard about the audience I gave the duc de Choiseul at Rheims. People have talked about it so much that I wouldn't be surprised if old Maurepas was afraid he was going to be sent home for a rest. You may well believe that I didn't see him without first telling the King, but you will never guess the stratagem I used not to look as if I were asking for his permission. I told him that I felt like seeing M. de Choiseul and that I was only puzzled about the day. I managed it so well that the poor man settled himself the hour at which it would be most convenient for me to see him. I think I used my prerogative as a woman to the full.

At last we are going to be rid of M. de la Vrillière. Although he was hard of hearing, he still heard that it was time he left, for fear he might find the door locked against him. He will be replaced by M. de Malesherbes. . . .

I have made a great loss . . . in Mme de Cossé. . . . Mme de Chimay has replaced her.

I have quite another project in mind. The maréchale de Mouchy will be leaving, I'm told. I do not know who I will take in her place; but I have asked the King to take advantage of this change to appoint Mme de Lamballe as Superintendent. Imagine how happy I am; I will make my intimate friend happy and will enjoy it even more than she. This is a secret; I am not yet telling the Empress. Only the Emperor knows; insist that he tell no one—you can easily see why.* . . .

Marie Antoinette to Maria Theresa
Versailles, 14 July 1775

Madame my very dear Mother,

My dear Mama's kindness and love penetrate my soul, but right now they make me feel even worse: for the last four days I have been suffocated by Monsieur and Madame's joy. It isn't that I don't find it very natural; I approve of it so thoroughly that I have hidden my tears so as not to take away from their joy. Three days after my sister Clotilde's departure, they will go and spend two weeks in Chambéry† in the deepest incognito. How dreadful it is that I cannot hope for the same happiness!

We are on very good terms with Monsieur and Madame; they are both very reserved and very quiet, at least in appearance. Madame is Italian in body and soul;‡ Monsieur's character is exactly similar. Our habits are formed; we will always live together without division or trust, and I think the King feels as I do on this subject. . . .

We are awaiting the comtesse d'Artois's delivery from one moment to the next; she is still in the best of health and goes

* Count Rosenberg was so horrified by the tone of this letter that he felt compelled to let the Empress see it; both she and Joseph II were in turn deeply shocked.
† One of the residences of the Sardinian Court, Chambéry was the capital of Savoy.
‡ Marie Antoinette means she is a hypocrite and a liar.

out every day, although she is now four days into her ninth month.

We will have very few fêtes, even though they will celebrate both the birth and [Madame Clotilde's] marriage. Money will be saved; but, far more essential, a good example will be set for the people who have suffered so much from the high cost of bread. Luckily hope is returning; the wheat fields look very good, and bread is sure to be cheaper once the crop is in. . . .

I am delighted with my sister Elisabeth;* she has shown, on the departure of her sister and on several other occasions, the most charming courtesy and sensitivity. When at the age of eleven, one has such a tender heart, that is very precious. I will see her more now that she is in Mme de Guemeénée's care; the poor girl may leave in two years. I am sorry that she is to go as far as Portugal; it will be a help for her to leave while she is still so young; she won't feel the difference between the two countries as strongly. May God grant her that her sensitivity will not make her unhappy! As for my sister Clotilde, she is delighted to be leaving. It is true that she expects to visit Chambéry† every two years and see members of the family from time to time; I don't imagine she will have a great success in Turin, but then they'll make her do anything they want: she is easygoing, not very bright, and cares greatly about nothing. . . .

* Louis XVI's youngest sister.
† While Italian was spoken in Turin, the capital of Sardinia, French was spoken in Chambéry. As for Marie Antoinette's appraisal of her sister-in-law, it is accurate. She only fails to mention Mme Clotilde's enormous size, which resulted in her being generally called Gros-Madame, Fat Madame. . . .

Maria Theresa to Marie Antoinette
Schönbrunn, 30 July 1775

Madame my dear daughter,

The courier goes a day earlier as it is carrying money to the [Austrian] Netherlands; I wanted to tell you at the earliest possible opportunity how the too magnificent present of the hair of my dear children pleased me: it is perfectly worked and does honor to the artisans of Paris and to my dear daughter, who wanted to treat her old Mama.

But how little that pleasure lasted! I cannot hide from you that a letter you sent to Rosenberg upset me most dreadfully. What style! What frivolity! Where is the kind and generous heart of the Archduchess Antoinette? All I see is intrigue, low hatred, a persecuting spirit, and cheap wit—intrigue of a sort that a Pompadour or a Barry would have indulged in so as to play a great role, something which is utterly unfitting for a Queen, a great Princess of the House of Lorraine and Austria, who should be full of kindness and decency. Your too early success and your entourage of flatterers have always made me fear for you, ever since that winter when you wallowed in pleasures and ridiculous fashions. Those excursions from pleasure to pleasure without the King and in the knowledge that he doesn't enjoy them and that he either accompanies you or leaves you free out of sheer good nature—all that caused me to mention in my letters my justified concern. Now I see it all too confirmed by your letter.

What a tone! "The poor man!" Where is the respect and the gratitude you owe him for all his kindness? I leave you to your own thoughts and say no more, although there would be much more to be said.

Nor do I mention the secret you are trying to keep in regard to your appointment of the Lamballe. I wrote you what I did for your own good. Two Piedmontese sisters-in-law, one of which has provided an heir to the throne, and the other leading the wisest and quietest life which earns the approval of all sensible people, and all foreigners, and you want your Superintendent to be another Piedmontese? . . .

Your happiness can vanish all too fast, and you may be plunged, by your own doing, into the greatest calamities. That is the result of your terrible dissipation, which prevents your being assiduous about anything serious. What have you read? And, after that, you dare to opine on the greatest State matters, on the choice of ministers? What does the abbé do? And Mercy? It seems to me that you dislike them because instead of behaving like low flatterers, they want you to be happy and do not amuse you or take advantage of your weaknesses. You will realize all this one day, but it will be too late.* I hope not to survive that dreadful time, and I pray to God that He end my days sooner, since I can no longer help you but cannot bear to lose or watch the sufferings of my dear child, whom I will love dearly till my last breath.

Marie Antoinette to Maria Theresa
Versailles, 12 August 1775

Madame my very dear Mother,

I could never dare to write my august Mother if I felt half as guilty as she thinks me. To be compared to a Pompadour, to a du Barry, to be covered with the most dreadful epithets does not fit your daughter. I wrote a letter to a man I trust, whom you trust, and to whom, on so respectable a precedent, I felt I could give my own trust. Since he has been in ce pays-ci, he knows the value of certain sentences, and I

* A remarkable forecast!

(172)

could therefore fear no ill effect from their use. My dear Mama feels otherwise; I can only bow my head and hope that in other circumstances she will judge me more favorably and, I dare say it, as I deserve to be.*

The comtesse d'Artois gave birth on the sixth at three forty-five as easily as possible: she only had two or three strong pains and in all spent only two hours in labor. I spent the entire time in her room: I need not tell my dear Mama how I suffered in seeing an heir who isn't mine; but I still managed not to forget any attention due the mother and child. Will my dear Mama accept the love and respect of a daughter who is very sorry to have displeased her?

Maria Theresa to Marie Antoinette
Schönbrunn, 31 August 1775

Madame my dear daughter,

Your situation has seemed such to me that I felt able to use the comparison† which you rightly call dreadful. I did so only with great effort; judge, therefore, my position, and the alarm of my heart and love when I see you giving in to seduction and adulation. My comparison did not reach personal behavior.‡ God save me from even doubting you on this, I could not bear it; I was referring only to cabals, intrigues, and protections; and in these matters your wrongs would be greater than theirs: you were placed at birth by God, whereas they had to try and sustain themselves. . . .

I must admit that this easy delivery of your sister-in-law's has touched my heart a little because of the same consider-

---

* This kind of evasion is, henceforth, Marie Antoinette's unchanging strategy.
† To Mmes de Pompadour and du Barry.
‡ The Empress means that she believes her daughter to have remained chaste.

ation you mention; we must still always prefer and wish for an heir within the family itself. It has been a long time now since you have said anything on that important question . . . it seems to me that you care less than you once did and are not making enough efforts. I am pleased with the attention and care you had for the mother and child; there I recognize my dear daughter, and that rightly brought you approval and love. . . .

Marie Antoinette to Maria Theresa, 31 August 1775

Madame my very dear Mother,

Your dear letter revived me. The idea that my dear Mama disapproved of me was most upsetting to me; I hope that I will never deserve such feelings for these suspicions. As for protections and recommendations, I think that in ce pays-ci it is impossible to avoid them; it is even a matter of etiquette that the members of my Household be given no special favors unless I have asked for them; the essential point is that my protection must always be well-placed, and I will always do my best. It would be unreasonable if I were to be annoyed at my condition;* but I think a great deal about it and speak to the King about it quite often, although always with sweetness and measure. I am trying to make him feel he should have the little operation,† which has already been mentioned and which I believe to be necessary.

The comtesse d'Artois is still in the best of health; she went to Mass in the chapel last Sunday at the end of her five weeks. The King gave her a thousand louis‡ for her deliv-

---

* The nonconsummation of her marriage.
† Circumcision.
‡ Twenty-four thousand livres.

ery, and her husband diamond bracelets, with the case also in diamonds with the portrait of his son.

My sister the princess de Piedmont left from Choisy on the twenty-eighth; we had all gone there with her the evening before. She was not much upset by the separation. That is quite natural; she never saw much of us, and Mme de Marsan, who was in name and reality her dear friend, had completely subjugated her. . . . I have grown to know my sister Elisabeth much better; she is a charming child, intelligent, full of grace and character. When her sister left, she displayed the most charming sensitivity, and all much beyond her age; the poor little thing was desperate, and since her health is very delicate, she fainted and had a very strong nervous fit. . . .

The comtesse de Noailles has resigned;* the King granted me Mme de Lamballe as Superintendent; Mme de Chimay, who was dame d'atours, becomes dame d'honneur; and Mme de Mailly, who was one of my ladies, is now dame d'atours. She will be replaced by Mme de la Roche-Aymon, the niece of the Grand Almoner, to whom the late King had promised the position. I hope that what my dear Mama will learn about Mme de Lamballe will convince her that there is no fear to be had of her connection with my sisters-in-law. She has always had a good reputation and is not at all Italian. She is established here for life, and so is her brother. I think both realize that France is now their true country. . . .

---

* The comtesse de Noailles was greatly disliked by the Queen as a stickler for etiquette. What Marie Antoinette does not say was that appointing a Superintendent set a new lady over the dame d'honneur, who until then had been the senior officer of the Household. As such, it was an obvious insult—hence Mme de Noailles's resignation. The dame d'atours was the Mistress of the Robes.

Mercy to Maria Theresa, 18 September 1775

I managed to convince HM to give up an idea about which she cared greatly, that of giving an appointment as dame d'honneur to her favorite, the comtesse de Polignac. . . . The princesse de Lamballe will soon enter into the office of Superintendent . . . Since this last is a kind of creation, I begged the Queen at least to allow the attributions of the office to be such as to cause as little expense as possible.

. . . The Queen was worried about the letters she has received [from Your Majesty] and even more about the tone of her answers. "My mother," she told me, "sees things from afar. She does not evaluate them from my standpoint, and she judges me too severely; but she is my mother, she loves me, and when she speaks, I can only bow my head."

Marie Antoinette to Maria Theresa
Fontainebleau, 17 October 1775

Will Madame my very dear Mother accept still my homage for her birthday? I am ashamed of offering it so late: it is certainly not forgetfulness: I thought that the courier would come four days earlier. I need all my dear Mama's indulgence for that mistake. . . .

The maréchal du Muy's death is dreadful, especially for his wife, whom everyone loves for her sweetness and politeness. My dear Mama would be touched by the terrible state she is in. She only found out that they were operating on her husband when she heard his shouts; as she came into the room, she fell on the doorstep, where she stayed during the entire operation, which lasted for thirty-five minutes. He suffered unbelievable pain and died within twice twenty-four hours. It is feared that the maréchale will not long survive him; that is her only desire. The King had given her a 10,000-franc pension when she married; he has just now given her 30,000; there is no example of this kind of generosity to the widow of a minister who was in place for so short a time; she deserves this exception, and she can never be as well treated as I wish her to be.

I will have nothing to reproach myself with when it comes to the choice of a new War Minister; I am pleased with the attentions and respect shown me by M. de Maurepas, who first told me what he thought before he had come to any conclusion and then told me about the decision he was suggesting to the King. It is M. de Saint-Germain, who had left the service of France for that of Denmark. This is being kept absolutely secret until his answer is received. It is not known whether he will accept. I have nothing to say, either for or against, since I only undertook to respect the secret and do not know him at all.

Monsieur and Madame returned on the second of this month, very pleased with their trip. Some people amused themselves by spreading rumors, according to which we were on bad terms; I can assure my dear Mama that this is not at all true and that we are very friendly.

Mercy to Maria Theresa, 19 October 1775

When the Queen had firmly decided to reestablish the office of Superintendent of her Household, I insisted at first on having its extent defined, along with its rights and prerogatives, and on having any abuses reformed. In fact the old accounts showed that there had been many . . . so new regulations were needed, and the abbé de Vermond undertook to draft them according to our conversation. This work was very simple, very clear, divided into eight articles; ev-

erything was arranged so as to prevent any conflicts of juris-
diction [with the other ladies of the Household] and any
troubles which might arise from this. The Queen approved
these regulations and endorsed them in her own hand; the
minister was all the more pleased that he saw the abuses had
been rooted out and the expenditure reduced. At last, at the
moment when all was settled, the princesse de Lamballe, by
being appealing, by weeping, got the Queen to listen to her,
and told her that the duc de Penthièvre* would not let his
daughter-in-law take on an office which had been shorn of
part of its old prerogatives and that therefore she, the princesse de Lamballe, could only take this office if it were exactly the same as under Mlle de Bourbon.†

I will not recount here the efforts I made to convince the
Queen to stand by her earlier decision. . . . Nothing I said
made any impression; HM gave in to her affection for the
princesse de Lamballe.

Marie Antoinette to Maria Theresa, 12 November 1775

Madame my very dear Mother,

. . . It is very certain that not only is there no tiff between Monsieur and myself but also, what is more, that
none is rumored, and everyone has noticed how well I treat
him and his wife. I will, however, tell my dear Mama that
she is a little wrong about him. It is quite true that he does
not suffer from the vivacity and turbulence of the comte
d'Artois, but with a very weak character, he is given to
much dissimulation and sometimes to dishonorable behav-

---

* Her father-in-law.
† Mlle de Bourbon, who had died in the 1730s, had been the last Superintendent. She was the King's cousin, and instead of the normal 45,000 livres
salary, she received 150,000 livres.

ior; in order to further his interests and gain money, he uses little intrigues which would make an honest private person blush. For instance, isn't it shameful that he should have bought from Mme de Langeac, M. de la Vrillière's mistress, a forest that this minister had snatched from the late King through Mme du Barry? Unfortunately for Monsieur, all these maneuvers are becoming known and leave him without the public's respect or affection. He had even had the reputation of being a wit but has lost it because of several of his letters, which were not very honest and were very clumsy.

The King seems more friendly and trusting to me than ever, and I have nothing more I can possibly want from that side. As for the important question which worries my dear Mama, I am very sorry to have nothing new to report; the laziness is surely not on my side.* I understand better than ever how important this point is for my future; but my dear Mama must realize that my situation is a difficult one and that patience and sweetness are my only weapons. I am still hoping, and the King often sleeps with me. . . .

Mercy to Maria Theresa, 15 November 1775

HM . . . does not know how to reconcile the princesse de Lamballe to the comtesse de Polignac because these two favorites, who are jealous of each other, have been presenting the Queen with respectful little complaints disguised as the marks of the most loving sensitivity. I told the Queen that since she had publicly shown her friendship for the two favorites, I thought that she should treat them well, each according to her position . . . but there is also another rea-

---

* Again this is about the nonconsummation of the marriage.

son which I could not mention and which is much more weighty.

The princesse de Lamballe is backed by M. le comte d'Artois, by the duc de Chartres,* her relative, and by all the circle at the Palais Royal, whose intrigues I greatly fear. The comtesse de Polignac is pushed by the baron de Besenval,† several young courtiers, an aunt with a rather bad reputation,‡ and other equally dangerous friends.

It seems difficult, therefore, to say which of these two parties could become the most dangerous and best to have them balance each other and mutually cancel out their influences.

Marie Antoinette to Maria Theresa, 15 December 1775

Madame my very dear Mother,

Since my last letter, I have had another cold, which I have shared with everyone. We have had terrible fogs which brought a general influenza about. It starts with a headache, goes on with a fever and cough. My influenza is over, but I still cough a little; my sisters have also had it, and one day all four of us had a fever at the same time, along with the comte d'Artois; as for the King and Monsieur, they have escaped until now, but every day new people are catching it.

M. de Saint-Germain is starting on great reforms in the troops and the King's Guards; he intends to increase the

* The duc de Chartres was a distant cousin of the King's; he was married to Mme de Lamballe's sister-in-law and lived at the Palais Royal in Paris.
† The baron de Besenval was an elderly Swiss officer possessed of a golden tongue and a great fund of gossip; as such, he kept Marie Antoinette amused and gained great influence over her.
‡ That lady, the comtesse d'Andlau, had lost her position as lady in waiting to Madame Adélaïde after she had given the teenage Princess a number of pornographic books.

army by 40,000 men without its costing the King anything more.

I have never forgotten what my dear Mama told me about the Piedmontese character;* it suits Monsieur perfectly, who in this way has certainly made the right marriage. I do not know what he is plotting now; we were on very good terms, and I had even been complimented for some time on my attentions to him and his wife. Then he decided to try and become one of my intimates, and to further himself, he wrote (that is his usual trick but until now it has not helped him). His letter is addressed to a gentleman of his Household, but at the same time he told him to show it to a man I trust. It is very verbose, very base, very false; in spite of all that, I thought I should seem taken in by it and pretended I believed it all. I spoke to him about it before he had said anything, reproaching him in a friendly way about the fact that he had thus used a third person. Since then we have remained on friendly and cordial terms; but in fact I can see we are both equally insincere; I am all the more convinced that if I had to choose a husband among the three brothers, I would still prefer the one God has given me: he is true, and although he is awkward, he shows me every possible attention and kindness. It is true that there have been many rumors about the operation. Until now, nothing has happened, and I very much doubt that the King will decide to go through with it. Unfortunately the physicians are making his indecision worse; mine, without believing it necessary, thinks it would be very useful. The King's, who is an old fool, says there are many drawbacks to having it performed and many drawbacks to not having it performed. My role is rather difficult and I think it best to say nothing. . . .

We are in the midst of an epidemic of satirical songs. They

* That is, that the Italians were liars and intriguers.

(181)

are being written about everyone at Court, men and women alike, and the frivolity of the French did not spare the King. The need for the operation has been the main theme against the King. As for me, I haven't been spared; I have very liberally been gratified with both tastes, those for male and female lovers. Although nasty writings are usually quite successful here, these are so dull and so gross that they have been taken up neither in the public nor in society.

How happy the Grand Duke* and his children will be! Why must he arrive precisely at the moment when I hoped to see the Emperor? . . .

My dear Mama knows how I feel about the baron de Breteuil, and so she can imagine how pleased I am to see her content. I would like to get him the blue ribbon,† but the King will not name any for quite a while, and I think it impossible to have him make an exception.

The maréchale du Muy is still inconsolable; it is much feared that she will not be cured of the state of languor in which she is plunged. . . .

Mercy to Maria Theresa, 17 December 1775

I proved to the Queen that the princesse de Lamballe was costing the State more than 300,000 livres,† including the way her brother has been treated here and all the new ex-

* Leopold, Grand Duke of Tuscany, Marie Antoinette's brother, was about to visit Vienna.
† A broad blue ribbon, or sash, was one of the insignia of the Order of the Saint Esprit, the French equivalent of the Garter or the Golden Fleece. It was naturally much coveted.
† This sum was all the more striking in that the government was then engaged in an economy drive and that Mme de Lamballe was herself immensely rich. This heedless dissipation of the State revenues, along with her well-known taste for diamonds, did much to make the Queen unpopular.

penses caused by the recreation of her office as Superintendent, that these expenses are completely useless and occur only to satisfy the Queen's affections.

Marie Antoinette to Maria Theresa
Versailles, 14 January 1776

Madame my very dear Mother,

My health is excellent, thank God; never can it be so easy for me to sacrifice a few amusements, in obedience to her, so as to preserve my health than in this moment when my soul is overcome by the happiness she holds before me.* . . .

Neny's accident touches me deeply; his loss could not be repaired, and even if my dear Mama were able to find as good and faithful a man, I am sure that she would always regret an old servant.

My dear Mama is perfectly right to denounce the frivolity of the French, but I am really pained that she has conceived a dislike for the whole nation. The character [of the French] is very flighty, but it is not evil; pens and tongues say many things which the hearts don't believe. The proof that they feel no hatred is that upon the smallest occasion, they say kind things and even praise much more than one deserves. I have just now seen this. There has been a terrible fire in the Palais, where trials are held in Paris. The same day I was to attend the Opera; I didn't go and sent two hundred louis for the most pressing needs. From the moment of the fire, the same people who had been repeating the talk and the songs against me were praising me to the skies.

We have here so great a quantity of snow that the like

---

* There seemed to be a possibility that Maria Theresa would visit Brussels, then the capital of the Austrian Netherlands; Marie Antoinette would have joined her there. In fact the trip never took place

hasn't been seen for many years; so we go sledding just like in Vienna. We did it here yesterday and today. There is a great ride into Paris; I would have loved to go, but since no Queen has ever done so, there would have been talk and I preferred giving it up to being bothered by new tales. . . .

I am no more pleased than my dear Mama with the advice of the physicians. The King sent for Moreau, the surgeon of the Hôtel-Dieu of Paris. He said about the same as the others—that the operation was not necessary and that there was every hope without it. It is true that there is a considerable change in the King and that his body seems to gain in consistency. He has promised me that if nothing happens within the next few months, he would decide to have the operation on his own accord. . . .

Mercy to Maria Theresa, 19 January 1776

Although in the course of the last year the King has given the Queen, on different occasions, more than 300,000 livres worth of diamonds, she still felt a great desire for earrings which were shown to her and for which the jeweler asked 600,000 livres.* I did not conceal from the Queen that it would be more prudent to defer so great an expense; but the temptation was too strong and could not be resisted. In truth the Queen took many precautions. . . . HM will pay for this purchase over four years so as not to take too much all at once from her funds.

* $2,700,000.

Marie Antoinette to Maria Theresa
Versailles, 27 February 1776

Madame my very dear Mother,

The nomination of the blue ribbons pleased me greatly. The baron* is right to be pleased; although he deserves much, it is a great favor to include him in the first nomination made by the King; but he owed that attention to my dear Mama, and even if I had had no other reason to protect Breteuil, I could not have remained silent. The King did it with a very good grace, as he did for the duc de Civrac, former marquis de Durfort, who is lucky to have been sent to Vienna. I think him a very good man, but his merits have caused no great sensation here. The King has treated me very well in this first nomination of blue ribbons: he is giving one to the marquis de Tessé, my First Equerry and a man of very noble birth, and to M. de Mailly, the father-in-law of my dame d'atours.

I may not wish for the death of the King of Prussia,† but we must always suspect his intentions, and it would be a very good thing if his bad health prevented him from plotting and lighting fires everywhere, as he has done up until now. Breteuil left in a good frame of mind, and I feel sure that his reports and dispatches will always be such as to maintain the union between my two families. The Duke of Wurtemberg arrived here a few days ago. I was rather surprised by the easy tone with which he spoke to me, as if indeed he knew me well. He drags his mistress everywhere; she is a rather ugly countess. I saw her at the Opera Ball; I don't know what they have become; I think they have left.

The King has made some edicts which may occasion some disputes with the Parlement. I hope that they won't go so

* De Breteuil.
† Frederick II. Maria Theresa, with some reason, particularly hated him.

far as under the last reign and that the King will maintain his authority.

I have had a pleasant time over Carnival; but two days after Maundy Tuesday, I suffered from a cold and a sore throat. I am beginning to go out today; unlike many others, I had neither fever nor headache. . . .

Marie Antoinette to Maria Theresa
Versailles, 10 April 1776

Madame my very dear Mother,

. . . I am very touched by what my dear Mama thinks about the children I might have had; I have ever greater hopes and am convinced that the operation is no longer necessary.

It is quite true that I went to a ball at night, and Madame didn't, but that is because her health, which has not been good for some time, will not let her stay up late.

I will send my dear Mama by the next courier the design of my several coiffures; she may find them ridiculous, but here one is so accustomed to seeing them that no one pays attention anymore, since everyone wears the same kind of coiffure.

I was only able to see Mercy for a moment when he gave me the letters. The next time he comes, I will ask him for details on the abbey of Messines.* My dear Mama cannot imagine how great a pleasure I take in looking after something she cares about. Even if I were to devote all my time to it, I could still never repay her kindness and her love.

* A dispute had arisen between a French abbey near the border with the Austrian Netherlands and the Austrian Abbey of Messines. A matter of very little consequence, it was resolved in favor of Messines.

Mercy to Maria Theresa, 13 April 1776

Every week the comte d'Artois and the duc de Chartres organize several horse races and the Queen, who has developed an extraordinarily strong taste for this spectacle, has yet to miss one. . . . A kind of platform has been built for HM, from which she watches the show and where there is always a great concourse of ill-chosen people, many informally dressed young men which, together with the confusion and the noise, is hardly in keeping with the dignity of a mighty Queen. . . . These races often take place on Tuesday, and the Queen then fails to receive the Ambassadors [whose audience day it is] and who recently were prevented from paying court to the Queen during three entire weeks.

The Queen excuses everything from those who amuse her. The more or less favorable way she receives people depends almost entirely on this.

WITH THE NEXT letter, the evolution of Marie Antoinette's character becomes quite plain: until now she had answered her mother's reproaches with evasions and half-truths. Here for the first time, rather than admit her responsibility for Turgot's dismissal, she lies outright—as Mercy points out in his letter of May 16, 1776.

Lying to the Empress remained a private matter. Unfortunately Turgot's dismissal marked the clear beginning of Marie Antoinette's interference in matters of State. It is true she had engineered the early firing of Louis XV's ministry, but Louis XVI would have done this within a few months anyway. Now a great and useful servant of the State was forced out simply because he had offended the Queen by suggesting it was time to replace the comte de Guines as French Ambassador to Great Britain. Thus major political interests were compromised for the pettiest of personal vendettas. Inasmuch as the sheer incompetence of later Finance Ministers helped bring about the Revolution, it can fairly be said that Marie Antoinette herself bore a large part of the responsibility for the cataclysm which destroyed the monarchy.

Marie Antoinette to Maria Theresa
Versailles, 15 May 1776

Madame my very dear Mother,

. . . M. de Malesherbes left the ministry yesterday; he is replaced by M. Amelot. M. Turgot was dismissed the same day; M. de Clugny will replace him. I can tell my dear Mama that I am not sorry about these dismissals, but I had nothing to do with them.* . . .

Although that business about Messines is of little importance, two ministers, MM. de Vergennes and de Saint-Germain,† are concerned with it; I saw them again this morning and was promised it would soon be resolved. Will my dear Mama allow me to kiss her? My respect and love.

Mercy to Maria Theresa, 16 May 1776

The princesse de Lamballe, because she multiplies her claims and defends them with arrogance, creates endless conflicts within the Queen's Household whose ladies are complaining about the Superintendent's despotism. There are continual quarrels with the dame d'honneur, with the dame d'atours. The Queen is constantly forced to adjudi-

* In fact she was directly responsible for the two ministers' dismissal.
† The Ministers of Foreign Affairs and War.

cate, to listen to complaints. HM is fed up; her service is badly done and all are displeased. . . .

The Queen has returned to her taste for that comtesse de Polignac. . . . It is in her circle that intrigues of all sorts are born and that HM's dissipation is encouraged.

. . . In the business of the comte de Guines, the King finds himself caught in an obvious contradiction with himself. In letters which are complete opposites, written in his own hand to the comte de Vergennes and the comte de Guines, he has compromised himself and his ministers with the knowledge of the public, which is also aware that all this is being done by the Queen's desire and through a kind of violence with which she has cowed the King.

The *Contrôleur-général* [Finance Minister], who knows the Queen hates him, has decided to resign; the Queen's plan was to demand of the King that M. Turgot be dismissed and even sent to the Bastille on the day the comte de Guines was made a Duke, and it took the strongest and most persistent efforts to moderate the Queen's anger, which is due only to Turgot's suggestion that the comte de Guines be recalled. The Contrôleur-général enjoys a great reputation for honesty and is much loved by the public; it is a shame that his retirement should be in part the Queen's work. . . . The Queen is kept so beside herself, in such a frenzy of dissipation that, together with the King's extreme indulgence, there is sometimes no way to make her see that she is unreasonable.

Maria Theresa to Marie Antoinette
Laxenburg, 30 May 1776

Madame my dear daughter,

. . . You have forgotten the drawings showing how you

dress; we are being shown outfits so exaggerated that I cannot believe that the Queen, my daughter, should wear the like. Please also add how women of a certain age are arranged; it is not that I want to be critical, but I cannot believe that reasonable people dress as we are told over here, and I want to defend the French nation and only attribute these childish displays to the young, with whom one must be indulgent. What you tell me about the business of Messines shows how anxious you are to please me; I am delighted, but the two ministers are only doing their duty in not settling lightly anything that affects the King's service.

I am very pleased that you had nothing to do with the dismissal of the two ministers,* whose reputation among the public is excellent and who only failed in my opinion because they tried to do too much at once. You say that you are not sorry: you must have some good reasons; but for a while now the public has not been praising as much and blames you for all kinds of little intrigues which are not suitable to your position. Since the King loves you, his ministers must respect you; when you ask for nothing that goes against a sound policy or the proper order of things, you earn respect and love at the same time. All I fear for you (since you are so young) is that you may become too dissipated. You have never liked reading or applying yourself; it has often worried me. I was delighted when I saw that you cared about music; that is the reason why I have so often pestered you about your reading. For more than a year now, I have heard no more of your reading or music; I only hear instead about horse rides, hunts, all without the King and with many ill-chosen young people, which worries me greatly because I love you so dearly. Your sisters-in-law are behaving very differently, and I must tell you that all these noisy pleasures which the King doesn't share are not

* A perfect example of the Empress's attempts at correcting her daughter without affronting her.

proper. You will tell me, "He knows all about them and approves of them." I will answer that he is kind and that you must therefore be all the more careful and share your amusements with him. In the long run you can only be happy if you two are linked by a loving and sincere union and friendship. . . .

Marie Antoinette to Maria Theresa
Marly, 13 June 1776

Madame my very dear Mother,

We have just been very worried for the comte d'Artois. His measles, which came out on Thursday morning, has made us move to this place on Saturday. He was more ill than is usually the case; his cough was so strong that he spit up a little blood; the headache was violent, and a rather high fever, which lasted for several days, made us fear that he might be in danger. All the paroxysms ended yesterday; he is about to start a convalescence which will demand much care. The comtesse d'Artois, who is still progressing well in her pregnancy, has remained at Versailles; they made her move to another apartment so that she would be safe from measles. Besides, her quiet ways spared her most of the worry, and it has not been difficult to conceal her husband's state from her. She is expected to give birth in about six weeks.

Since everybody was moving out of Versailles, I had my nephew* moved to my house at Trianon. We worried about my sister Elisabeth for a moment; she had some fever and a headache, but it was only due to a large tooth which came out; she is now with us and in the best of health.

* The comte d'Artois's son, the future duc d'Angoulême.

I wasn't able to have the drawings of the coiffures before the courier left; my dear Mama must have received them through the baron de Breteuil's courier. Coiffures for women of a certain age are like all other articles of clothing and adornment, except for rouge, which old women still wear here and often more than the young ones. For the rest, after forty-five, they wear softer, less noticeable colors, the dresses are less closely fitting and heavier, the hair is less curled, and the coiffures are less high.

It is a great sorrow to me that my dear Mama should believe to my disadvantage reports which are often false and almost always exaggerated. I cannot imagine what people mean by little intrigues not suitable to my position; I let the ministers be appointed without being in any way involved; I told my dear Mama frankly that I wasn't sorry that the others were gone; that was because they displeased almost everyone. Besides, my behavior and even my intentions are well enough known and very remote from all plots or intrigues. Some people may worry about what is being said between the King and myself; but just to please them, I will not give up the trust which must remain between my husband and myself; and I hope that public opinion is not so opposed to me as my dear Mama has been told. My taste for music has not ended; I spend as much time on it and with as much pleasure. Until our trip to Marly, I had a weekly concert in my apartment during which I sang with several others. I started again reading Laurent Echard's *Roman History* a little while back.

There have been no more horse rides for two months now. The King hunts twice a week at Saint-Hubert. I always have supper there with him and sometimes hunt as well. I pay great attention to older people when they come and pay court to me. I admit that there are not very many in my own little group; but how can people tell my dear Mama that it is composed of ill-chosen young people when in fact most of the places [in my Household] are occupied by people of very noble birth who are all between thirty-five and forty-five years old and more?* . . .

The comtesse d'Artois has a great advantage, that of having children; but that is perhaps the only reason why anyone ever thinks about her, and it is not my fault if I do not have that same merit. As for Madame, she is more intelligent, but I wouldn't exchange my reputation for hers. . . .

Maria Theresa to Marie Antoinette
Schönbrunn, 30 June 1776

Madame my dear daughter,

I will admit that the comte d'Artois's measles worries me; that illness is more catching than smallpox. I don't know whether the King has had it. As for Madame Elisabeth, I do not doubt that she will catch it. For you, I fear nothing, so long as you do not approach them too soon. Before four weeks one can never be sure; the consequences are often worse than those of smallpox for the eyes, and especially for the chest, and that is what I would fear most for you; you have already suffered twice from violent colds, which come from being overheated and affect the chest. I am always pleased when I hear they have you drink milk. I do not at all find your apologia too emphatic; I am delighted, my heart is always at one with you and believes only with difficulty whatever is against you; but, as your mother and your

* Mercy had complained, rightly, about the fact that Marie Antoinette was now surrounding herself exclusively with a small group of frivolous, pleasure-mad young people, paid no attention to anyone over thirty (she nicknamed them "centuries"), and spent her time gossiping about the amorous adventures of her friends. Her denial, here again, is an absolute lie; and while there were indeed a few mature people in her official Household, she managed never to see them for more than a few moments.

friend, I feel I must warn you about what people say so that you can be on your guard in the midst of so flattering and so frivolous a nation. . . . I am delighted that you go on with your reading and your music; they are necessary resources, especially so for you. I must say that the drawings of the French outfits are very extraordinary; I can't believe that they are actually worn, and even less at Court. What you did for your nephew is like you; you will never do wrong on these sorts of occasions; I recognize there the mind and the heart of my dear Antoinette. . . .

Please thank the King for having ended the Messines business so quickly and with such consideration for me. I am wholly obliged to you: thus the pious settlement which I care about can be established; at my age one can no longer speak in terms of years, but my love will only end with my life. Always yours. . . .

Marie Antoinette to Maria Theresa, 14 July 1776

Madame my very dear Mother,

Our measles are happily ended: that of the comte d'Artois was more frightening at first; he had so strong and continual a cough that he spit up blood; he is completely cured. Monsieur's measles was not as bad and was not cause for worry; but he is not as fully recovered as the comte d'Artois and they made him take milk, which didn't agree with him. We stayed at Marly not only during my brothers' measles and convalescence, but also until there was no more measles in Versailles, where there had been a lot; thanks to these precautions, a purgation, and the diet the King followed, he was preserved and his health is excellent.

We await the delivery of the comtesse d'Artois from one moment to the next; her health has been very good all through her pregnancy, except that for the last few days she has been complaining about a few pains; that is what makes us think she will soon be giving birth.

Mme de Chabrillant, M. d'Aiguillon's daughter, died at Aiguillon where she went to see her father. As soon as I found out her life was in danger, I thought that if M. d'Aiguillon were to lose his daughter, it would be inhuman to force him to stay in the place where his daughter had died. I asked the King to give him the liberty of going anywhere he wants, except the Court; the King granted it to me. . . .

The decision about Messines pleased me; the King will never be more agreeable than in those occasions which relate to my dear Mama. . . .

Mercy to Maria Theresa, 16 July 1776

The Queen's taste for jewelry is not yet sated. HM has recently given herself diamond bracelets worth nearly 300,000 livres.* In exchange the Queen gave the jewelers some stones which they appraised at a very low value; for the balance she had to make a large deposit. . . . Thus it is that besides the old debt of 300,000 livres for the earrings, HM still owes 100,000 livres and she has nothing left for current expenses. Given this, the Queen, most unwillingly, asked the King to give her 2,000 louis (48,000 livres). The Monarch greeted this request with his usual kindness; he only allowed himself to say softly that he wasn't surprised the Queen was out of money, considering her taste for diamonds.

* $1,350,000.

Marie Antoinette to Maria Theresa, 26 July 1776

Madame my very dear Mother,

The courier who goes to Madrid gave me two great satisfactions—that of receiving my dear Mama's news and that of knowing that my brothers and sisters had arrived. . . .

The prince de Ligne* presented me with a request which I cannot refuse mentioning to my dear Mama. He has several estates in France and is about to win a suit which will give him those that are disputed. He fears, with reason, that he may not be able to keep them once he is no longer in France; he would like to settle his second son here, but before doing anything, he knows that he needs my dear Mama's permission, and he has asked me to obtain it. If you are kind enough to grant this, I will be delighted and will take the child in my regiment† until a better place is found.

The Emperor's trip pleases me greatly, no matter when he may come; but he doesn't like balls and entertainments much, so Carnival will be the worst time for seeing and examining everything as he likes to do. . . .

Marie Antoinette to Maria Theresa, 16 August 1776

Madame my very dear Mother,

You will already know about the happy delivery of the comtesse d'Artois: her health is excellent, and neither she nor her daughter suffered from any accident.

We have lost the prince de Conti;‡ he was a man of great

---

* The prince de Ligne was the head of an illustrious Belgian family and thus the Empress's subject. Witty, handsome, charming, and utterly civilized, he was popular throughout Europe.
† Children of great families were often given a (theoretical) military command and went on to be promoted without having served.
‡ The King's distant cousin, he had hoped to become Prime Minister in the 1740s; upon being disappointed, he had systematically opposed the policies of Louis XV and Louis XVI.

wit but very dangerous because of his endless intrigues with the Parlements.

I was delighted to see Count Dominique Kaunitz* last Tuesday, but since it was during a Court ceremony, I only saw him for an instant, and he came back yesterday to see me privately. I took great pleasure in talking to him and especially in being fully reassured about his father's health, about which I was very worried; I know what a loss he would be to my dear Mama. . . .

I envy the Grand Duke and his wife's happiness; but I cannot help thinking of the moment when they will leave, which will be very bitter for them, and my dear Mama's love will also surely suffer from it. . . .

Mercy to Maria Theresa, 17 August 1776

In spite of all the efforts I have made to convince the Queen to give up a plan I think very detrimental to her service, HM has decided . . . to give her First Equerry, the comte de Tessé a *survivancier*† in the person of the comte de Polignac, the favorite's husband. . . . The comte de Maurepas was one of the main agents of this business, which clearly proves that the comtesse de Polignac belongs to the minister's party, and that it is through her he is always so well informed of the Queen's thoughts and plans. The custom here is to give a survivancier only at the request of the office holder; forcing him to take a survivancier means that he will be upset. The comte de Tessé did not deserve this. Although very limited, he is honest, quiet, zealous, and most

* Son of Prince Kaunitz, the Austrian Chancellor.
† A *survivancier* was sometimes appointed to succeed the holder of a Court office. He usually received no salary and was the son or heir of the office holder.

exact in fulfilling the duties of his office. He is married to a Noailles and thus linked to that powerful family. . . . None of these considerations affected the Queen's compliance and predilection for her favorite . . . The Queen, in order to preserve the appearance that she is equally kind [to Mme de Lamballe], saw to it that the Poitou governorship was given to the duc de Chartres.

Maria Theresa to Marie Antoinette
Schönbrunn, 2 September 1776

Madame my dear daughter,

Your short letter, to which I even found a difference in handwriting, worried me since you say you have a migraine; but that of Mercy of the twenty-first told me two days later that you had a bout of tertiary fever but that your physician is not worried and will allow the fever to continue as long as it gets no worse, so as to destroy the humors which sometimes ail you; in spite of this very proper reasoning, which reminded me of our great van Swieten and which Stoerck also approves, I would prefer to know that you are completely cured and fear that you do not take sufficient care of yourself, especially in the autumn.

I owe you an answer about the prince de Ligne for the settling of his second son in France. I am always delighted to oblige those whom you protect, but he must ask for my permission through the Brussels government and Prince Kaunitz, before anything can be done; that is what the duc d'Arenberg did. I must only warn you that the prince de Ligne is full of wit and pleasant qualities, but that his character does not come up to them because he is frivolous, and that he has boasted much about his last trip to Paris.

All the news from Paris* tell us that you have spent 250,000 livres on some bracelets, that in order to do so, you have upset your finances and are now in debt, and that in order to remedy this, you have sold some of your diamonds for a very low price, and it is supposed you urge the King to these useless profuse outlays which have been rising again lately and put the State in distress. . . . These kinds of anecdotes pierce my heart, especially for the future; but there are two other circumstances which did much to console me. It is to you that people attribute the comte d'Artois's good behavior to his wife, and not enough can be said of yours to her. I recognize my kind and loving daughter in this, and also in that story of the grandmother from whom you have taken a child: all these anecdotes bring me back to life, but that of the diamonds has humiliated me. That French frivolity with all these extraordinary adornments! My daughter, my dear daughter, the first Queen [in Europe] would become frivolous herself! I cannot bear that idea. . . .

Marie Antoinette to Maria Theresa, 14 September 1776

Madame my very dear Mother,

My fever has been over for eight days; now I am not sorry to have a few hours of it, although it is very painful. The quinine I took afterward caused a great melting of humors and a sort of overflow of bile. I have had to be purged; I am very well now and have taken some more Peruvian bark. My dear Mama can be sure that I will follow doctor's orders, were it only because of her kindness and the worry she feels for her child. We usually have a beautiful autumn at

* It was really Mercy.

Fontainebleau; I will not abuse it and will always be home very early.

The prince de Ligne has rejoined his regiment; I let him know my dear Mama's intentions. Although he is very likable, and much liked here, I still know that he is frivolous.

I have taken, as survivancier of M. de Tessé, M. le comte de Polignac, who is Colonel of the King's Regiment and a man of a very good family. He is married to a woman I love greatly. I wanted to prevent a request from the Noailles, who are already much too powerful a tribe here.* . . .

I have nothing to say about the bracelets; I did not think people would try and bother my dear Mama with such trifles. . . .

Mercy to Maria Theresa, 17 September 1776

The Queen, reading Your Majesty's letter, said to the abbé de Vermond, "Well, now my bracelets have reached Vienna! I will bet that information comes from my sister Marie."

"Why?"

"This is jealousy; that's the way she is."

Vermond then asked if the Empress seemed annoyed. "So-so—you'll see," and he was given the letter.

[Because of the Polignac appointment, the Queen's horses now cost 200,000 livres a year more than those of the late Queen.] At first the public was pleased that the King had given Trianon to the Queen; now it is worried and alarmed by the money which is being spent there.† She ordered the

* As so often, Marie Antoinette is trying to deceive her mother: the Noailles could not have asked for the survivance, as there had never been one for the office of Equerry; and, uniquely, M. de Polignac was given a large salary to do exactly nothing.

† The Queen was creating a completely new, expensive, English-style garden and building a small theater.

gardens redone so as to have an English-style landscape which will cost at least 150,000 livres. The Queen has had a theater built at Trianon. So far she has only given one play there, which was followed by a supper, but the evening was very costly.

. . . The Queen's income has been more than doubled, and yet she now has debts. . . . She has bought many diamonds, and her gambling is expensive; she no longer plays ordinary games where one cannot lose much. Lansquenet and sometimes pharaon* have become her normal games. . . . Her ladies and the courtiers are worried and upset by the losses they risk when paying court to the Queen. It is also true that these high stakes displease the King and are concealed from him as much as possible.

Maria Theresa to Marie Antoinette, 1 October 1776

Madame my dear daughter,

I am reassured that your long fever has ended and that you tell me yourself that you are in good health. . . .

Could I do enough when I received that much desired portrait of the King? I would be sorry if you were not better than I, both in appearance and in mind: you are young in a country with natural talents; you should grow and become perfect; it is only your frivolity I fear, and I cannot conceal my fears on that subject. You go over the bracelets very quickly, but it is not such as you want to consider it. A sovereign abases herself in so adorning herself, and even more so if, in order to do so, she spends very large sums of money and at what a time? I see your spirit of dissipation only too clearly; I cannot stay silent; I love you for your

* Pharaon was a card game played for high stakes at which large sums could be won or lost in a moment.

own good, not to flatter you. Do not lose through frivolities the credit you earned earlier; people know the King is very moderate [in his expenditure], and the fault will therefore be considered as yours alone. I do not wish to survive such a change. I am all yours.

Marie Antoinette to Maria Theresa, October 1776*

Madame my very dear Mother,

I am very ashamed of the apology I must offer my dear Mama for the lateness of my wishes and my respects for Saint Theresa's day; the trip to Choisy and the departure to Fontainebleau had confused me a little, and I hoped that this courier would arrive earlier. . . .

My dear Mama can be completely reassured about my health; I followed the prescriptions and precautions enough so that the doctors no longer fear a return of the fever. My dear Mama may be sure that if there had been the least change in my state, I would have told her so right away.† I am sorry about it but must agree that there is no retrogression and that I still have a good hope. . . .

Maria Theresa to Marie Antoinette
Vienna, 31 October 1776

Madame my dear daughter,

I hope this will arrive before the tenth, as you wish, so there will be time to send it back before your return from

---

* There is no exact date because Marie Antoinette simply forgot to send the Empress her wishes; omitting the date was an attempt to hide this.
† The Queen is referring, as usual, to the nonconsummation of her marriage.

Fontainebleau; otherwise we would have missed a whole month, and I must tell you that I always await the arrival of these couriers with a loving impatience. Your excuses about forgetting my name day are accepted without rancor; but, my dear daughter, it is not once a year that I wish you to think of me, but every month, every week, and every day, so that you forget neither my love nor my advice and the examples I give you.

I must admit that I am worried by this life of constant dissipation, those promenades, those rides which even Queens much older than you never tried, although they were still young and accompanied by their husbands; the point that upsets me the most, that all this should be done without the King, that it is your will alone, and his overly great good nature, which may end some day, especially if excessive spending is added.* It is on those occasions that I would like you to think of me, and I am sure and know your heart, if it has not been entirely changed by flattery and frivolities, that this thought alone would stop you because of the pain that this behavior would cause me, which may end of itself but perhaps too late for your happiness and your reputation; these are my only care and will be as long as I live.

Marie Antoinette to Maria Theresa, 12 November 1776

Madame my very dear Mother,

The kindness of my dear Mama for my birthday and her extreme indulgence about my forgetfulness are the most poignant of reproaches. How could I forget, even for one moment, everything my dear Mama has done for me? Her

* This almost incoherent sentence is typical of the way the Empress wrote when she was upset.

example will always be my pride, and I would be too happy if I could imitate it, although from afar.

Our trip went very well; the King hunted too often for me to accompany him every time, but I went along very often. On Wednesday I will go with him to a famous horse race; we are still closely united and very good friends. . . .

Mercy to Maria Theresa, 15 November 1776

The Queen decided that she wanted to play some pharaon; she asked the King that he allow her to have some of the player bankers [i.e., men who held the bank against whom the other players betted] from Paris come out [to Fontainebleau]. The Monarch answered that since gambling was prohibited, even in the Houses of the Princes of the Blood Royal, allowing it at Court would set a bad example; but with his usual kindness, the King added that it would be all right as long as the game was played for one evening only. The bankers arrived on October 30 and played the whole night and the morning of the thirty-first at the princesse de Lamballe's, where the Queen stayed until five in the morning, after which HM gave orders to play again that evening and far into the morning of November 1, All Hallows Day.* The Queen herself played until almost three in the morning. The worst of it was that it happened on the morning of a solemn feast, so people have been talking. The Queen got out of it by joking; she told the King that he had allowed a session of gambling without specifying its duration, and that it had therefore been allowable to make it last thirty-six hours. The King burst out laughing and answered, "Go on, you are all worthless, the whole bunch of you!" Monsieur

* All Hallows Day is one of the most revered religious feasts in Catholic countries.

and Madame attended the two sessions, but they did not stay up as late; M. le comte d'Artois stayed until seven or eight in the morning.

One of the worst consequences of all this dissipation is that the King almost never spends the night with the Queen. . . . I have spoken very strongly about this to the Queen and have pointed out to her that it was important to her influence and her safety that the Court not know that the King was sleeping apart from her.

Maria Theresa to Marie Antoinette
Vienna, 30 November 1776

Madame my dear daughter,

I am delighted to know you are back [at Versailles] and quieter for the winter; in the long run your health will not withstand all those runs and late nights; even if it were always in the King's company, I would say nothing, but always without him and with not only the worst society in Paris, but also the youngest so that the Queen, the charming Queen, is almost the oldest of this whole company! These gazettes, these sheets which made my days so pleasant, which reported the good actions, the most generous ways of my daughter, are now changed; all I find there are horse races, gambling, and late nights so that I will no longer read them, but I can't stop the people who talk about all this. . . . The Emperor means to go to France. I can imagine what a consolation this will be to you, and you will profit of the time he will spend with you, and from his advice. . . .

Marie Antoinette to Maria Theresa, 16 December 1776

Madame my very dear Mother,

In truth I could consider myself unhappy because of what people say about me. While some of them convince my dear Mama that I only see people as young as I, here for the last year the very young think I treat them badly and neglect me, and not fifteen days ago there was talk of a little intrigue for them not to attend my balls. Still they all come and there were even children who looked as if they were out of school. I thought I had told my dear Mama that I went to the great race at Fontainebleau with the King and that I hunt with him as often as I can. . . .

Our balls began this month; I dance with pleasure, but I intend not to tire myself as I did these past years. . . .

My dear Mama can imagine how pleased I will be to see the Emperor; I have been hoping for him for so long that I won't count on it yet. Besides my satisfaction, my greatest happiness would be that having seen things as they are, he can free my dear Mama of the prejudices people are trying to give her against me. These upset me greatly, and I can only be happy by convincing her that I will retain to the last day of my life my respect and gratitude for her unparalleled kindness.

THE EMPEROR JOSEPH II, Marie Antoinette's brother, was her opposite in almost every way. He cared nothing for amusement, fashion, or the usual indulgences of a crowned head. A curt, often disagreeable man, he was also extremely conscientious and hardworking, a model ruler in many ways, and the archetype of the enlightened despot. He disliked the routines of the Court, which he considered a waste of time, but traveled as widely as he could in order to learn the way other countries functioned. Highly intelligent

though he was, he often made enemies of people whose feelings he failed to understand. There was a substantial
chance, therefore, that he would antagonize Marie Antoinette, of whose behavior he strongly disapproved.

Maria Theresa to Marie Antoinette
Vienna, 2 January 1777

Madame my dear daughter,
    This year begins so happily for you that I hope you will
long feel its effects. In a month you will see the Emperor;
that is a momentous time for you. You know his heart and
his wisdom. From the first you may expect everything: it
will not fail you, since he takes a real pleasure in seeing you;
from the other you may draw great resources. I hope that
you will speak to him with that trust and love which he
deserves and which must tighten forever the links between
our Houses and families while confirming the most loving
friendship between the sovereigns: those are the sole means
of ensuring the happiness of our States and our families. I
hope the King will like him and that once the first awkwardness is past, trust and friendship will occur. . . .
    P.S. You will speak to your brother about your marriage
with complete sincerity. I can answer for his discretion and
for the fact that he is well able to give you good advice. That
point is of the greatest importance for you.

Marie Antoinette to Maria Theresa
Versailles, 16 January 1777

Madame my very dear Mother,
    I am overwhelmed with the hope of seeing my brother

soon; I need not say so, my dear Mama knows it well, it will be hard for me not to install him near me.* People will be surprised, but I will sacrifice all to his preferences. He will be lodged and will live as he pleases; seeing him and talking to him will be such happiness for me! I count on his friendship, he can be sure of mine, and even if his is as great, I still have much more to gain than he does, since he will tell me about my dear Mama, who is so far from me. I am sure that the Emperor's trip will be good in every way; I know his discretion and will confide in him. After the first moment, which may be a little awkward, the King will be pleased to see him and speak to him: good things can only ensue, for the business of the State and for myself. My health is very good, Carnival is short, and besides I am taking care of myself; I hope to be less tired than the last years. I would like to have the same hope for my dear Mama's Lent; her health and the happiness of pleasing her are my deepest desires. May I kiss her?

Mercy to Maria Theresa, 17 January 1777

I found the Queen worried and embarrassed by the state of her debts, whose total amount she does not know herself. I added them up and they came to 487,272 livres.† The Queen, who was a little surprised to see her finances in so bad a condition, realized that she would have great difficulty with her current expenses and decided reluctantly to ask the King whether he might take on at least some of these debts. As soon as the Queen began talking about this, the King,

* The Emperor, who was traveling incognito, did not want to be hampered by Court etiquette from seeing the country as it really was; he therefore ordered Mercy to find him an apartment in the town of Versailles and refused all invitations to the Palace itself.
† That is, more than two years' income—over $2 million.

without a moment's hesitation, agreed to pay the entire amount. He only asked for a few months' delay as he wanted to pay this from his privy purse and without the intervention of any minister.

For a long time now Versailles has not been as empty as this winter, and it could become more so still. . . . Although HM treats everyone kindly and graciously when they are before her, it is still true that the small group of those the Queen calls her friends discourages most of the courtiers and takes away from them the occasion and the possibility of coming to pay their court.

Maria Theresa to Marie Antoinette
Vienna, 3 February 1777

Madame my dear daughter,

Your letters of the sixteenth and the twenty-fourth gave rise to different feelings in me; that which expressed so vividly your expectation of your dear brother's arrival gave me great pleasure; at the same time it made me sorrier to see it canceled.* The King's letter touched me deeply; you may tell him so if you think it right. . . . The Emperor and the King are so young; both have such a great and good heart that my hopes will be well founded if they know each other and feel that mutual trust which will be so necessary and useful to them in their political lives. . . . I have ordered [Mercy] to inform you and decide with you how your ministers should be handled. Here are the greatest questions which I mention only in passing. The dissensions between the Turks and the Russians, between Spain and Portugal, as well as the war in America may well cause a general confla-

* In fact the trip was merely delayed.

gration into which I would be drawn in spite of myself, especially since with our wicked neighbor* we must be especially circumspect; his usual hatred of us has grown even stronger ever since we dared, in Poland and elsewhere, to oppose his unjust principles.† He does everything he can to win favor or at least, at every Court, he tries to blame the way we act; no calumny is spared, especially in France, and that is the reason which makes me doubly sorry that the meeting cannot take place. . . . I will not conceal from you that your private life is not spared either, and I have mentioned several things to Mercy which really afflict me: your amusements, games, and promenades; that you are on bad terms with the King, sleeping separately because you stay up gambling all night, which he didn't want you to do; that you were struck by the Emperor's arrival; that you didn't want him to come at all; and even that you were now delighted because your pleasures would not be interrupted.‡ All these hints come from Berlin through Saxony, Poland, etc., and everywhere, and I must admit that for the last few months they have caused me great pain. . . . The gazettes confirm only too thoroughly all these different amusements which my dear Queen attends without her sisters-in-law and the King, and that has given me many a sad moment. . . .

* Frederick II of Prussia.
† This is a prime example of the Empress's double standard: she blames Frederick for policies like the partition of Poland, which she herself did not hesitate to follow. It is, however, true that calumny was one of Frederick's most constantly used weapons.
‡ As usual the Empress was thoroughly informed.

Marie Antoinette to Maria Theresa
Versailles, 17 February 1777

Madame my very dear Mother,

I can absolutely reassure my dear Mama's kindness. My health is very good and held up well through the Carnival; for the last three days, however, I have been taking cooling broths and expect that they will make me feel even better than before. I saw Mercy yesterday; he talked to me about everything my dear Mama mentioned. I am more disgusted than surprised by the nastiness and wickedness of the evil neighbor; he himself may be fooled on some points by his minister here; he has long been known as a man of little scruple who, to make himself look good, does not hesitate to send his master all kinds of stories. The distance is a great resource, and certainly no one here would dare to say that I am on bad terms with the King or that I sleep separately from him. There are too many witnesses to the contrary. As for my feeling on the Emperor's trip, surely they didn't hope anyone would believe it.

I must admit to my dear Mama that I took advantage not only of the balls I gave, but also of those at the Opera in Paris; but I only went there after telling the King and making sure he would not be displeased. He told me in the friendliest way that I could go there as long as it amused me;* besides I only went with Monsieur, whose arm I always held at the ball. At the last the comtesse d'Artois also came. It is very sad for me that my dear Mama should be affected by these rumors.

Although I have very little experience of politics, I cannot help being very worried about what is happening everywhere in Europe. It would be very terrible if the Turks and

* Hiding behind her husband's permission was one of Marie Antoinette's favorite tricks: in fact Louis XVI always allowed her to do anything she wanted, even if it upset him or seemed unwise—and the Empress knew it.

the Russians went back to war. At least here I am very sure they want to keep the peace. If my brother had come, I think, like my dear Mama, that his acquaintance with the King would have been very useful for the general good and quiet. It would be the greatest good fortune if these two sovereigns, who are so close to me, could trust each other; they could settle many things together and would be protected from the lack of skill and the personal interests of their ministers.

The Grand Almoner is at death's door; Prince Louis [de Rohan] will replace him in that office. I am really annoyed by this, and it will be much against his own inclination that the King will appoint him; but two years ago he allowed himself to be surprised by M. de Soubise and Mme de Marsan into a half promise, which they converted into a full one by thanking him, and which they have just now used to the full. If he behaves as he always did, we will have many intrigues.* . . .

Maria Theresa to Marie Antoinette
Vienna, 4 March 1777

Madame my dear daughter,

I must thank you. The handsome, magnificent table arrived here ten days ago in perfect condition; everyone has admired it. You tell me about cooling broths, the gazettes speak of the waters of Plombières; I would prefer a steadier way of life to medicines. I am glad that it is not true about your sleeping apart; but I wish that during the day you were only wherever the King is himself. . . .

The office that Rohan must have afflicts me; he is a cruel

* The Queen was all too right: the Affair of the Necklace proved it a few years later.

enemy, both for you and because of his principles, which are of the most perverse. Under an amiable, easy, and taking exterior, he has done much harm here, and now I must see him next to the King and you! Nor will he honor his office as a bishop.

I do hope, like you, that war will be avoided, but in the long run I am afraid, and that is one of the reasons why I want the two brothers-in-law to meet and be linked by feeling and interest. I kiss you sincerely.

Mercy to Maria Theresa, 18 March 1777

Nothing is changed in the endless compliance, the friendship, and the attachment which the King displays toward the Queen on every occasion. On this capital point there is nothing to be desired; besides that, it is fair to say that the royal family is characterized more by peace among its members than by their union. Mesdames are no longer seen outside their apartments. . . . Madame Adélaïde, and even more Madame Sophie, dislike the Queen; Madame Victoire has always remained on good terms with HM.

The Queen's immoderate taste for gambling is all the more regrettable in that it has angered the public and may cause other grave consequences. These games, although they are still forbidden, have started up in Paris again ever since the Court gave the example of disobedience to the law. These games have been attended with such great losses, with so much cheating that the government has had to renew the prohibition. . . . The Queen showed the King she was annoyed by this; he was almost afraid to tell her about the orders he had given; so at the moment the Queen pays no attention to these and plays some pharaon almost every day.

. . . The Queen loses large sums almost every day. . . . The money which the King is giving her to pay off her debts is at least in part absorbed by her considerable gambling losses, and if this disorder continues, the Queen will find herself doubly embarrassed since her debts will have grown while she took unfair advantage of the King's kindness. This subject requires the most serious advice from Your Majesty.

Mercy to Maria Theresa, 18 April 1777

Although I expected the Emperor's visit to have good results, I dare to say that those I see are beyond my hopes. The Emperor has so perfectly understood and used the right way in which to make a strong impression on his august sister that the ideas he explained to her cannot fail to bear fruit. . . . His Majesty attacks her prejudices but without going too fast; he gives precise reasons, draws consequences from earlier examples so that . . . the Queen's mind is subjugated.

Joseph II to Leopold, Grand Duke of Tuscany
Paris, 29 April 1777

. . . Yesterday I saw the ceremonies on a Sunday in Versailles in public—the lever, the Mass, the grand couvert.* As for me, I was hidden in the crowd and watching everything. I must admit it was amusing and that since I put on this kind of act so often myself, I gain from seeing [it] played by

---

* The lever, an immensely complicated ceremony, started with the King's official awakening and ended when, fully dressed, he went off to Mass; the grand couvert was when the King and Queen ate in public.

others. The Queen is a pretty woman, but she is empty-headed, unable as yet to find her advantage, and wastes her days running from dissipation to dissipation, some of which are perfectly allowable but nonetheless dangerous because they prevent her from having the thoughts she needs so badly. The building is handsome and deserves a visit; there are also some very interesting men whom it is very satisfying to know.* . . .

Joseph II to Leopold, Grand Duke of Tuscany
Paris, 2 May 1777†

[The ministers are the masters.] The King is only an absolute sovereign when he passes from one form of slavery to the next, he can always change his ministers, but he can never, unless he is a transcendent genius, become the master of the way his government is run. You can imagine how the State's business is done; as for me, I can see clearly that all the detail which is connected to personal intrigues is taken care of with the greatest attention and interest while the important business of the State is completely neglected. All the magistrates and the nobles who hope one day to reach a ministerial position are always shouting against the men in power so that they will be changed, but if one tries to attack the kind of dreadful despotism that each exerts in his office, all come together to resist since each hopes to hold the office eventually.

The King is badly educated, his appearance goes against him—but he is honest, not devoid of knowledge, only weak

* The relative moderation of this letter is due to the fact that it was sent through the regular post and would therefore probably be read by the French government.
† Unlike the preceding one, this letter was sent to the Grand Duke by an Austrian Embassy courier: the Emperor could therefore write freely.

to those who know how to intimidate him and therefore lead him by the nose; he leads a very uniform life without curiosity, without overall views, in a [state of] continual apathy. Besides this, he is a strong man and looks as if he should be able to father a child; on this subject there are deep mysteries; he has, I am told, very firm erections; he even puts it in, but he doesn't move and then withdraws without having ejaculated.

The Queen is a very pretty and amiable young woman, and could be seen as such anywhere, but she thinks only of having fun; she feels nothing for the King; she is drunk with the dissipation typical of this country, so that in a word she fulfills neither her function as a woman nor as a Queen as she should, for as a woman she completely neglects the King; she makes him do what she wants, more through her authority than in any other way; she spends time with him neither during the day nor at night; finally she has taken on this a very hazardous determination for it is built on false principles; as Queen she is tied down by no etiquette, she goes out, she runs around alone or with a few people without the outward signs of her position, she looks a little improper, and while this would be all right for a private person, she is not doing her job, and that may well have consequences in the future. Her virtue is intact, even strict, but less through forethought than inborn disposition; in a word it has all been all right until now, but in the long run she will find herself resourceless and things may go badly; that is what I have been telling her, but although I am perfectly satisfied with her friendship and her sincerity—she listens, she agrees—the whirlwind of dissipation which surrounds her prevents her from thinking of anything but going from pleasure to pleasure. All the people who surround her encourage her in this frenzy; how could I, alone, prevent it? Still I have made some progress, especially about her gambling, which was dreadful.

Monsieur is undefinable, better than the King, and without any warmth at all, and Madame, ugly and ill-mannered, is not a Piedmontese for nothing, she is full of intrigues. The comte d'Artois is a thorough dandy; his wife, who only produces children, is a complete idiot; Madame Elisabeth is neither pretty nor ugly; I seldom see her as I am determined to remain unmarried. Mesdames aunts are kindly women who no longer matter. . . .

Joseph II to Leopold, Grand Duke of Tuscany, 9 June 1777

. . . I really minded leaving Versailles for I have truly become very fond of my sister and I saw her sorrow at our parting which made mine worse. She is an amiable and honest woman, a little young, thoughtless, but at bottom with feelings of honesty and virtue, an understanding of her position, and really respectable. With all that, she is clever and sees things so clearly that I have often been surprised. Her first reaction is always the best, if she stayed with it and thought about it a little more, and if she listened a little less to the people who urge her on, of which there are armies, and in different camps, she would be perfect. The desire to have fun is very powerful in her, and since people are aware of it, they prey on that weakness, and those who give her the largest amount of, and the most varied pleasure are listened to and treated well.

Her situation with the King is very odd; he is only two thirds of a husband, and although he loves her, he fears her more; our sister has the kind of power to be expected from a royal mistress, not the kind a wife should have, for she forces him to do things he doesn't want to do. He is weak but not stupid; he has notions; he is able to judge but is apathetic in body and mind; he can hold a reasonable conversation, has no desire to learn, no curiosity, and is impotent neither in body nor mind, but the *fiat lux** hasn't come, all is without form. Just imagine, in his marital bed—here is the secret—he has strong, well-conditioned erections; he introduces the member, stays there without moving for perhaps two minutes, withdraws without ejaculating but still erect, and says good night; this is incomprehensible because with all that he sometimes has nightly emissions, but once in place and going at it, never, and he is satisfied; he says plainly that he does it all purely from a sense of duty but never for pleasure; oh, if only once I could have been there, I would have taken care of him; he should be whipped so that he would ejaculate out of sheer rage like a donkey. My sister, with all this, has little temperament; and there they are, together, two complete blunderers. That is about how things are except that the government, which depends on an octogenarian minister,† goes as best it can and is devoid of a real system; there is no courage, no firmness of mind; in a word they try to move forward without worrying about what happens on the right or left. . . .

Marie Antoinette to Maria Theresa
Versailles, 14 June 1777

Madame my very dear Mother,

It is true that the Emperor's departure has left a void I cannot fill; I was so happy during that short time that it now all seems like a dream. But what will never be one is all the

* The Emperor is referring to the beginning of Genesis; *fiat lux:* let there be light.
† Maurepas; he was actually seventy-six.

good advice he gave me and which is engraved in my heart forever.

I must tell my dear Mama that he gave me a thing I asked for repeatedly and which pleases me greatly: he has left me written advice. This is my main reading now, and if ever (which I doubt) I could forget what he told me, I would have this paper always before me, which would soon bring me back to my duty.

My dear Mama will have seen by the courier who left yesterday how beautifully the King behaved in the last moments my brother was here. In all I can assure my dear Mama that I know him well and that he was truly affected by this departure. Since he is not always a master of form, it is less easy for him to show his feelings on the outside; but everything I see proves that he is truly fond of my brother and feels very friendly toward him. At the time of this departure, when I was most desperate, the King showed me attentions and thoughtful tenderness that I can never forget and which would make me love him if I didn't already do so. . . .

Mercy to Maria Theresa, 15 June 1777

The first moment of the [Emperor's] and the Queen's meeting was extremely touching; they hugged and remained silent and full of emotion for a long time. Then they went to a back cabinet, where they spent almost two hours alone; there, their hearts opened; the Queen's was much moved; it became even more so because of two things the Emperor said to her as a proof of his satisfaction in finding her as she was. He told her that if she were not his sister and he could marry her, he would not hesitate to wed again so as to have so charming a companion. The second thing he told her was that if the Queen were to be widowed and childless, he wanted her to come and live again with Your Majesty and with him. This so touched the Queen that she was able to open her mind to the Emperor and spoke to him directly about the most essential aspects of her position.

. . . The last time I went to Versailles, I found the Queen still sad and moved by her august brother's departure. She talked to me in the most serious tone about her plans for improving her behavior.

Marie Antoinette to Maria Theresa
Versailles, 16 June 1777

Madame my very dear Mother,

My separation from my brother gave me a severe jolt; I suffered as much as possible and can only be consoled by the fact that he shared my sorrow; all the family was touched and moved. My brother behaved so perfectly with everyone that he takes with him the regrets and admiration of all the estates; he will never be forgotten. As for me, I would be unfair if my sorrow and the emptiness I feel left me nothing but regret. Nothing can pay for the happiness I felt and the signs of friendship he gave me. I felt very sure he only wanted my happiness, and all his advice proves it; I will not forget it. He only lacked the time needed really to know the people with whom I must live. . . .

The comtesse d'Artois may be pregnant again. That is an unpleasant outlook for me after more than seven years of marriage; it would, however, be unfair to show bad temper. I am not without hope; my brother will tell my dear Mama all about it. The King talked to him on this point in a friendly and trusting way. . . .

Maria Theresa to Marie Antoinette
Schlosshof, 29 June 1777

Madame my dear daughter,

. . . I had foreseen the jolt that it would cause you and worried about it: in fact I am told that your nerves suffered from it. I hope it will not have any consequences, since you say nothing about it, and Mercy doesn't either. How flattering and consoling for me is the general approbation which this dear son has earned. I was a little afraid that his rigid simplicity and his philosophy might be unpopular and that on his side he would not like the country; but I have the consolation of seeing the reverse of that . . . but what pleases me most of all is what you tell me about the friendship and trust between the two brothers-in-law. . . . You may contribute most to this happy beginning by following your brother's advice. . . . The Emperor was touched by his liking for you; he found great pleasure in your conversation and your friendship. I do not betray him in conveying his own words, which I could never say better: "I left Versailles with difficulty because I was really fond of my sister; I found a kind of sweetness of life which I had given up, but the taste for which I see I retain. She is amiable and charming; I spent hours and hours with her without realizing that time was passing. Her sensitivity when I left was great, but she held herself in check; I needed all my strength to find legs to walk away."

. . . I expect the most happy consequences from all this, even for the state of your marriage for which I am given hopes: but it is all postponed to the return when we will speak about it. I must admit it annoys me a little for everything depends on your having children; and I quite approve of the way you feel about your sister-in-law's pregnancy.

Mercy to Maria Theresa, 15 July 1777

The Queen is still behaving according to her new plan; she still has not strayed far from the thoughtful decisions she had taken. . . . She still does not gamble outside her apartment, but that is only half progress because the stakes for which pharaon is played every evening at the Queen's are still very high.

Marie Antoinette to Maria Theresa
Versailles, 19 August 1777

Madame my very dear Mother,

My health is entirely good now, and my dear Mama's kindness would guarantee my cure if it were not already complete. My side is also fine, and I did not suffer from it at all during this fever. The idea of taking the waters of Carlsbad almost makes me regret my recovery; it would be a very great happiness for me if I could ever find myself so close to my dear Mama: what she says about all this fills me with gratitude. I can imagine my dear Mama's joy at seeing the Emperor sooner than she thought; he wrote me he would surprise her and arrive in Vienna on the second. I was quite sure he could never go to the camp without spending at least a few days in Vienna; I am very relieved to know his travels are at last over. . . . According to everything he wrote me, he seems pleased with what he saw; everywhere he went, people were equally enchanted with him; all the letters that come from there speak only of him.

I am very worried about what my dear Mama is good enough to tell me about Ferdinand; I knew nothing of his health, and I am ashamed to admit that since we are both very lazy, I have not had his news in a very long time. I am very impatient to hear about the Queen of Naples's delivery. I very much want her to have a boy; but it seems to me that she hardly expects that. As for my own state, it is unfortunately always the same; that is why I don't bother my dear Mama with it. But I do not despair; there is a slight improvement, which is that the King is more eager than before, and that is a lot for him. Otherwise he is in good health, and I have only reasons to be pleased with him. . . . We are close to the moment of the cardinal de la Roche-Aymon's death, and prince Louis [de Rohan] will succeed him. I will not conceal from my dear Mama that I find it very upsetting, and the King himself is not happy about it; he was horribly deceived in this. That is the misfortune of being young and having no one reasonable to rely on. . . .

A LTHOUGH on the whole the Emperor's visit was not a success—people thought him boorish and generally odd—it did produce one wholly positive change: after years of hesitation, Louis XVI decided to undergo circumcision, an operation which in an age without anesthesia was both painful and frightening. As soon as he recovered, it became obvious that at long last he had become able to have sex, and Marie Antoinette wrote her mother the following ecstatic letter.

Marie Antoinette to Maria Theresa, 30 August 1777

My dear Mother,
    Vergennes tells me he is sending a courier to Breteuil. It is a thrilling occasion for me. I am in the most essential happiness of my entire life. It has already been more than eight days since my marriage was perfectly consummated; the

proof has been repeated and yesterday even more completely than the first time. At first I thought of sending my dear Mama a courier. I feared that it would be such an event as to cause talk. I will also admit that I wanted to be quite sure. I do not think that I am pregnant yet but at least have the hope of being so from one moment to the next. I have so many proofs of love from my dear Mama, how happy she will be now! I enjoy her happiness like my own. May I kiss her with all my heart?

Maria Theresa to Marie Antoinette
Schönbrunn, 30 August 1777

Madame my dear daughter,

Thank God that awful fever is gone! All you tell me about Carlsbad is charming; I kiss you for it. Our dear Queen behaved well: here is a second fat boy, and he has been named Francis,* which is a charming attention. . . .

What you tell me about the greater eagerness of your dear King pleases me greatly. The good Stoerck, who cares so much about you, after having spoken to the Emperor, has assured me that a man of thirty can still change but that one must try never to give up and that for that reason a wife must never waste an occasion and even look for them with every kind of obliging behavior. So, no sleeping separately, no night parties, especially no more gambling. . . .

I am so glad you play billiards or company games. The Emperor has told you everything there is to say on this subject. I can only add that you will soon be sorry. You are losing sums that the King and you can use better, and if you win you should be sorrier still: we are therefore always a

* Maria Theresa's late husband was named Francis.

dupe [when we gamble]. A generous effort on yourself, by
forbidding it at Court, would greatly honor you and heap
me with consolations. I know through my own experience
what danger and unpleasantness one risks on those occasions and the little efforts it would cost you [to stop] would
be richly repaid later. . . .

P.S. The news of your brother [Ferdinand] is no better
yet; I sent him a doctor to find out what is what. You can tell
Vermond that the Emperor confirmed his assiduity and zeal
in your service, and such he has been ever since I have
known him.

Marie Antoinette to Maria Theresa
Versailles, 10 September 1777

Madame my dear Mother,

The birth of a son to the Queen of Naples has pleased me
more than I can say; I certainly love my sister with all my
heart . . . but I must confess that I rejoice even more about
her newborn baby because I hope soon to have the same
happiness. Since the letter I wrote my dear Mama was given
to the baron's courier, I had a moment in which I hoped I
was pregnant; that hope vanished, but I have every confidence that it will soon return. Ferdinand's state worries me;
from so far I cannot tell, but it seems to me that given his
condition the air of his natal city would do him good, and I
very much wish he would spend the winter in Vienna.

The King doesn't like to sleep in my bed.* I urge him not
to proceed to a complete separation. He sometimes spends
the night with me. I do not feel I should insist he come more

* Marie Antoinette is again lying. What the King didn't like was being
awakened in the middle of the night when his wife finally went to bed.

often because he visits me every morning in my private study. His friendship and his love grow every day. . . .

Mercy to Maria Theresa, 12 September 1777

The Queen's passion for gambling is worse than ever, and it has given rise to several problems. . . . The gaming is sometimes tumultuous and mannerless; the bankers have reproached a few young women of the Court for their lack of exactness in the way they play; one evening there was a rather loud dispute of this kind between the comtesse de Gramont and the duc de Fronsac. Such scandals, which cannot be kept quiet, give rise to much talk. Besides, the Queen is losing more and more, her finances are completely exhausted, and therefore her old debts are not being paid off, nor is there ever any money for charity. . . .

The comtesse de Polignac is more in favor than ever. The Queen can no longer do without this young woman's company and tells her all her thoughts.

Maria Theresa to Marie Antoinette, 3 October 1777

Madame my dear daughter,

Two of your letters, those of the first of last month, and of the twenty-second, have abated somewhat the great joy you gave me in that of August 30. I am not sorry about the irregularity of your period, as long as you are not used to its being late. It is a sign that nature is changing, and we must hope that God, who after so many years has granted us one important point, will also grant us the rest. I am sorry that the King doesn't like to sleep with you; I consider this a very essential point, not to have children but so as to be more closely united and trusting in each other by thus spending, every day, a few hours alone together. But you are right not to insist on it; just keep paying attention to it so as to bring it little by little to where we want it; but, my dear daughter, to do that you will have to make an effort, you must go to bed at the time which suits the King and arise also at his time. . . .

I am delighted with Lassone's* letter and reassured to know that you are in such good hands. If he could write every month to Stoerck when you have your period, or even directly to me, for on this I do not trust my young Queen, who often forgets even more important matters. You must take precautions, neither excessive nor too public. I do not forbid you horse rides as long as you go sidesaddle, but no long excursions, even less any overheating. The jolts of a carriage that is being driven fast are much more dangerous, especially if followed by fright or a fall. My dear daughter has so sensitive a heart that she is moved to tears if the slightest mishap afflicts the least of her servants. I praise God and do not want to change you on this point; just avoid these occasions. A first pregnancy is always important for the others; if you start with a miscarriage, it is the end and must be avoided. Given your constitution, I should not fear that you were liable to them, but once you get used to them, there is no remedy. . . .

The Emperor has finally returned from his eternal camps in good health and, as for me, I tenderly kiss my dear little woman whom I love.

* Marie Antoinette's chief physician.

Mercy to Maria Theresa, 17 October 1777

I cannot get over my amazement at the short duration of the impression made by the Emperor on the Queen, and after having seen her for two months fully convinced of the useful truths which had been told her, it is unbelievable to see how quickly everything is back to a state usually worse than it was before the Emperor's visit. I have reason to believe that the advice written down by His Majesty has been discarded and burned.

The comtesse de Polignac and the duc de Coigny are more favored than ever, and that produces daily the most deplorable results; these two people are constantly wrenching from the Queen favors which cause continual complaints among the public. The duc de Coigny's protégés are given all the financial offices and the comtesse de Polignac's creatures are given money which is taken away from those who have a right to expect it. No minister dares resist the Queen's desires.

. . . When the Queen writes that the King prefers to sleep alone, she is telling less than the truth. He has nothing against sleeping with HM and has ceased doing so only because the Queen stays up gambling so late.

Marie Antoinette to Maria Theresa
Fontainebleau, October 1777

Madame my very dear Mother,

. . . We have been in Fontainebleau for eight days; the King has had a cold the entire time, but it has not prevented him from going out. I took advantage of the time to take for eight or ten days some baths which I needed very badly because I was overheated; I will be purged at the end of the week. After that, I hope the King will return as usual; I even expect that I will convince him to come and sleep here a few times since his apartment is closer than at Versailles. I realize the advantage in his spending the night so as to create greater trust, but that can only come little by little. My dear Mama may be sure that I will neglect nothing to carry this essential point and that I would rather sacrifice my amusements than to fail. Besides, I hardly ever stay up late at night any more, and I hardly went out all summer, both for my health and because I know a little better how to spend my time at home than in the past. I read, I embroider, I have two music masters, one for voice, the other for the harp; I have started drawing again—all that keeps me busy and entertains me. Now is the moment of my greatest dissipation during our stay in Fontainebleau; but I can assure my dear Mama that my ordinary way of life will be very little changed. As for gambling, I have only played cards in my apartment for the last two months; it is absolutely necessary that I do so once or twice a week;* if my dear Mama could see things for herself, she would realize that it cannot be otherwise. Besides I no longer play cards elsewhere, and if I go out, I only play billiards and do not gamble. . . .

I hardly ride at all; in the last three months I think I cannot have ridden more than four times, especially lately. It is not that I thought it would hurt me. But the prejudice here is that it stops one from having children, and I never ride when I have my period. I cannot even be driven in a carriage the first two days, as it is too strong for that.

---

* It is quite true that etiquette prescribed royal card playing, but Marie Antoinette was playing pharaon, a sort of *chemin de fer*, for huge stakes and the whole night through.

Maria Theresa to Marie Antoinette
Vienna, 5 November 1777

Madame my dear daughter,

. . . I was delighted with your last letter; you go into important questions in detail, and nothing can bore me if it comes from you. The smallest subject is a most important one for me because I love you so dearly and care only about your well-being. I am very glad you are still playing music, embroidering, and especially reading, especially since the King is not given to those noisy pleasures which last only for a while, end of themselves, and leave a great void, often with unpleasant consequences. If I weren't aware of their drawbacks, why should I want to deprive you of them? I would rather urge you on with all my heart. Gambling is surely one of the worst pleasures, it brings bad company and bad talk. . . . We must give in neither to ourselves nor to others, who find it too useful to fool us, for that game is nothing but that. I think it very prudent of you not to tire yourself by riding horses, but I would be sorry if you gave it up completely; you do it so well, and it keeps you close to the King, whose sole amusement it is. . . . But I must tell you that I am very impatient about the King's nonchalance, and if it continued at Versailles, all my hopes would be at an end. I would hate to give them up now. . . .

Thank God that the Queen, your sister, is over her worries; her children are cured. . . . She fears her return to Naples, where smallpox is causing great ravages. In her place, I must say, I would also be worried. . . .

You will receive yourself a letter from Ferdinand which I gave the courier. He was delighted, you know his heart; he is well able to feel, but his health worries me terribly; he has lost a lot of weight and is as thin as Leopold was but with a much worse face and constant nervous attacks and indigestions. . . .

Marie Antoinette to Maria Theresa
Choisy, 18 November 1777

Madame my very dear Mother,

. . . Although I spent my time very pleasantly at Fontainebleau, I am not sorry the stay is over. The King will hunt less, will be less tired, and I hope he will finally live with me in such a way as to ensure my position and my happiness.

Playing pharaon really had a drawback at Fontainebleau because of the crowd, but it won't be the same at Versailles, and I will take measures so that there is nothing to be said against card playing at Court. Ferdinand wrote me he was very well; I will admit that I am not reassured, especially after what my dear Mama wrote. . . .

Maria Theresa to Marie Antoinette
Vienna, 5 December 1777

Madame my dear daughter,

At every courier I expect good news, but it is too long delayed. I hope the weather will be abominable so that the King won't hunt so much and get tired and so that the Queen will not gamble every night well into the small hours. It is bad for your health and beauty, very bad, and separates you from the King, who goes to bed early, and very bad for the present and the future. You are not doing your duty, which is to adapt yourself to your husband. If he is too kind, that is no excuse for you and only makes you the more wrong, and I tremble for your future. Have no illusions, that game brings with it the worst company and actions everywhere in the world. It is well known. Pharaon holds you because you want to win, and one always ends up a dupe: add it up, in the long run if you play honestly, you cannot win. . . . If I get nowhere writing you, I will go to the King himself to save you from greater dangers. I know the consequences too well, and you are losing much of your popularity, especially abroad, which I feel terribly because I love you so dearly. . . .

Marie Antoinette to Maria Theresa
Versailles, 19 December 1777

Madame my very dear Mother,

I hoped, four days ago, that the courier would take my dear Mama the news of my pregnancy. Ever since we returned from Fontainebleau, the King has made it a custom to sleep with me and has very often fulfilled his duty as a true husband. My period came back yesterday, which annoys me, but given the way the King now lives with me, I am very confident that soon I will have nothing to desire.

I don't want to bore my dear Mama with all the stories and exaggerations that have apparently reached Vienna about my card playing. I only play at the public, etiquette-required, card games of the Court, and starting this week we will only play twice a week until the end of Carnival.

The balls begin this week; as I had a very heavy cold and was beginning to have diarrhea, I went to the ball but did not dance.

The Duke of Braganza arrived a week ago; I have not yet seen him; I am very impatient to do so in order to talk with him about all that is dear to me in my country. How happy I would be to see my brother and sister-in-law here! As for lodging them, there would be no problem; especially if they come in the spring or early summer, they would be very comfortable in my house at Trianon, and in Paris Mercy has a house fit to receive them. I think there might be more problems as regards the etiquette, but that doesn't seem impossible to arrange in advance; I will talk about it with Mercy when he comes. The most urgent and most essential thing is my brother's health, about which I am always worried; if once he could be really convalescent, I think the French air might do him good. . . .

Unlike his mother, the Emperor greatly admired Frederick II and was anxious to emulate his achievements. One of Frederick's most visible characteristics since the beginning of his reign had been that he always seized what territory he could, whether he had a right to it or not. Now Joseph II thought he saw his opportunity. The Elector of Bavaria was about to die, and his closest heir, the Elector Palatine, was a very distant cousin. Exhuming claims which dated back to the fifteenth century and had long been forgotten, the Emperor negotiated a settlement with the prospective heir: as Holy Roman Emperor, he would sanction the installation of the Elector in Bavaria, but as ruler of Austria he would receive lands amounting to a third of Bavaria. When at the end of December 1777 the old Elector died, the Emperor, suddenly and without warning, seized the coveted territory.

Europe was horrified, and so was Maria Theresa, who thought that her son had made a dangerous mistake, especially when Frederick II, now posing as the defender of right, prepared to declare war on Austria, thus realizing the Empress's worst nightmare. When, shortly afterward, Vergennes, the French Foreign Minister, sent out a circular deploring the annexation, Maria Theresa could hardly contain herself: Austria was not only behaving in an immoral fashion, it was also being abandoned by its ally. Because she was painfully aware of Frederick II's military genius, the distraught Empress began to fear the worst.

Being a practical woman, however, she promptly took two steps. First, without telling the Emperor, she entered into negotiations with Prussia (but in the end they failed); and second she determined to gain the backing of France. For this she had a willing tool in the person of her daughter, so Marie Antoinette was told to get to work on the King, who must order his ministers to reverse their policy and start supporting Austria; and since needs must, she discovered she could write Marie Antoinette about politics after all. From January 1778 on, long, frantic letters repeat that the alliance must be maintained, that France must support Austria unconditionally (even though Maria Theresa knew perfectly well that she was in the wrong). Although Mercy, as usual, deplored Marie Antoinette's frivolity and lack of follow-through, there was no doubt that within her limitations she was doing her best. In spite of this, war did break out; but neither side was really anxious to fight, there was no major battle, and the compromise Peace of Teschen was finally arranged.

All this had a marked effect on Marie Antoinette. She now developed a steadier interest in politics, which led to frequent and highly visible interventions. Since unfortunately she quite lacked her mother's talents in judging men and options, she forced a series of incompetents on the hapless Louis XVI, advocated foolish or impossible policies, and made it plain that the King was indeed the "poor man" of her earlier letter.

Maria Theresa to Marie Antoinette
Vienna, 5 January 1778

Madame my dear daughter,

The very idea that a courier may bring me news of a pregnancy overwhelms me with consolation and impatience; at sixty, one cannot wait long, and my love for you and even for the King makes me dither. Do not neglect any occasion, my dear daughter, as you did at Fontainebleau.

How I fear that eternal Carnival which may create new obstacles! I must declare war on all these continual dissipations, which deprive us of so essential a point and bring on so much talk unfavorable to my dear Queen. Your balls are perfectly proper; you must amuse yourself, and so must the others; but those of the Opera are not right at all. You already felt last year their drawbacks: they gave me much pain; but this year, when we have such hopes that you may become pregnant at any time, you would be unforgivable to take risks, to go at night in this season to Paris, which no Queen of France has ever done, leaving the King alone at Versailles. . . .

We have just heard about the death of the Elector of Bavaria; I am very sorry about it; Mercy knows all about this so that he can inform you, and I ask that you listen to him carefully. The peace of Europe is at stake. . . . At this instant, I am told that the Grand Duchess has just happily given birth to a Prince. I sincerely share her joy but could not hear the news without wishing that God may grant me the same consolation from my dear Queen within the year. . . .

Mercy sent me the measurements of a painting you would like to have for Trianon; it is the opera performed for the Emperor's wedding. I take the greatest pleasure in the world in serving you; but I need an explanation: there are two, one the opera, the other the ballet, where my little

Queen was with her two brothers. I expect you would like to have the last or perhaps both. You will; but in that case I still need measurements for the second painting and must know where the light comes from, whether it is to be framed or laid directly on the wall like a tapestry. I will try to see to it that you receive it before eight years, which is how long I have impatiently been awaiting your portrait; but I will not let them go before I receive that dear and much desired portrait from you. I am vind:ctive; but I will make peace easily as soon as I see your face. I kiss you.

Marie Antoinette to Maria Theresa
Versailles, 15 January 1778

Madame my very dear Mother,

I am ashamed and upset to have to tell my dear Mama that I had my period yesterday morning, and what hurts me even more, if possible, is the disappointment to my dear Mama's love. I must, however, retain every hope because of the way the King lives with me.

Mercy, who is ill, has already sent me information concerning Bavaria. I see with pleasure that all goes amiably and that the alliance and friendship between the two families will not be weakened. When the Elector had just died, I had a moment's worry. I am very happy because I was very quickly freed from it; I needed that for I know that the mere idea of a quarrel would make my life miserable.

All the balls have begun everywhere; I dance very moderately at those in Versailles, and as for those in Paris, I didn't go.

My dear Mama overwhelms me with her kindness about the paintings; I never would have dared to ask for them, although they will give me immense pleasure. You embarrass me greatly by putting me in a position where it will look as if only my desire is speeding those portraits begun and missed by so many painters. . . .

I hoped to send with this letter a porcelain box which I thought my dear Mama could use for her smaller dinners. The package is too fragile to go by courier. I beg my dear Mama to accept it with that kindness which I so want to deserve and retain to the last day of my life.

Mercy to Maria Theresa, 17 January 1778

HM is gambling for even higher stakes than before. Toward the end of December, she lost 300 louis [7,200 livres] in one evening; the King paid them the next day, and very often he discharges these debts which the Queen herself could not meet. . . . These ruinous pleasures upset the Queen's finances so that she can no longer contribute to charities. . . . The public has noticed it and resents it.

. . . The Queen often has some difficulty in keeping up the appearance of friendship between the princess de Lamballe and the comtesse de Polignac. As the latter's favor grows, that of the Superintendent withers away so that she has now become a bore and an annoyance to the Queen.

Maria Theresa to Marie Antoinette, 1 February 1778

Madame my dear daughter,

Your letter of the fifteenth, which told me about your period, gave me no pleasure; but nothing is lost as long as there isn't an interruption or a separation as in Fontainebleau, but Carnival must not create one. In the long run the responsibility would be yours, which would upset me more than I have been for these past eight years. You mustn't think too much about it—that is often an obstacle. Your sister, the Queen, is, I fear, again pregnant; I regret it—they come one after the other, and she suffers greatly while she is carrying.

Mercy's illness could not come at a worse time; this is a moment when I need all his activity and all your feelings for me, your House, and your country, and I count entirely on what he may have to tell you on several major questions, on the insinuations that will be made in every quarter that our policy is dangerous; especially that will be said by the King of Prussia, who is not scrupulous about these assertions, because he has long wished to be on better terms with France . . . that would be a change in our alliance *which would kill me.* * . . . The King of Prussia fears only you, which I must admit pleases me greatly and doubly for you and for us. Our alliance, the only natural one, the only one useful to both our countries . . . is very important to me, and I hope, through everything Mercy will explain to you, that you learn its usefulness and goodness.

I am impatiently waiting for the measurements for the paintings to be sent you. This occupies me, as well as the porcelain box you are sending me. We have excellent weather, but many people are sick. I kiss you, my dear daughter; why can't I say soon: my dear Mama! Everyone here is praying for you. I am always all yours.

* Emphasized by the Empress.

Marie Antoinette to Maria Theresa
Versailles, 13 February 1778

Madame my very dear Mother,

Mercy comes tomorrow and I await him impatiently. It is most essential for me to speak to him so that I can learn enough to clear the clouds that could be created for the King in a moment like this one, and put him more on his guard than ever against the King of Prussia's perfidious insinuations; he certainly forgets nothing: there have already been five couriers from him within a month. . . .

Our relations with England are worsening severely; they have attacked several of our ships, and finally we no longer think it necessary to hide our dispositions preparatory to revenging ourselves for their insults; many ships are being armed, and troops with artillery have just been sent to Brittany; Our preparedness may make them wiser; it is not yet sure that we will have a real war.

I have just seen Mercy; from all he told me and from what I see myself, I hope that the little clouds people have created will soon vanish so that they will cause no alteration in our alliance and close friendship, which is so useful for Europe, and to which no one can be more devoted in every way than I.

I don't know whether Gluck will arrive before the courier. I wrote through him to my dear Mama that my period came on the eighth. That is six days early.

Ferdinand's better health is a wonderful piece of news; I hope it will continue. . . .

Mercy to Maria Theresa, 18 February 1778

The Queen spoke rather heatedly to her husband about the Bavarian situation, the King of Prussia's maneuvers, and the danger of a coolness in the alliance. The King answered, "It is your relatives' ambition which is causing all the trouble; they started with Poland, now they are doing it again in Bavaria; I am sorry for this because of you."

"But," the Queen answered, "you cannot deny that you were told about the situation and agreed to what has been done."

"I had so little agreed," the King answered, "that we have just given all French ambassadors the order of informing the Courts to which they are accredited that this dismemberment of Bavaria is carried out against our wishes and that we disapprove of it."

. . . A single sentence of Your Majesty's letters touches the Queen and motivates her far more than two hours of my political explanations. I had a recent proof of this through the very strong impression due to a sentence where Your Majesty speaks of the King of Prussia and says, "We cannot live at the same time; it would cause a change in our alliance *which would kill me.*" I saw the Queen grow pale as she read those words, and that is what prompted her desire to act.

Maria Theresa to Marie Antoinette
Vienna, 19 February 1778

Madame my dear daughter,

It is five in the morning, the courier is at my door, and I write you in all haste. I had not been warned of his departure; he is sent early so as to obviate the black and malicious insinuations made by the King of Prussia; I hope if the King knows all this, that he will not let himself be influenced by wicked people; I count on his justice and his love for his dear little wife. I go into no detail; the Emperor and Mercy have already; I can only add that there may never be a more important occasion to hold firmly together and that our system depends upon it. Imagine, therefore, how strongly this affects me! . . .

Maria Theresa to Marie Antoinette
Vienna, 6 March 1778

Madame my dear daughter,

Your letter of the thirteenth consoled me because of all the obliging and loving things you say about our business in Bavaria, about which I care deeply, but I cannot yet say anything about it and will rely on what Mercy will tell you and also on what the King's ministers must have said abroad on this subject. This is no complaint or reproach; unfortunately this whole business was insufficiently prepared or foreseen: but it matters to both of us that we be thought so closely linked that nothing untoward appear. . . . I love the King too well to want him to do anything contrary to his interests or his glory; I would rather sacrifice mine; but if we want to do good, we must do it together: otherwise we can achieve nothing solid.

I have a bad toothache and a swollen face, even to the eyes, but no fever at all; it mostly makes it difficult to write. Gluck arrived after the courier and brought me the news which does not please me and of which I will soon be fed up.

Here is the explanation for the two paintings you want; they are already working on them, but they won't be finished for a year: if you are pleased with them, you will write me so that they can go on. . . .

Maria Theresa to Marie Antoinette
Vienna, 14 March 1778

Madame my dear daughter,

The courier of the second returned yesterday and reassured us a little about the King's intentions. In our critical situation I am sorry to alarm you, but it is for a good reason and the need is pressing. Mercy has been told to speak clearly and ask for advice and help. Once fighting has started, it will be much more difficult to conciliate things. You know our adversary, who tries to strike great blows at the outset: imagine my situation when my beloved sons are involved. All my firmness abandons me at that thought, and I feel only that I am the mother [of several children], and that of the State as well, in which so many subjects will suffer; one can feel for that situation, but never express it well enough. I am all yours.

Marie Antoinette to Maria Theresa
Versailles, 18 March 1778

Madame my very dear Mother,

I would be very worried if my dear Mama were not kind enough to say that she has no fever. I am very impatient to know that she is cured of the ache and swelling. I spoke yesterday at some length with Mercy; he seemed rather pleased with the conversation he had just had with the ministers; as for me, I am delighted with the King; he sincerely wants to maintain the alliance. He told M. de Goltz* that he wanted no part of his master's business. The King sent a message to the King of England to say that he had signed a treaty with the Americans. My Lord Stormont received on Sunday an order from his Court to leave France. It looks as if our navy, on which we have been working for a long time, will soon be active. God grant that those movements do not bring a land war about! . . .

Lent has brought us back to our normal way of living. The King sleeps with me three or four nights a week and behaves in such a way as to give me great hopes.

I am deeply moved by my dear Mama's kindness in regards to the paintings. The size is perfect; they will greatly increase the pleasure I take in visiting Trianon. May I kiss my dear mother with all my soul?

Mercy to Maria Theresa, 20 March 1778

I must not conceal from Your Majesty that despite the strongest, almost daily protests, I am far from getting the Queen to take the kind of precise and continued actions which the situation demands, and although HM takes the liveliest interest in it, I always meet with the obstacle of her dissipation.

Marie Antoinette to Maria Theresa, 25 March 1778

Madame my very dear Mother,

I hope that with this courier Mercy will only give my dear Mama reassuring news. As for the King personally, he

* The Prussian envoy.

cares greatly about the alliance, indeed as much as I could possibly want; but in so important a moment I did not think I should limit myself to speaking with the King. I saw MM. de Maurepas and de Vergennes; they answered very properly when I asked them about the alliance and seem really to care about it; but they are so afraid of a land war that when I mentioned the case where the King of Prussia might start hostilities, I was unable to obtain a clear answer. . . .

Maria Theresa to Marie Antoinette
Vienna, 6 April 1778

Madame my dear daughter,

. . . I am lovingly grateful to you for the interest you take in my position. Never has an occasion been more important, and without forcing or risking what is proper for France, the King can be of the greatest help to us by showing firmly the friendship he feels for us and the alliance. Unfortunately the talk of several of the King's ministers to foreign Courts has made people believe the reverse. The Emperor is about to leave: see if I can think about anything else. I await the courier that Mercy promises us with the most extreme impatience.

MARIE ANTOINETTE'S reaction, when something displeased her, was always to order it changed: she was the Queen; let everyone else obey. That is exactly the manner in which she now treated both Maurepas, Prime Minister in fact but not in name, and Vergennes, the Foreign Minister. Not surprisingly her manner and her commands were both resented. When the King was then seen to reverse himself at his wife's bidding, it helped neither his reputation nor hers.

Marie Antoinette to Maria Theresa
Versailles, 19 April 1778

Madame my dear Mother,

My first impulse a week ago, which I regret not following, was to write my dear Mama about my hopes. I was prevented by my fear of causing too great a sorrow if my hopes were to vanish; they are still not completely assured, and I will only count on it at the beginning of next month, the time for the second period. In the meantime I think I have good reason to feel confident; I have never been late, on the contrary always a little early; in March I had my period on the third; today is the nineteenth and nothing has happened. Other than that, I feel perfectly well; my appetite and the time I sleep have grown. I must also soothe my dear Mama's alarms and worrying by giving her a faithful account of the way I live. Since the beginning of my hopes, I stopped all riding in carriages and have limited myself to short walks. I am told that when the second missed period is past, it will be healthier not to stay in so much. My dear Mama can count on my being very moderate and careful about all my movements.

Mercy brings me my letters: that is already one great worry the less about the departure of the courier; but the Emperor's letter and his departure give me many more alarms. After speaking with Mercy on the bad state of affairs, I sent for MM. de Maurepas and de Vergennes. I spoke rather strongly to them and think I impressed them, especially the latter. I was not too pleased with these gentlemen's arguments; they only try to use shifts or evasions and to get the King used to them. I expect to speak with them again, perhaps even in the King's presence. It is cruel, in so important a business, to deal with people who are not true. . . .

I forgot to say that I was forbidden to attend the Corpus Christi ceremonies because of the fatigue, which here is rather great. I saw to it that the poor received everything they are usually given. I went to all the Masses of the week, except that I went to one of the loges instead of accompanying the King, so as not to wear Court dress. Yesterday coming back from Evensong, I vomited a little, which increases my hopes. I would be too happy if the [Bavarian] business could be settled and free me from worry and the greatest misfortunes that could happen to me. I cannot think of them without trembling, especially for my dear Mama, whose heart is so sensitive and kind and who really deserves to be happy after she has ensured all the world's happiness. May I kiss her lovingly?

Maria Theresa to Marie Antoinette
Schönbrunn, 2 May 1778

Madame my dear daughter,

The courier of the nineteenth of this month brought me consolations which I needed badly in the present circumstances; the immediate effect was that I installed myself here in Schönbrunn; I had difficulty moving because I was so upset. You send me a great, unexpected piece of news; may God be praised, and may my dear Antoinette be consolidated in her brilliant position by giving France an heir! No precaution is excessive; I am delighted that you no longer run to Paris at night, that you have even given up billiards. I see thereby that you omit nothing and sacrifice even the least dangerous of your amusements; but I tell you, my dear daughter, that two months aren't enough: you need thirteen full weeks, especially for a first pregnancy, in order to be sure. Continue, therefore, these same precautions for five more weeks. I think that after that, and once you feel the child, you shouldn't sit or lie on chaise longues too much, except for an accident, God forbid! Then you would follow Lassone's advice blindly; he is entitled to my trust. . . .

If only you could see the joy here about the great news! There cannot be more in Paris. . . . The news had filtered through five or six days before the arrival of the courier, and I am very obliged to you for the regrets you mention at not having written earlier. This is a mark of your love and your desire not to cause me to feel joy in vain. Another time, however, if something important happens, I beg you not to spare me. It all matters very much to me; I do not easily allow myself to feel joy, and for the last thirty-six years have grown accustomed to sorrow; that has become second nature to me; a moment's pleasure is therefore very valuable to me. But then, how much I must tell you, my dear daughter, on what you write, and the faithful Mercy even more, about how you worked for us, using all your energy and charms.* The ministers in Bavaria and Ratisbon† are already speaking differently, and I dare say that if things had not been spoiled at the beginning, they would never have arrived at the point they have reached, there would never have been a war and the alliance would never have been strained: our goal was and always will be not aggrandizement, but a more solid situation. . . .

I am rather pleased with the news from Bohemia; all are in good health in spite of endless fatigue, bad weather, and

* The Empress means that the Queen seduced Louis XVI into backing Austria.
† The Imperial Diet, the council gathering all the German Princes, sat at Ratisbon.

(247)

worse roads. I am very pleased that you were careful not to wear Court dress, [did not tire yourself during the feast of] Corpus Christi; even your nausea pleases me and I hope it will all go on. Try not to think too much about it: this is easier to advise than to do, but you must try as much as possible not to worry. Everybody wishes you well; everybody prays; but in case our hopes are disappointed, nothing is lost. It is enough that it should be possible and God will give His blessing to you and the wise and virtuous King, my dear son. I kiss you.

The Queen of Naples's joy will be extreme; I bet that she will be moved to tears.

Marie Antoinette to Maria Theresa
Versailles, 5 May 1778

Madame my very dear Mother,

I am truly outraged by that dishonest dispatch they concealed from Mercy so that we could neither anticipate it nor stop it. I showed my displeasure as soon as I found out about it. It is incredible the talent the ministers have here for drowning business in a deluge of words. Still, thanks to what Mercy had told me and because of the thoughts I cannot keep from having at every moment about the most important event of my life, I pressed them so that they had to change their tone a little.* I do not understand politics enough to judge, but Mercy, who seems not too pleased about the contents, likes its style and appearance much better. It seems according to all the letters that there is still a hope of avoiding war. What happiness if we worried in vain!

* The first dispatch categorically declined to support the Austrian position; the second announced an attempt at conciliation with Prussia, France offering itself as mediator.

My health and hopes are still good, and they are thought so sure that a new Household is being appointed for my sister Elisabeth because her education cannot continue with that of my children. . . .

Marie Antoinette to Maria Theresa
Versailles, 16 May 1778

Madame my very dear Mother,

. . . I still am in very good health, except for an occasional feeling of stifling, which cannot be avoided. I saw my male midwife this morning (Vermond, one of the abbé's brothers); I myself feel more confident in him than in any other; besides, he is the best and Lassone thoroughly approves of him. He felt me and was very pleased; he said I could go for short carriage rides as long as it wasn't too fast and that I must not go out on the days when I would have had my period; according to his calculation and mine, I am entering the third month; I am already beginning to put on weight visibly, especially around the hips. I lived for so long without hoping to be so happy as to bear a child that I feel it now all the more strongly and that there are moments when I think it is all a dream; but the dream continues and there is, I think, no more doubt.

I am deeply moved by the joy in Vienna about my pregnancy that my dear Mama was good enough to relay. . . . I forgot to tell my dear Mama that when I missed my period for the second time, I asked the King for 500 louis, which makes 12,000 francs, which I thought right to send on to Paris for the poor who are in debtors' jail because of the months they owe wet nurses, and 4,000 francs here in Versailles for the poor. It was a way of being charitable as well as a notification of my condition before all the people. . . .

How kind my dear Mama is to show that she approves of the way I have behaved in all the current business! Alas! I deserve no gratitude: my heart alone acts in all this. I am only sorry I cannot go directly into the minds of all the ministers to make them understand that what was done and said in Vienna is thoroughly fair and reasonable: but unfortunately none are more deaf than those who don't want to hear; and besides, they have so many words and sentences which mean nothing that they are already dizzy before they can say something reasonable. What I mean to do is to speak to them both before the King so that they will at least use the right tone to the King of Prussia; and in truth it is for the convenience, even the glory, of the King that I want it, for he can only gain by supporting allies which must be so dear to him in every way. Besides, he is behaving perfectly to me because of my condition and is most attentive. . . . We are going tomorrow to Marly for three weeks: it will give me a chance to walk a great deal and to amuse myself; there will be many people. . . .

Maria Theresa to Marie Antoinette
Schönbrunn, 17 May 1778

Madame my dear daughter,

The consolation of your pregnancy, announced even by the King, and your two letters of the fourth and fifth all give me great consolation. I cannot sufficiently thank God for having granted me still the favor of seeing you, my dear daughter, solidly established for the future. All my wishes for my dear family have thus come to pass; I can close my eyes peacefully. . . . Mercy tells me how obligingly and tenderly you have been working for your family and country. The future will show that France's very interest and consideration demanded this, and if at the beginning it had spoken with the firmness now bringing about a great improvement, I am very sure that all would be peaceful, but these terrible possibilities face us* and once begun won't end so easily, and for the sake of humanity I hope all can still be arranged for peace. . . . The King [of Prussia] boasts from time to time of being on good terms with your ministers; he also claims that he communicated to them the secret correspondence between the Emperor and himself. That is another one of his tricks: at their Neustadt meeting the two Princes agreed to write each other on important occasions; the Emperor agreed, as I had asked him, to use this way of averting the storm that was about to burst. . . . Mercy will have the honor of communicating both these letters and our current situation to you. Now that you show both affection and zeal for our interests, I find it necessary to inform you more and more thoroughly. . . .

You can see by [Frederick II's] behavior just how far we can trust him or his word. France has seen this on many an occasion, and no European Prince has been spared his perfidy; and that is the man who would be the protector and dictator of all Germany! . . . For thirty-seven years he had made Europe wretched through his despotism, violence, etc. As he renounces all recognized principles of truth and honesty, he disdains every treaty, every alliance. We are the most exposed [to his attacks] and we are abandoned. . . . The future is bleak. I will not be alive then, but my dear children and grandchildren, our holy religion, our good peoples will suffer only too much. . . .

* The Empress, semihysterical and writing in a completely confused style, is referring to the possibility of war.

Marie Antoinette to Maria Theresa
Marly, 29 May 1778

Madame my very dear Mother,

. . . I still feel perfectly well and have not the slightest discomfort. We have been at Marly for ten days. It is a charming place; I take advantage to do a lot of walking, especially in the morning. It is very good for me and does not tire me much, although I am growing amazingly larger since I do not wear a corset except for what I need to hold myself up. I saw Mercy these last few days; he showed me the proposals sent by the King of Prussia to my brother. It is impossible to see anything more absurd than his proposi- tions; they are so much so in fact that it seems to me people here realized it as well; at least I can answer for the King. I have not been able to see the ministers. M. de Vergennes has not come here; he is ill: it will have to wait until we go back to Versailles.

I had already seen the correspondence between the King of Prussia and my brother. . . . His [Frederick II's] impru- dence, his bad faith, and his nastiness are visible in every line. I was delighted with my brother's answers; it would be impossible to be more graceful, more moderate, and yet stronger. . . .

I cannot tell my dear Mama how moved I was by her letter; the trust she shows me overwhelms me. Oh God! I wish I could give all my blood to make her happy and able to enjoy the peace and happiness she so truly deserves! . . .

Maria Theresa to Marie Antoinette
Schönbrunn, 1 June 1778

Madame my dear daughter,

This letter will arrive very close to the thirteenth,* that day so dear to me which now concerns me more than ever. The saint† will be tormented for you. You cannot believe how interested everyone is in you; they couldn't be more so if it were the Emperor [who was about to be given an heir]. What a pleasure it is to be loved, but how much nicer still to deserve it; that is our only reward! . . .

Choosing the people who will look after that precious child is another focus for your care and my worries. By giving too much attention, one can do very ill, and I wish that the women had no orders to give and merely followed the doctor's orders, as we do here; it worked so well for me. I fear cabals and recommendations; and with children, especially the first year, everything depends on the care they are given: I mean reasonable and natural care: not to swaddle them tightly, not to keep them too warm, not to give them too much pap or other food, and most important to find a good healthy wet nurse, which is not so easily done in Paris; and it is about the same for country people because of the universal corruption.

I am delighted with the alms for which you asked the King; I am also delighted, as you write me, with the King's feelings for us and with your vivacity of expression, which shows clearly how much you care for him and for us. . . . We have begun to talk, and you will again find that the King of Prussia has not changed, even on this occasion, and he is being listened to, he wants an alliance between France, Russia, and himself to settle the future and resist us; he expects, if peace is achieved (which I still wish very ardently, and I

* Marie Antoinette's name-day.
† The saint in question is Anthony.

can't urge you enough to work on it), that it won't last long, and, so as to stop or crush us, he is flattering you so as to be tied to you. . . .*

The unfortunate acquisition of Galicia fooled us a little because it was so easy; but it has given us a good lesson and we won't come back so easily.† Immense expenses, worries, the loss of trust everywhere are no small reminders of the hurried decisions taken then. . . . The weakness and ill will of the [French] ministers and most of the nation, which was only too manifest, will not be taken into account; it will even be forgotten, because we count entirely on the hearts of the King and his amiable Queen, and our close love for them makes their glory and interest seem ours as well. . . .

There is still time to put everything in order and to come together properly; but if this occasion is wasted, it will be too late. Take advantage of my old gray head to receive my most loving advice for the welfare of our kingdoms, families, and that of my dear children, whom I love and kiss tenderly.

Marie Antoinette to Maria Theresa
Versailles, 12 June 1778

Madame my very dear Mother,

. . . My dear Mama may not be completely pleased with the answer given to M. de Goltz. . . . Not only was I kept from knowing the decision once it was made but even after it was communicated to Mercy, and he is the one who told me. I was not able to hide from the King the fact that I was upset at his silence; I even told him I would be ashamed to

---

* This letter has been cut down by about two thirds, but Marie Antoinette read her mother's repetitions in full.
† The Empress is referring to the first partition of Poland.

admit to my dear Mama the way in which he was treating me as regards an affair of such interest to me, and of which I spoke to him so often. I was disarmed by the way he answered me. He told me, "You see that I am so wrong that I don't have a thing to say." In fact he did have excuses because during our whole stay at Marly he was bothered by the intrigues of M. le prince de Condé, who wanted to be named to the command of the whole army, and by those of the maréchal de Broglie who, thinking he was needed, wanted to usurp the King's authority by appointing all the officers who are to serve under him.* Luckily they were all disappointed, and the King was firm. I thought it right to ask the King to speak to his ministers about the dishonesty of their silence to me: it seems essential that they do not grow accustomed to it.

Mercy has just visited me: he showed me the King of Prussia's new proposals. They seem to me, although he has changed a few words, as absurd as the others. He is simply trying to fool us.

I feel very well, and the stay at Marly, where we had the finest weather possible, did me much good. I was lodged downstairs; as a result I went for walks at all hours of the day, especially in the mornings around nine or ten. I am growing much larger; I was childish enough to measure myself; I have already taken on four and a half inches. My dear Mama is very kind to worry about the future little child: I can assure her I will take great care of it. The way they are brought up now, they are less hampered; they are not swaddled, they are always in a crib or held in the nurse's arms, and as soon as they can be outdoors they are accustomed to it little by little until they are almost always out. I think this is the best and healthiest way to raise them. Mine will be lodged downstairs with a small grill to separate him from

* An army was then being formed which was to serve as the expeditionary corps on a projected invasion of England.

the terrace, and he may thus learn to walk faster than on a
parquet floor. . . .

Marie Antoinette to Maria Theresa
Versailles, 7 July 1778

Madame my very dear Mother,
     . . . I feel very well. I was bled two weeks ago, which did
me much good. Only the extreme heat we have been having
for the last few days is very uncomfortable; but it is raining
today, so I hope not to stifle so. The courier is leaving; may I
kiss my dear Mama? The regular monthly courier will
come, and I will write in more detail then.

Marie Antoinette to Maria Theresa, 15 July 1778

Madame my very dear Mother,
     I cannot tell my dear Mama how moved and worried I am
in this great misfortune;* but my dear Mama's sensitive
heart is my greatest torment. . . . No, God will not allow
so unjust a man to triumph! The Emperor's presence, the
two commanding generals, and especially the courage of all
the Austrians reassure me greatly. I had, this morning, a
really moving scene with the King. My dear Mama knows
that I have never attributed what has happened to his heart,
but rather to his extreme weakness and his lack of self-confi-
dence. Well, today, he came to my apartment; he found me
so sad and so alarmed that he was moved to tears. I must
admit that it really pleased me; it proves how much he cares
for me, and I hope that now he will make his own decisions

* The imminent outbreak of the war.

and behave as a good and faithful ally. I also saw M. de Maurepas after the courier's arrival: I showed him how indecent M. de Goltz's behavior had been, and finally I convinced him to send the declaration that was made here a month ago to the charge d'affaires in Berlin so that he shows it in its entirety to the King of Prussia, just such as it had been sent to Vienna and should be.

My dear Mama is too kind to worry still about my health. It is very good, and I daresay that right now it depends only on hers. I therefore beg her to spare herself. . . .

Maria Theresa to Marie Antoinette
Schönbrunn, 2 August 1778

Madame my dear daughter,

. . . Everything drags and seems still unlikely to come to this end I so desire that would quickly take the Emperor and my sons out of their cruel situation, which has been made still worse by the junction of the Saxons,* who number 30,000, and thus give the King [of Prussia] 40,000 men more than we have, and force us to stay on the defensive. . . . I am still awaiting an answer in a few days which will settle our hopes and our fears, and I did not want to delay this courier further, since I will send you another as soon as I see more clearly or hear about a change. . . .

What you write me about that conversation with the King brought tears of consolation to my eyes, but even more what Mercy tells me about your dear tears and how moved you were. I recognize my dear Antoinette's admirable heart! The idea of shunning the theater is very touching at your age, and in a country where it is thought impossible to live

* With the Prussians.

without it; but please follow Mercy's advice on that. We may be sad but never dejected. Our cruel enemy would enjoy it too much; the more critical the circumstances, and the more we must hold up so as to take the necessary measures. I cannot tell you what a consolation it was, how the fete at Trianon you canceled has honored you in all the private letters; Breteuil especially was delighted and talked about it everywhere. Your pregnancy, which gives me such consolation, demands that you stay away from sad ideas, I beg you; otherwise, in that condition, I can become a prey to melancholy. . . .

Maria Theresa to Marie Antoinette
Schönbrunn, 6 August 1778

Madame my dear daughter,

Mercy will tell you about my cruel situation as a sovereign and as a mother. Since I want to save my states from the most cruel devastation, I must, at whatever cost, try to end this war; and as a mother I have three sons who are not only exposed to the greatest dangers but will be killed by exhaustion since they are not accustomed to this sort of life. By making peace now, I will not only be blamed as being terribly pusillanimous, but I also strengthen the King [of Prussia] even more, so the remedy must be prompt. I must say that my head is weak and my heart has long been completely destroyed. . . . Since Prince Henry [of Prussia] came over the border with Saxony in force, Laudon did not think he could resist and has retreated to Kosmanos, behind the Iser, thus giving five of our best provinces to the enemy, who does nothing but pillage. We even had a few little losses here and there in the course of the retreat, but he wanted to be near the larger army so as to be linked with it. . . . I ask you to reinforce Mercy to save your House and your brothers. I will never ask the King [of France] anything which could bring him into this wretched war, merely a show of selecting or assembling some troops and generals to come and help us in case the Hanoverians or others join our enemies.* It would not suit France to have us enslaved by our most cruel enemies. . . .

Marie Antoinette to Maria Theresa
Versailles, 14 August 1778

Madame my very dear Mother,

I have spent two weeks in the most dreadful anguish because I did not receive any news. I imagined all kinds of horrors. The arrival of the courier, which I was awaiting with such impatience, only made my worries worse along with the cruel uncertainty which is devouring me. But can I even think of my own ills when my dear Mama is in so awful a situation! It is true that for the last three weeks that thought cancels and absorbs all my other feelings.

I had decided yesterday that I would ask the King to offer his mediation; and in order to decide him to do so, I preferred seeing him at the moment when I knew he would be with MM. de Maurepas and de Vergennes. We had just begun to talk, and the King seemed well disposed when the baron's [de Breteuil] dispatches arrived; they were read in my presence. I will not hide from my dear Mama that M. de Maurepas now and again created difficulties about the baron's dispatches. All were very surprised at the change for

* In her panic the Empress is in fact asking Louis XVI to prepare himself for war, a move altogether contrary to French interests. Marie Antoinette unhesitatingly supported her.

the margraviates;* I believe that in the evening Mercy clarified the question thoroughly with M. de Vergennes. . . . In consequence, next Monday, M. de Vergennes must write a strongly worded letter to the chargé d'affaires in Berlin. They are also thinking of sending a negotiator to Germany. I think I managed to block M. Odune because Mercy said he wouldn't do.† The great point is to make our ministers speak the true language of the alliance; they promised they would, but we will have to keep watching and fighting if this unhappy business is not over immediately. My great consolation is that the King is with us in heart and soul.

I am very lucky in that although I am pregnant at such a dreadful time, my health is still excellent. My child moved for the first time on Friday, July 31 at ten-thirty at night; from that moment it has been moving often, which causes me great joy. . . . Since that time I have grown much larger, and even more than one usually is at five months. I certainly deserve no praise for canceling the fete at Trianon; I could not possibly have looked cheerful. A few days afterward, I went back to my usual way of life. My head cannot keep up with the thoughts that crush me; they are, however, necessary to answer people's questions and reasonings. Through the philosophers and intrigues of all kinds, the King of Prussia has managed to gather many partisans, and I find myself forced, at certain moments, to appear cheerful. . . . It has been decided that my child will be named and baptized as soon as it is born. If my dear Mama is kind enough to be the godmother, I hope she will be kind enough to send her power of attorney and the names she will want to give. The King of Spain will be the godfather.

* As the result of his negotiations with Maria Theresa, Frederick obtained the two tiny principalities of Anspach and Bayreuth for Prussia.
† In thus personally selecting diplomats on the advice of the Austrian Ambassador, the Queen makes her allegiance crystal clear: she had earned the insulting name, l'Autrichienne, by which the people were to call her.

Madame my dear daughter,

I was about to send you a courier when Kleiner arrived and brought me your letter of the fourteenth. You can imagine how sensitive I am to all you say and do. You guessed only too well that the negotiation would fail. I must admit I hoped it would succeed, especially if we gave Bavaria back to the Elector while the King waited for the margraviates until the agreed time.* . . .

That your health should remain so good is the greatest grace and consolation God can give me; but I must tell you that knowing how sensitive you are I am not entirely reassured. You can at least cry easily, and that has always given me relief during the disasters I have met. I wish you my health. What you tell me, how the movements of your child make you happy, moved me to tears. I am very touched that you want me as godmother. . . . Whenever anything at all important comes up, I will send you a courier or messenger; similarly if my health were impaired, but it is very good. . . . I asked the Emperor twice to send you and Naples the latest news, but he answered he could not give you more than is in the papers. The public has been complaining about it and not without reason, but I myself know nothing more. There was a little coldness between us† because of the negotiation, but I hope it will soon change. . . . I must tell you that this dispute increases my sufferings, and I hope to see it ended as soon as possible, and I trust that for the essential, we are agreed in this business; it was only about the means that we had a difference. . . .

* Here again, Maria Theresa goes on at great and repetitive length about the need for the alliance; this letter has been heavily cut to avoid tiresome repetition.
† By negotiating behind his back, Maria Theresa made Joseph II look like a fool; naturally, the Emperor resented it—hence the coolness.

Marie Antoinette to Maria Theresa
Versailles, 3 September 1778

Madame my very dear Mother,

It is thus decided that we* are to be the prey of the anguish and horror of war. The King of Prussia has thrown the mask away and his partisans are reduced to blushes. At this time the [French ministers] seem really decided to blame the King of Prussia openly. Mercy is more pleased with his last conversation with the ministers; he will write my dear Mama about it. I saw MM. de Maurepas and de Vergennes. M. de Maurepas seemed changed much for the better about this business; God grant that it last! They spoke to me clearly about M. de Goltz and his lies; they will no longer see him separately, and they have not told him about the dispatch to the chargé d'affaires in Berlin. M. de Pons† has gone back to Berlin, and all will now go through him and not M. de Goltz. I suggested to the ministers that they send a letter to all the [French] ministers in Germany so that they can broadcast the King's opinion of the King of Prussia's behavior; but they want to wait until they receive the answer they expect from Berlin.

My health is still very good; I will be bled tomorrow and hope not to be again except perhaps at the end. . . . It is not surprising that in a business‡ like this one, and such as I know him, my brother may have been so affected as to be wrong; but my dear Mama is too kind not to understand it and will attribute it to the circumstances. . . . I cannot blind myself; we have everything to fear from that cruel enemy because we know he allows himself to use all kinds of means. I am a little reassured by the courage of my dear

* The Austrians, that is: once again the Queen makes her allegiance very plain.
† The French envoy to Prussia.
‡ The Bavarian succession.

Mama's good and faithful servants, who will be further encouraged by my brothers' presence and example. . . .

Maria Theresa to Marie Antoinette
Schönbrunn, 9 September 1778

Madame my dear daughter,

I start by what I care about the most, that our armies are always face to face, that they suffer much in these mountains where there is already snow, as well as many discomforts and illnesses: but ours is better in every way than that of the King. . . . The Emperor is still in good health, thank God; but Maximilian has caught a tertiary fever, which I hope will not last; he has had to retire to a castle four hours away from the army. Yesterday the Grand Duke [of Tuscany] arrived here; his wife will follow on the twentieth. I find him, as ever, thin but strong. I needed a little help in these circumstances; they expect to stay here for the winter or as long as these unhappy circumstances will last. Try, my dear daughter, to end them as soon as possible: you will save your mother, who can stand no more, and two brothers, who must be crushed in the end, your country, a whole nation that loves you so much. . . .

All we ask is that a firm language be used everywhere, especially by the [French] ministers within the Empire who, I must say, have always spoken a language which, if not quite contrary to our system, was at least very weak and confirmed our enemies in the belief that France is not closely linked to us.* . . . We must take advantage of this moment in which the inconveniences and miseries of this campaign are still vividly felt. . . .

* This letter has been heavily cut to avoid the endless repetition which worked so well on Marie Antoinette.

Marie Antoinette to Maria Theresa
Versailles, 17 September 1778

Madame my dear Mother,

I may be having illusions, but the last courier has somewhat stilled my worries. It is already a great achievement before all Europe to have negated the King and his brother's activity. Although other people's ills do not relieve our own, still on this occasion I regard it as a great good because it will force our enemies to leave Bohemia. Here they still seem firmly disposed to mediate the peace. . . . I will still work to make sure they write to the German Courts to let them know what we have told Prussia. . . .

I am worried about Maximilian's fever. I expect he is very annoyed to be kept away [from the army] right now. I am delighted to know that the Grand Duke is in Vienna; he will be a great help to my dear Mama. . . . My health is still very good, in spite of the inconveniences inseparable from an advanced state of pregnancy. I am beginning to be a little heavy; but since I walk every day, I hope to be well until the end. I was bled a week ago; they could only get a very small quantity of blood because my veins are small, so I may have to be bled again in a month.

Marie Antoinette to Maria Theresa, 17 October 1778

Madame my very dear Mother,

. . . I was very worried about Maximilian and realize how happy you must be to see him again and convalescing well. As for the King of Prussia's leaving with his troops in such a terrible state, that is an incalculable advantage which must be very humiliating for him, and it will encourage all Austrians, if need be, since they are already fighting for a beloved sovereign and have the Emperor as an example at their head. . . . I am very sorry about the weakness and variations of M. de Maurepas. I spoke to him several times and rather firmly; but I thought I should contain myself and not break with him completely so as not to place the King in a difficult position between his minister and his wife. I will speak to him again as soon as possible so that he at last carries out the word he had given about writing all the ministers in Germany. . . . The King sincerely wants to bring peace to Germany, and I am sure he would manage it if he could act by himself and was not slowed down by his ministers. . . .

We have been at Marly for the last ten days; I feel very well and walk as much as I can. Lassone will send my dear Mama every detail about my health. May I kiss her lovingly?

Mercy to Maria Theresa, 19 October 1778

Although the Queen certainly displays the greatest zeal and interest in the current problems, still the distractions caused by the normal life of the Court often prevent that assiduity which is so necessary if she is to succeed on the most important points. When the Queen has spoken to the King on something she wishes done, when she has convinced her husband and the ministers apparently agree with her views, she no longer thinks it necessary to come back to it. . . . Thus it happens that the ministers, who are convinced that the Queen forgets from one day to the next what has happened twenty-four hours earlier, do not constrain themselves in their actions.

Maria Theresa to Marie Antoinette
Vienna, 2 November 1778

Madame my dear daughter,

I am writing you on the day and at the moment you came into this world: you can imagine how moved I am, since I can only be thankful for the consolations [you give me]; may God give them back to you a hundredfold and make you happier, not as a mother but as a sovereign. I have nothing more to say since my letter of the fourth. . . . I appreciate your zeal and your love, but I sometimes fear that you may expose yourself too much without accomplishing anything; that might bring you into disrepute among those who think badly or who distract you with words when the facts show that they are not doing with any exactitude what they had promised us they would do. What a difference between the King of Prussia's ally and ours! Not only does Russia, on every occasion, speak the same language as its ally, but her plain declaration, which the last courier brought you, is embarrassing us greatly, and so we cannot hope, though we must wish, for peace. The King of Prussia's movements this last fortnight denote grand views; suddenly, after having encamped his troops in Silesia,* he gathers all his troops and throws himself with all his strength on our piece of Silesia which is completely open and can be taken by anyone. He pillages as usual and even seems ready to go on to Moravia,† which I don't think likely because of the season and the state of the roads. . . .

---

* That is, within Prussia; Frederick had taken most of Silesia from Austria in 1741.
† Deeper within the Austrian possessions.

Maria Theresa to Marie Antoinette
Vienna, 25 November 1778

Madame my dear daughter,

I will be very short; this letter will find you very near your time. I still hope that God will grant us the consolation of knowing that you have given birth between the eighth and the fifteenth.* All the rest is indifferent: a son will follow a daughter. I hear that you expect to breast-feed your child; that should depend on the King and your doctor; in their place I must tell you that I wouldn't let you, but it is very good of you to offer. We are having our nine days' prayer in the Saint Xavier chapel, and the crowd there is really touching. . . .

This courier is sent off for the business of the mediation. Luckily the Emperor is in perfect health but thin. . . . We need peace, the sooner the better, and without a congress; there are too many interests to be disentangled. The mediators should tell us to put everything back the way it was last year, in 1777: as for the Bavarian succession, the dispute with Saxony and other interested parties should be left for the Empire to decide.† All would be quickly solved and we would still lose the most: the immense expense [of the war] and the devastation of our poor provinces. . . .

Mercy to Maria Theresa, 20 December 1778

The Queen gave birth to a Princess this morning at half past eleven. Labor began at half past midnight; at first the pains were mild and came with long intervals of rest and mo-

* In fact Marie Antoinette gave birth to a daughter on December 20.
† Maria Theresa means the Imperial Diet, which was likely to have a pro-Austrian majority.

ments of sleep. The severe and lengthy pains only started around eight, and the waters flowed at that time. The Queen stood it all with great courage. I saw that august Princess in the last moments of the delivery and again a few moments after it was over. The effort she made not to complain or cry out caused a slight convulsive movement of the nerves; it was thought best to bleed her, and the accident ended immediately. The Queen is as well as possible, and her august child, who is large and strong, is in the best of health.

M ERCY DID NOT tell the Empress that because it was the custom for Queens of France to give birth in public (so as to preclude any substitution in the case of a stillborn baby or even a girl), Marie Antoinette's bedroom was packed with people pressing against the balustrade at the foot of the bed. Not only, therefore, did the Queen have to suffer all the normal pains of childbirth, but she had to do so in front of a noisy, pushy crowd: some men even climbed up on the furniture the better to see her. Right after the baby was born, the room became so hot and so close that the Queen fainted. At that point, in a remarkable feat of strength, Louis XVI tore open windows that had been nailed shut for the winter. The attending physician revived the Queen by bleeding her, and the spectators were at last sent out of the room.

Mercy to Maria Theresa, 16 February 1779

I cannot conceal from Your Majesty that when the King and Queen went to Paris, the public's reception was not what one might have expected. There were some shouts of "Long live the King! Long live the Queen!" in some parts of the city; in others a deep silence prevailed, and it has been noticed that the crowds were due much more to curiosity than to affection. . . . The Queen's dissipation, the expenses she causes, the look on her part of an immoderate desire for amusement in a time of calamity* and of war†—all that has alienated many people.

Maria Theresa to Marie Antoinette
Vienna, 1 April 1779

Madame my dear daughter,

. . . I received the news that your brother and sister-in-law had safely arrived back [in Florence]; they found their children in excellent health, but your brother Maximilian worries me greatly. Ever since his illness when he was with the army, he had had swellings, deposits, especially on the legs. He neglected them, hid them as much as he could so that he could have fun dancing, riding, playing tennis, etc., which is very appropriate at his age; but the swelling suddenly grew and he was given Baden [mineral] water. He took it and became worse so that he has been in bed for the last three weeks and they have already had to make three incisions. He is no better and will have to bear a few more; I only hope that the bone is not affected and that he will not remain a cripple at the age of twenty-two. He accepts his situation with patience and courage so that I am doubly moved. . . .

As for the peace, I couldn't be more worried. It seems to me that our fair hopes are disappearing; it is not our fault,

* The crop had been particularly bad that year.
† France was backing the fledgling United States in their fight for independence.

but then they cannot expect us to let our Elector be skinned while our adversaries, with the protection of the King of Prussia and of Russia, triumph over us; there will have to be a little justice and equality.

What you write about your dear daughter pleases me greatly, and especially the King's love. But I must admit to being insatiable; she needs a companion, and he must not delay too long. My dear daughter, neglect absolutely nothing you can do and, especially now in the warm season, do not go on too many rides; that would be absolutely contrary to our wishes and those of every good Frenchman and Austrian; and believe me always your loving Mama and friend.

P.S. Your big portrait delights me! Ligne says it looks like you; but it is enough that it shows your figure, with which I am very pleased.

IN APRIL 1779 Marie Antoinette caught the measles and decided so to arrange her enforced isolation as to enjoy herself thoroughly. Being contagious, she could not see the King—no doubt rather a relief—but instead of seeking the company of women friends, she chose to be guarded by four men. Two of these—Besenval, who was in his sixties, and Guines, who was enormously fat—could hardly be called attractive; but the other pair, the duc de Coigny and Count Esterhazy, were young and handsome. People naturally drew the obvious conclusions: the Queen, they said, was secluding herself with her lovers. In fact this was quite untrue: Marie Antoinette remained sexually virtuous; but it was imprudent at the very least for a pretty twenty-four-year-old Queen to behave as she did.

It is quite true that the King, who never refuses anything which might please his august spouse, had allowed the ducs de Coigny and de Guines, the comte Esterhazy, and the baron de Besenval to stay with the Queen [while she has the measles]; but his consent was arranged by the Queen, who failed to see the consequences it might have. The result has been some deplorable rumors, bad jokes in which the courtiers tried to decide which four ladies would be chosen to keep the King company if he should also be ill. No sooner did the four above-mentioned persons settle in but they wanted to watch over the Queen during the nights. I strongly opposed this ridiculous idea; I made Lassone, the doctor, forbid it. . . . Finally the abbé de Vermond and I made such a fuss that it was decided to have the gentlemen leave HM's bedroom at eleven and only return to it in the morning. Besides the bad effect produced by so unusual an arrangement, I must also worry about all the dangerous ideas suggested to the Queen during her conversations with these persons. . . . She had demanded, out of concern for the King, that he never come to see her. Her companions dared criticize the King's obedience to the Queen's wishes so that she became angry at her husband. I trembled when I thought of the consequences this might have, and on the tenth day of the illness, together with the abbé de Vermond, I asked the Queen to write a few pleasant words to the King. That proposal was rejected with much anger. I owe it to the abbé de Vermond to say that it was he alone who brought the Queen back to her senses. She wrote a few words to say that she had suffered much, but that what annoyed her the most was to be deprived for a few days more of the pleasure of kissing the King. The note had all the effect I expected; the King was delighted.

Marie Antoinette to Maria Theresa
Versailles, April 1779

Madame my very dear Mother,

The measles I have just had were more painful than usual in this country; I was about to be purged, which I needed badly, and still had a little milk. All is happily over, my eyes were not affected, and there are no fears for my chest. I have as yet only been purged once; I am moving to Trianon today to have a change of air until the end of my three weeks, at which time I will be able to see the King again. I stopped him from closing himself in with me; he has never had measles and, especially in a moment when he has so much business, it would have been unfortunate if he had caught the disease. We write each other every day; I saw him yesterday from a balcony outside. May I kiss my dear mother? I am not strong enough to write more: I have asked Mercy to do the rest.

Maria Theresa to Marie Antoinette
Vienna, 1 May 1779

Madame my dear daughter,

I cannot yet announce the signing of the peace (we need so many papers and assistance from outside), but it is arranged, which is a great relief;* please tell the King that I am grateful for his good offices; I owe them in part to you, my dear daughter, because of the love he bears you and the efforts you made. Try to see to it that in all future great and small events we agree at the outset. . . .

* The Peace of Teschen was signed on May 13, 1779. It gave Austria a few border areas in Bavaria, while Frederick II received the margraviates of Bayreuth and Anspach which had previously been ruled by relatives.

I am very touched by your concern for your brother. . . .
Thank God, he is better; for the first time in six weeks, I saw
him yesterday standing on his own two feet. My joy was
inexpressible, but the last two incisions are still open; the
first three are closing, but now he has a pain in the other leg,
which has a tumor that is shrunk by the remedies they have
applied to his thigh bone, but that pulls on his knee. I admit
that I am still very worried, for it is always the same tumor
that has been in his blood since the campaign because of his
tremendous exertions. He also takes medicines, is on a strict
diet, and is docile and good-tempered, never complaining,
not even worried; and I must admit I wouldn't have his
strength, but it makes him all the dearer to me and to us. It
is touching to see him; he has held up so well since the
beginning. He has organized his time, reads a great deal,
plays music, works at his military science and Hungarian,
and tries to accept his situation; I am extremely pleased with
him.

The Emperor also worried me a little. For the last ten
days he has been suffering from hemorrhoids, with no fever
or crisis, just the inconvenience and melancholy it causes.
He wanted neither to go out nor to see people, but now that
is over. He is extremely worried when he misses something. . . .

Marie Antoinette to Maria Theresa, 15 May 1779

Madame my very dear Mother,
How great is my happiness in learning that this much
desired peace has at last been concluded! It was due my dear
Mama, and I wanted to feel that we contributed to it from
here. Certainly my greatest care will henceforth be to up-

hold the union between our two countries (if I may so express myself). . . .

My health is now fine; here is a letter from Lassone, which will give you more detail than I could myself. I still have stomach pains but am beginning to suffer less. My dear Mama may be sure that I take every care, eat very little, and never stay up late. As for horses, I haven't ridden one since my illness and, in any event, expect to ride very little.

I wish I could tell my dear Mama that I hope to be pregnant. But I don't count on it yet. It took me a long time to get over my measles, and the last time I had my period (on the twenty-sixth), I almost had a hemorrhage. That leaves me little hope that I am pregnant now. But you may be sure that it won't be my fault if it doesn't happen soon.

Maximilian wrote me himself. I am delighted to know that he is better; but I will always be worried until his tumor is completely gone. It is very rare for someone his age to be as reasonable and patient as he has just been.

My daughter is very well; she is beginning to recognize the people she sees the most often; I am still away from her, since I am at Marly and she at Versailles, but I go there as often as I can. . . .

Maria Theresa to Marie Antoinette
Laxenburg, 1 July 1779

Madame my dear daughter,

Your letter of the fifteenth found us here at Laxenburg where we remain still. The air has been very good for your brother who now, to my great consolation, walks without crutches, just [uses] a very light cane. But everything isn't cured yet; it will still take much time and care. That is all the easier with him that he is agreeable to everything and does not even pride himself on it.

What you tell me about your charming daughter fills me with joy. . . .

I sincerely wish peace for the King: maritime wars are even more cruel and costly.* Our reconciled friend† tries to hurt us; and through his intrigues and very subtle and mendacious insinuations, he tries to turn everyone against us; he uses everything he can imagine, prejudices and cajoleries. . . . I count on the King's feelings and the honesty of his ministers, but some little liaison or something crooked could take place. . . .

I would rather seem importunate than not to recommend you to beware. . . . Unfortunately the ancient prejudices in our two nations are not as erased as I would wish, and against them only our constancy and friendship can triumph for the good of our Houses, peoples, and holy religion. . . . My dear daughter, you can do much if you follow these principles and if you listen to and follow Mercy's advice; he has all my trust and is surely as attached to you as anyone of your Frenchmen or ministers. I kiss you with all my heart. God preserve our hopes!

Maria Theresa to Marie Antoinette
Schönbrunn, 1 August 1779

Madame my dear daughter,

Your letter of the sixteenth afflicted me greatly because all our fine hopes were gone; and I must admit that I really counted on them. Nothing is lost; you are both very young, in good health, and you love one another, so it will easily be

* France and the United States were at war with England.
† Frederick II.

made up, but it is better to have than to hope. Thank God you had no hemorrhage, inconvenience, or weakness! You must follow Lassone's advice, and although I am opposed to separations, if he recommends one, I think you should do so, naturally if the King agrees, otherwise not; but I must tell you that I remember the past, that you were only too eager on this point, and I would not want it to become usual again. Your happiness depends on it—that of your people, that of your family.

I will admit that I am trembling for the fleets and in spite of your great superiority, I do not feel safe. Combined operations* are very difficult because the right moment must be seized, and it already seems to me that something has been lost, and too much time left to the English, all of which will cost you double. . . .

Marie Antoinette to Maria Theresa
Versailles, 16 August 1779

Madame my very dear Mother,

I cannot find the words to tell my dear Mama how grateful I am for her two letters and the kindness with which she wants to use every means to give us peace. It is true that it would be a happy event and that my heart wants it more than anything in the world; but unfortunately I see no hope for it right now. All depends on this moment; our fleets, French and Spanish, being combined, we have a wide margin of superiority.

They are now in the Channel!—and it is not without trembling that I think that from one moment to the next fate will decide. I also worry about the nearness of the

* The French and Spanish fleets were to join in an invasion of England.

month of September, for then the sea is no longer practicable. . . . The King is touched, as he should be, by all the marks of good will you have given him, and I do not doubt that he will always be eager to take advantage of them rather than relying on the intrigues of those who have so often betrayed France. . . .

My health is excellent. My period has started at the right time and is not too strong. I will start living as usual again, and in consequence I hope soon to tell my dear Mama about new hopes for pregnancy. She can be reassured about my behavior; I am too aware of the necessity of having children to neglect anything I can do. If in the past I was wrong, it was childishness and frivolity, but now my head is much more even and you may be sure that I am aware of all my duties. Besides, I owe it to the King because of his love and, I can say it, his trust in me, which grows ever stronger.

Madame's pregnancy is mere gazettes' gossip. She is always in the same state. There was a moment when we thought it was no longer so—even Monsieur was boasting greatly—but the passage of time proved that it was all empty words, and I think he will always stay as he is. . . .

I am very sorry that the improvement to Maximilian's leg has not continued; it is dreadful to be so inconvenienced at his age; his patience is really moving, and I hope that little by little he will get better. I am sending my dear Mama the portrait of my daughter; it is very like [her]. The poor child is beginning to walk in her basket. Several days ago she said, "Papa"; her teeth are not out yet, but you can feel them all. I am delighted that she started by naming her father; it will tie him more closely to her. He always goes to see her regularly, and as for me I need nothing to make me love her more. . . .

The Queen's fondness for the duc de Guines has been brought to such a point that it will not be easy to stop its progression. The duc de Guines is intelligent; he is clever and good at intrigues. He has already been so forward as to give the Queen several memoranda in which several good and useful ideas are blended with many traps designed to further his ambitious plans.

. . . The Queen would be greatly shocked if people thought that she was being led by someone. . . . She honestly thinks people unaware of the influence the duc de Guines has over her, and that in turn makes her much more willing to listen to him. If only she could be shown that it is not so, it is very sure that she would become much more distant to him, and nothing could help that happen more than to have Your Majesty tell her august daughter that people everywhere are saying that the Queen is so much under the duc de Guines's influence that she decides nothing without his advice.

Maria Theresa to Marie Antoinette
Schönbrunn, 19 August 1779

Madame my dear daughter,

I cannot refuse the King's Ambassador* the appreciation he deserves: you recommended him to me and he served the King with zeal, judgment, and promptness; on every occasion he showed himself very attached to the system so happily linking our two Houses. He deserves your favor, and whatever the King does for him I will consider a mark of

* The baron de Breteuil.

friendship for us. . . . If it suits the King's service and his convenience, we will see him here again with pleasure. . . .

Maria Theresa to Marie Antoinette, 1 September 1779

Madame my dear daughter,

Your letter of August 16 gave me great joy because of what you tell me about your health, the King's return, the hopes you give me of a companion for the dear child whose portrait you sent me; she is charming, strong, healthy and has caused me the greatest joy. I have her portrait opposite me on a chair and cannot let it go; but I think also that she looks like the King. I am writing you from the middle of the Danube; when I arrive at Schlosshof, I will send my letters back to Vienna for the courier. The weather is splendid; I expect to spend five days with your sister: your brother's condition, although he is better, will bring me back. I can only have peace when I am there. I had the pleasure of seeing him up on his feet before leaving; but he was already better in Laxenburg, and as long as the wound is not closed, I always fear bone splinters. His mood and his patience are the same as ever.

You will have heard about the accident of Vesuvius at Naples. The populace, which is horrible and fanatical, was much more dangerous than the eruption; there were 30 to 40,000 men who forced the opening of the church and carried Saint Gennaro in procession. The King and Queen had the greatest difficulty in leaving the theater where they were; the crowd kept as hostage the two horsemen who had been sent them to tell them to be orderly and wait until day for the procession: they did no harm but would not give up their demands. It is dreadful to have a people like that. I am glad your sister wasn't pregnant. The Emperor had already left when the courier arrived; he expects to be away for two months. The weather is admirable; I hope it will remain so.

I am not a little worried about the great events which must be occurring just now, and since the whole kit and caboodle is in the Channel, I must admit my fear that your great superiority won't be so effective there, and in case of mishap the English have a great advantage, since all their harbors are there, and France has none before Brest.* . . .

I cannot resist telling you an anecdote which is generally told and which at the beginning, like so many others, I thought unbelievable, but we hear from all over that you are so controlled by the duc de Guines that you decide nothing without his advice. In all his political missions the duc de Guines behaves in such a way as not to give you reason to complain; I therefore have no prevention against him, but the unfortunate circumstances in which he has found himself, together with his well-known reputation of being very ambitious, force me to tell you about these stories, since, my dear daughter, there would be great damage for you in letting people think that the Duke controls you in everything, please believe me always very lovingly. . . .

P.S. Forgive the ink blots and the poor writing; they are caused by the movement of the oars.

Marie Antoinette to Maria Theresa, 15 September 1779

Madame my very dear Mother,

The good weather we are enjoying here makes me hope that my dear Mama will have the same at Schlosshof. I took great pleasure in talking to the baron de Breteuil about my dear Mama and her health. It is a great achievement for the

---

* The Empress is referring to the projected invasion of England, which in the end never took place.

Ambassador to have deserved her favor and her approval. The King's health and mine are very good, and we are living together in such a way that I may soon have hopes, although as yet I can count on nothing.

The taking of Granada and the naval battle have pleased everybody here; unfortunately we need greater events to bring peace. The public is complaining strongly about the fact that M. d'Orvilliers,* with forces so much stronger than those of the British, has not been able either to find them in order to fight them, or to stop any of their trading ships from returning to port. It will all have cost a lot of money for nothing and I see no probability of peace talks for this winter. . . .

It is true that the duc de Guines is part of my circle, but he also belongs to the King's, who treats him very well. I rendered him a service in the cruel business which M. d'Aiguillon had started against him; naturally he is grateful. It is also the way things are done there that those who could not destroy him with their calumnies now out of jealousy should exaggerate the way we treat him. It is a custom in this country for people always to try and guess who is leading us: I have seen this too often over the last nine years to be surprised now.

My brother's condition gives me hope; but I will only cease worrying when he is fully recovered. . . .

Marie Antoinette to Maria Theresa, 14 October 1779

Madame my dear Mother,

We have given up the stay in Fontainebleau because of the expense of the war and also to receive news from the army

* The admiral commanding the French Channel fleet.

faster. We spent five days in Choisy, and we are going to Marly tomorrow for two weeks.

Our fleet was unable to find the English and did nothing at all; that is a wasted campaign which has cost a great deal of money. The worst is that illness has settled in the ships and is causing great damage. The dysentery which is epidemic in Brittany and Normandy has also done great harm to the land troops which were to be embarked:* it is a desolation. Illnesses are also afflicting the Spanish and cooling their zeal, all the more that they have difficulty recruiting new troops.

I am very much afraid that this setback will make the English more difficult, thus putting off any peace talks, which I do not expect soon. . . .

My sister Elisabeth will be inoculated at La Muette: she herself wanted it and decided to do it. My daughter is in the best of health. Since I was very heated, I took a few baths and was purged the day before yesterday. I will drink asses' milk while I am at Marly; my health is very good. The King lives with me in the most intimate way. I am still not yet pregnant, which is making me very impatient.

Marie Antoinette to Maria Theresa, 16 November 1779

Madame my very dear Mother,

The good news my dear Mama sends about my brother Maximilian gives me much joy. God grant that this dreadful leg ailment never come back! I hope he will continue to take the necessary care during the winter months.

My health is good, and the milk suited me very well. I had not been purged since the last which I was given to get rid of the last of my measles six months ago. I was heated and

* The invasion of England is what the Queen is writing about.

had a little cough, but without any chest pains; the milk took care of all that. I am neither fatter nor thinner.

The orders have gone to disarm the fleet and bring the troops to their winter quarters. . . . The nullity of the campaign postpones all thought of peace. The English will surely make the greatest efforts next year; but besides what they have suffered and lost this year, they will be severely hampered by the Americans and perhaps the Irish. . . .

As for the baron de Breteuil, knowing my dear Mama's good intentions, she can be sure that I will try to have him see their effect. He was very well treated, both at Marly and at Choisy.

My good health, the King's, and the way we live still give me reason to hope; but for this month, since yesterday, I am sure I am not [pregnant]. I am overwhelmed with my dear Mama's kindness and unique attentions and, at this moment, for my birthday, I do not remember without remorse the forgetfulness and lateness of which I have sometimes been guilty. If I dared, I would say it has always happened almost in spite of myself. My duty and my heart warn me in advance of the times, but my giddiness, I must admit it to my shame, sometimes makes me forget to send my letters off in time. If I had my own couriers, these mishaps would not happen. I ask a thousand pardons to my dear Mama: I have never been guilty in this way without being punished by an immediate repentance. . . . My daughter continues in excellent health: she now has four teeth.

Maria Theresa to Marie Antoinette
Vienna, 1 December 1779

Madame my dear daughter,
   Your letter of the sixteenth brought by the courier reas-

sures me completely about your health and that of your dear daughter but does not satisfy me in regard to a pregnancy which I await with impatience. Your daughter will soon be a year old; she needs a little companion, and we all want him.

What you tell me about the fleets is sad because it will delay peace, another year the English will no longer be surprised and it will all cost more efforts, money, and blood;* but at the moment there was nothing better to do. . . .

Your sister of Naples is suffering greatly because of her pregnancy; I fear she may again have only a daughter. Your brother of Milan's trip may be delayed since the Duke of Modena was very ill.† He is less so now, but at eighty-and-some-odd years, he cannot hope to get better.

I would like to scold you about that long compliment you made me at the end of your letter. I will never demand extraordinary attentions, but I must admit that the slightest mark of your love and remembrance wakes me up for a long time because I love you so dearly and care only about my dear children. The Queen of Naples spoils me a little by her attentiveness. . . .

Marie Antoinette to Maria Theresa
Versailles, 15 December 1779

Madame my very dear Mother,

I am very sorry not to give my dear Mama the news her love so fervently awaits. The way I live with the King keeps my hopes up, but until now I can count on nothing. It is a sad repetition; my period started again the day before yesterday. But they are good, neither too much nor too little,

* The Empress was entirely right that the project was abandoned.
† The Duchy of Modena, at his death, was to be inherited by the Habsburgs.

and I have been feeling well. For two weeks I had stomach pains, but they were not severe enough to prevent me from doing things as usual. I am lucky that they were no worse, for everyone here is sick, especially with dysentery.

We are awaiting M. d'Estaing, who has been at Brest for a week. The winds had scattered his fleet; his ship came in almost alone, but since then we have had news of the others. . . .

I am still sure that the King of Prussia is wasting his time with his intrigues to be the mediator. Mercy will tell my dear Mama about a French officer, a sort of adventurer with neither mission nor permission, who took it upon himself to speak of negotiations at Berlin. What proves our ministers' good faith in this is that M. de Vergennes warned Mercy even before he had any news; besides, I think the apocryphal negotiator will be ordered back to France.

I should be very sorry if M. le duc de Modéne's health stopped Ferdinand's trip; how happy he will be to join my dear Mama and the whole family! I feel it, even if I cannot hope for this myself; I may not say more. . . .

Maria Theresa to Marie Antoinette
Vienna, the First of the Year 1780

Madame my dear daughter,

I cannot begin the year better than by sending you my loving compliments and wishes—first for a Dauphin, and within the year. The générale Krottendorf has just died. I hope she will stop visiting you. . . .

. . . The public and our nobility are very much in favor of England; that is an old prejudice as being anti-Austrian is with you; but no one in the administration, the Court, or the ministry thinks that way, and I can answer for the mother and the son,* as long as the latter is encouraged in his present good dispositions, and provided that the behavior of your ministers within the Empire is not always contrary to those of the Emperor. . . . I am not at all pleased with the situation in America, or that of the fleet. This coming year, you will have forces twice as strong against you; England's resources are immense and their fanaticism unbelievable. You know what I wish as a partisan of France and the mother of their dear Queen: peace.

I did not make myself clear about Ferdinand's trip. He will go around Italy, to Florence, Rome, and Naples; but that slip brought me a charming explanation from you, since you thought him happy because he was coming here. With no compliment from either of us, I can tell you that this part of your letter moved me deeply, and I kiss you lovingly. I am delighted that Vermond is with you; I trust him completely because I know how attached he is to you. You have to be the way he is in order to remain in a great and tumultuous Court when one has no personal ambition; only your kindness keeps him there. Perhaps he could send me the book, the title of which I enclose; no bookseller here could get it for me. I have two volumes; the other two are missing.

Marie Antoinette to Maria Theresa, 15 January 1780

Madame my very dear Mother,

. . . It seems to me that Mercy has always been rather pleased with M. de Vergennes, most especially in the last conversation he had with him. Whenever he thinks I ought to speak, my dear Mama can be quite sure that I will do so as for the thing most essential to my happiness. Aside from the

* Maria Theresa and Joseph II.

circumstances in which there may be specific facts, I will avail myself of every opportunity to keep the King in his good disposition, which has always seemed to me very sincere.

M. d'Estaing returned here, suffering greatly from his wound, after a campaign which proved more difficult than useful. We are still not discouraged, however, and have every reason to believe that during the next campaign, we will be the strongest in America. M. de Guichen will leave shortly with a fleet of fifteen to eighteen ships and three to four thousand soldiers.*

The weather here is very cold and unpleasant; there are terrible fogs to which we owe an epidemic of colds; everyone is coughing in Paris and Versailles. I spent three days in bed with a fever. Only the King and Monsieur escaped the disease, and they looked after the rest of us, for we were each in our rooms without being able to go out; even my daughter was ill, but even though she is still teething, she did not have any fever. As for me, I hope to be completely cured; I am still taking ipecacuana† pills, but they do not prevent me from living as usual. I am no longer coughing; I am waiting for it to be a little less cold and will then think seriously about my health and the question so important to my happiness. I expect to take iron again next month and will perhaps have myself bled as a precaution. Vermond and Lassone think I could become pregnant more easily afterward. . . .

As late as 1780, a year when Maria Theresa's health declined sharply, the Empress was still trying to reform her daughter. Mme de Polignac is a case in point.

The comtesse de Polignac came from a good, but rela-

* The soldiers were placed under Rochambeau's command.
† A vomitive.

tively poor family and seldom attended the Court until she was noticed by Marie Antoinette. With the face of an angel and the sweetest of voices, she displayed just the kind of exaggerated sensitivity the Queen fell for every time, especially since the pretty comtesse kept explaining to Her Majesty that she wanted no favor other than to spend time in her beloved company. This, however, did not prevent her from asking favors for others—her husband, her daughter, her lover, the comte de Vaudreuil, her friends, her friends' friends. As a result the Polignac clan cost the State close to a million livres ($4,500,000) a year, M. de Polignac was created a Duke and given, as we have seen earlier, the reversion of the office of First Equerry, while in 1785 the Queen's friend was given one of the great offices of state, that of Governess to the royal children. Naturally the public resented all this, and Mme de Polignac was soon as unpopular as Mme du Barry had ever been.

Maria Theresa to Marie Antoinette
Vienna, 1 February 1780

Madame my dear daughter,

I am fully reassured about your health. The colds must have been worse in France than here. Thank God! you and your dear little girl were over it in three days. I am afraid Carnival may bring on a relapse, since the weather is dreadful, and the return from Paris to Versailles* displeases me greatly. It seems to me that Lassone is right to give you iron, which did wonders for the Queen of Naples, and being bled cannot hurt. I could always count on becoming pregnant when I had myself bled. Thus I am delighted with what you

* The Opera Ball was in Paris, so the Queen returned to Versailles late at night in an unheated carriage in the depth of winter.

write and expect to see within a few months the effects of this, which are so highly desired and so important for you. Besides, all the news from everywhere, written or printed, mentions the perfect union between the two of you, says the King shows you so much attention and affection on every occasion that it is wonderful, but also that some take advantage of it. They say that the Polignac, just because of her favor with you, has asked to be given the county of Bitche, which would then be made a dukedom. The public is surprised with this request, which denotes more avidity than attachment. They also say that you want to give her millions. I pay no attention to these rumors, not thinking them likely, but I think it necessary and useful that you know about them, especially at a time when the State is so heavily burdened. . . .

Your brother Ferdinand and his wife (under the name of the Count of Nellenbourg*) already arrived in Rome on the nineteenth. . . . The Holy Father received them with the most touching tenderness and attention, as well as all private people, but especially the cardinal de Bernis,† and the Grimaldi also did much; and I must admit that at this time it pleases me. Thus people see how tightly we are linked, and while this is engraved in our hearts, it must also be made public. Now they are in Naples, and I am a little worried about your sister's advanced state of pregnancy, knowing how active and agitated she is. This letter will reach you during Lent; please think seriously about your health, and do not spoil anything by riding too often. Once the other amusements are over, and with the return of the good weather, I fear that exercise. I kiss you lovingly, my dear and more than dear daughter.

* The Archduke was travelling incognito.
† The French Ambassador to the Holy See.

Marie Antoinette to Maria Theresa
Versailles, 15 February 1780

Madame my very dear Mother,

If my dear Mama has worried about Carnival, I am delighted to reassure her. It has ended without any inconvenience to my health or of any other kind. I think I can even say that the balls I gave every week in my apartment were a great success; they were well attended, for dancing and company, by all the best people from Paris and Versailles.

We have here a great number of princes of Hesse. Prince Georges is here with his entire family, his wife, his younger son, his two daughters, and his sister-in-law. I expect that the four women will come and see me some day this week. As for the two Princes, they have already come; Prince Georges's son especially is a great success here—he is very pleasant. As for the poor father, he has been ill ever since his arrival in Paris; he has gout, and on top of that, at the moment he has a swelling around the eyes, which is very painful.

I am too well accustomed to the inventions and exaggerations of ce pays-ci to be surprised about the gossip in regard to Mme de Polignac. It is quite usual here for the King to contribute to the dowry of members of the Court who are well born but not rich. The little Polignac* is to marry the comte de Gramont, who already has the reversion of the post of Captain of the Guard. Her mother thought of the County of Bitche but only for a moment, and as soon as she found out what it was worth, she was the first to tell me and gave up the idea of asking for it; the ducal title is just nonsense. As for the money the King will surely give the little

---

* Mme de Polignac's daughter. Marie Antoinette is simply lying; she had asked Louis XVI to give the huge and utterly unprecedented sum of a million livres to the Polignacs as a dowry; in the end the King talked them into taking a dukedom for their son-in-law instead. Soon afterward, the comte de Polignac was also created a duke.

girl a dowry, but people will say that she received more golden louis than she will have had écus.* It is a great joy for me to see that the King's way of thinking spares me any solicitation for my friend. He is quite convinced of the absolute honesty and nobility of her feelings. He will be delighted to do her good for her own sake; but I still appreciate the mark of friendship he gives me on this occasion.

The King has just published an edict, which is just a first step toward the paring down he wants to carry through in his Household and mine. If it is actually done, it will be a very good thing, not only for the money it will save, but also for the public opinion and satisfaction. We must wait for the actual happening before we can count on it; it has been tried and failed during the last two reigns. The King has the power and the good will; but in this country there are so many complications as to forms that if the right one is not chosen, the result will be new problems like in the past. . . .

Marie Antoinette to Maria Theresa
Versailles, 16 March 1780

Madame my very dear Mother,

. . . My health is now very good, and I must hope soon to become pregnant. I could not read without trembling what my dear Mama wrote me about the Queen of Naples—what a dreadful series of calamities. They say here that her daughter is very ill, and I am afraid her son may also catch smallpox; it is all the more unfortunate that they say it is the worst strain of the disease. . . . My daughter has not had even a moment's fever since she was born. She will soon be

*.A gold louis was worth twenty-four livres, an écu only three.

weaned and is so tall and strong she looks like a two-year-old. She walks alone, crouches, and stands without help, but she doesn't speak much. I must confide to my dear mother's tender heart a happy moment I had four days ago. There were several persons in my daughter's room; I had someone ask her where her mother was. That sweet child, although no one had said a word, smiled and came to me with her arms open. This is the first time she has shown she knows me; I must admit it gave me great joy, and I think I love her better since then.* But I realize I am speaking about her at length; my dear Mama's kindness and indulgence will forgive me this verbiage.

We received some terrible news last weel., that of the loss of an important convoy we were sending to Martinique. First they said all the ships had been taken [by the English], but now it seems sure that more than half has escaped. In spite of this improvement, the loss is still great, especially for the public opinion and the credit markets. Some eight to ten thousand well-trained troops were supposed to take ship for America at the end of the month; they will be gathered in Brittany; but I think this news will delay their embarkation. . . .

Mme de Hesse, daughter of the princess Françoise, went away yesterday. I saw her several times; she seemed very pleased with her stay. As for poor Prince Georges of Darmstadt, I still haven't seen him; he has been ill ever since he arrived. His wife came to see me with his two daughters. I liked the two young princesses; the younger, the wife of the hereditary prince, is very uncomfortable; she is pregnant and suffers a great deal. I am afraid she may finally miscarry; they are all leaving next month. They are here for a suit, but it will not be judged so soon. . . .

* This was all the more striking that Madame Royale, as the child was known, never saw her mother for more than a few minutes at a time and then not every day.

P.S. I reopen my letter to tell my dear Mama about the good news we have just heard. A convoy, worth more than thirty millions, has just arrived at Rochefort. It was escorted by a large ship and two frigates. It will greatly help credit.

Maria Theresa to Marie Antoinette
Vienna, 1 April 1780

Madame my dear daughter,

I start by thanking you for the word you added to your letter about the arrival in Rochefort of an important convoy. I cannot hide from you that I am much occupied and worried by your situation, which seems to me very critical, not because of [a lack of] resources in your monarchy, but because I think the English are so clever in this way* that no other nation can be their equal and that great efforts must be made merely to keep even with them. . . .

Everything you wrote me about your daughter pleased me, and I share with you a mother's feeling for the behavior of this dear child. How touching it is! But we need a Dauphin. I am impatient; my age does not leave me much time to wait. I would like to know if the générale has visited you since you were bled.

The Queen, your sister, has lost her dear Marianne, saved her son until now, but her second daughter was also ill of an inflammatory fever, and on top of that she is eight months' pregnant, with twenty-three bouts of fever, a cold on the nerves, and always moving about between Naples, Caserta, Portici, etc. I must say I am sorry for her. . . .

You did not answer to what I wrote you the papers said, that the King had given 800,000 livres to the comtesse Jules de Polignac as a dowry for her daughter, as well as a two-

* That is, at sea.

million [livre] estate besides paying her debts. There is even another anecdote, which I cannot believe, that a certain comte de Vaudreuil, who is supposed to be too closely linked with the comtesse,* was given, thanks to her, a 30,000-livres pension and an estate from the comte d'Artois, all through your intervention. I must warn you that this is causing a great sensation, quite bad, in the public and abroad, especially when Court expenses are being cut, which is necessary and praiseworthy. But these generous gifts, which are so excessive, on the other side make the cuts heavier and more unpleasant for those who suffer from them. I could not remain silent about these anecdotes which concern your reputation; because you have a kind heart, you let yourself be taken in by the greed of so-called friends, especially when things are as they are. If I did not warn you, who would dare? It was painful to write this, but your complete silence on this point showed me that the story was not false and that I had to tell you all this.

Marie Antoinette to Maria Theresa, 13 April 1780

Madame my very dear Mother,

The troops to be sent off to the Islands† are aboard their ships and only await a favorable wind to leave port. God grant they arrive easily! The embarkation already proved a problem; not enough transport ships had been gathered at Brest, and they were forced to leave two regiments behind. That of the prince de Salm is one, but it is hoped that they

* As usual, Mercy had done his job. Vaudreuil was Mme de Polignac's lover; and great sums were indeed spent on the comtesse, her family, and friends.
† The French possessions in the West Indies which were under attack from the British.

can follow very soon.* I hope he will do well; he has a good reputation among the military.

My daughter's weaning did not at all upset her health, she is still very well and interests me greatly; I yearn for her to have a companion, and I have reason to hope for one more than ever, since the King lives the right way with me and my health has been very good as a result of my bleeding. My period came as usual at the proper time; it should have been on the twenty-second, but it is always a few days early. . . .

I would give anything in the world to have a Prince Kaunitz† here in the ministry,‡ but unfortunately men like that are rare, and you have to perceive merit as my dear Mama does to find them.

M. de Vaudreuil is a nobleman who served in the army and whose relations are distinguishing themselves in the present war. He never asked for any favors and was rich enough not to care about financial help. He owns large estates in the [West Indies] but receives nothing from them because of the war. The King gave him 30,000 francs, not as a pension but only until the end of the war. He has asked the King to annul this because the comte d'Artois gave him an estate. I had nothing to do with this generous act; everyone here knows that my brother is sufficiently fond of M. de Vaudreuil not to need any further urging. I could say the same in regard to Mme de Polignac and the King; he likes her greatly, and although I am very happy and grateful for the good he does her, I have no need to ask him. The gazette and pamphlet writers know more than I do; I have never heard either about the two-million estate or about any other; if I knew more I would tell my dear Mama to whom I will always answer about everything. . . .

* In fact, he never did, but, soon after, he built one of the handsomest town houses in Paris, which today houses the Museum of the Legion of Honor.
† Prince Kaunitz, Maria Theresa's longtime and trusted Chancellor.
‡ The French ministry included Vergennes, one of the greatest Foreign Ministers in French history; and it was Marie Antoinette herself who had convinced Louis XVI to fire Turgot, a man whose work might well have prevented the Revolution.

I wrote the Queen of Naples recently; but because of her condition, I forbore to mention my sorrow and worry about her health and the loss of her daughter. . . .

Marie Antoinette to Maria Theresa
Versailles, 14 May 1780

Madame my very dear Mother,

I can only, my dear Mama, repeat the same sorry news about my condition. The King is always perfect for me, my health is rather good, except for being a little heated. I am in the middle of my period. For the last three months it has been going well, although it is seven days early month after month. But I am awfully sorry to have it still. The Queen of Naples's happy delivery is a great relief and the best consolation for the worries she gave us during her pregnancy. I hope that she will be the first to forget her past troubles and that her health will be greatly improved by it all. . . .

I send my dear Mama a little sample of eau divine; I was told that she no longer had any of good quality since my aunt's death. If this suits her, I will hope to be her purveyor in the future. May I kiss my dear Mama very lovingly?

Marie Antoinette to Maria Theresa, 16 June 1780

Madame my very dear Mother,

My dear Mama's sorrow makes mine even greater if possible. Ever since I have known that my uncle* was seriously

* Charles of Lorraine, the brother of the late Emperor Franz I, Maria Theresa's husband, was Governor of the Austrian Netherlands, today's Belgium.

ill, I have felt worry and sorrow like never before. He has always shown me love and friendship on every occasion. I am as attached to him as if I had the honor of seeing him and knowing him personally; and what a sad perspective to see the end of the last member of the House of Lorraine! His age is not so advanced as to preclude much hope, but they say he has no idea of his condition and scarcely thinks himself ill. He, who is so kind, so beloved in Brussels and in that whole country, refuses to do everything he is advised to try for his health. I am told he wants to allow the openings on his legs to close, and yet it is one of the best ways of saving him. My heart bleeds.

My brother Maximilian's election* must now be finished, or at least assured. I spoke this week to M. de Belderbush's nephew, who is the Minister of Cologne here, and asked him to convey all my thanks. Last week M. de Chalons, the King's Minister in Cologne, left here to rejoin his post. He was ordered to tell the Elector and the Chapter that the King would see [my brother's] election with pleasure; as for me, I asked him to convey my feelings for my brother, the lively interest I take in everything that concerns him, and the gratitude I will have for all those who will help in his election. I long for the Emperor's return [from Russia] so that my dear Mama will no longer be worried about him. . . . My health is good and reinforces my hopes for the future. What happiness it would be for me, knowing as I do that my dear Mama would share my joy! . . .

---

* As coadjutor to the Prince-Bishop-Elector of Cologne. He would thus succeed him automatically to this prosperous ecclesiastical Electorate.

Maria Theresa to Marie Antoinette
Schönbrunn, 30 June 1780

Madame my dear daughter,

I am very touched with what you have done as regards the election in Cologne: it is just like my daughter's loving heart for her family; but I am no less touched by what the King said about you and myself. Please tell him how moved I was. . . .

The condition of my dear brother-in-law is desolating. I was tenderly attached to him—he deserved it; he was kindness itself and made his province the happiest in the Monarchy. You say very truly that it is sad to see the end of the House of Lorraine; you are quite right; I had the misfortune of seeing the end of the Houses of Austria and of Lorraine,* they live on in you only, my dear children; may their virtues and kindnesses be eternal in you! You have there some outstanding examples. I have no more hopes for the Prince; he may linger but miserably; he refuses to acknowledge his condition—he fights against it. He wrote me a rather long letter by the courier of the twentieth of this month, which pleased me greatly, where he says only a few words about his condition.

I sent Mercy a summary of the news I have of the Emperor's trip. He writes only seldom, being burdened with fetes and displays, and he cannot speak frankly because the couriers go through Russia and Poland, and even right now those from Petersburg go through Prussia. It would not be the first time that a courier was lost.† . . . This trip really up-

* Charles VI of Habsburg, Maria Theresa's father, failed to sire sons and was the last male Habsburg. As for the House of Lorraine, Prince Charles was childless, while Franz I's children took on their mother's name and were thus known as Habsburg-Lorraine. Lorraine itself was ceded to France when Franz married Maria Theresa.
† Kidnapping couriers to steal their dispatches was known to happen, and in Prussia more often than elsewhere.

sets me, and another one* would make me more worried still, especially after the terrible riot, without example in a civilized country, which has just taken place. There it is, that liberty so often praised, that unique way of legislating! Without religion, without morality, nothing lasts. They speak of a great victory won in Carolina by the British. I would be sorry; it would make them even less willing to negotiate, and peace, for which I yearn, would be more distant.

You say that my attentions are inexhaustible; so is my love, and my children are my dearest occupation. They provide the only happy moments of my difficult life; the charming Queen of France contributes to this not a little, but we need a Dauphin. . . .

You want to take over the sending of my eau divine. All those that were sent were too strong. I am sending Mercy a little vial of my old one, as long as you are so pleasantly offering me some: that alone would make it good for me. I kiss you lovingly.

Marie Antoinette to Maria Theresa, Undated

Madame my very dear Mother,

I wrote my dear Mama as soon as I heard the sad news of my uncle's death, but since the courier from Brussels had already left, I am afraid my letter may have arrived very late. I dare not speak about it again so as not to reawaken so well founded a sorrow.

I talked to Mercy about the business of the election, which I hope and am impatient to see finished. He seemed

* The Emperor was planning to visit England; the riots are the anti-Catholic Lord George Gordon Riots, which raged through central London for several days.

very pleased about his last conference with M. de Vergennes. I intend to speak to M. de Maurepas, will warn him that M. de Goltz is distorting his conversations, and ask him to speak more clearly. . . . As for the [Emperor's] other trip, I hope he will think long and hard before visiting a country which is the enemy of all sovereigns,* and where the laws most essential to the peace and honesty of the public are overcome by the spirit of liberty and independence. The last riot made me tremble and gave me many thoughts. The taking of Charlestown is very regrettable because of the facilities and the pride it will give the English; it is still more so, perhaps, because of the Americans' wretched defense; there is nothing to be hoped from such poor troops. I told the King about my dear Mama's kindness; he was very touched and asked me to tell her and to repeat his respect and attachment for her. I am delighted that my dear Mama has sent the sample of eau divine; I will compare the two, to make sure; I am only sorry that I cannot send it before the next courier. May I kiss her?

Maria Theresa to Marie Antoinette
Schönbrunn, 2 August 1780

Madame my dear daughter,

You greatly touched me by your sorrow about your dear uncle, and by writing about it right away. Everything that comes from my dear daughter and her heart is very dear to me. I owe the success of your brother's election to the King and you alone; you were so obliging in this business that you are honored for it abroad, and our family is grateful. . . .

* The fact that the King of England could not govern without the assent of Parliament horrified all the continental monarchs.

I have just received a courier the Emperor sent on the twenty-third from Riga; he left Petersburg overwhelmed with politeness and amiability but nothing more. Mercy will tell you about it more in detail, and I do not think that the assertions he supposedly made that he wanted to help the English have any truth in them. I hope that M. Vérac* will tell you how it really was, and the Emperor's letter from Riga shows it wasn't so. That pleases me: I like to see my feelings continued in my children.

Your attack on the Emperor's other trip, which he would only make after a general peace, agrees with my thinking; but I must admit I was a little amused to see you so strong on this point. I am no less so, and for the last few years that nation [England] has been gaining terribly everywhere; one cannot be too careful in taking precautions and preventing their seduction and influence in everything. I am very sorry that this year's campaign is going no better than the others, after the King has spent so much and when the French are always so brave.

Enough politics, let us return to our loving interests. No appearance of a pregnancy, that really upsets me: we absolutely need a Dauphin. . . .

Marie Antoinette to Maria Theresa
Versailles, 15 August 1780

Madame my very dear Mother,

My dear Mama's heart will fully share the joy I have just felt when I received the letter of the Elector, who sent us a courier to announce my brother's election. My first movement was to send him one bearing my letter of thanks. M.

* The French Ambassador to Russia.

de Vergennes stopped me because the King has not yet answered and for other reasons of etiquette: but I insisted on giving the Elector a mark of my satisfaction. . . . I hope we will soon have good news from Munster; I await it impatiently. . . . The King of Prussia will be punished by his failure; he may intrigue all the more as a result. . . .

I realize how useful it would be if the King only sent reasonable people to Germany; I will do everything I can on the right occasions. I am less worried about the old anti-Austrian prejudice, which seems much weaker, than by a certain spirit of fear and weakness which sometimes holds our ministers and which naturally influences the behavior of the people they lead and who expect their promotions from them.

My health is good in spite of the heat and excessive drought we have here. I have hardly ever stayed up late for the last three months, and when it happened, it was always with the King, either at Saint-Hubert, where we have supper on hunting days, or at Trianon.

Maria Theresa to Marie Antoinette
Schönbrunn, 31 August 1780

Madame my dear daughter,

Thanks to your dear efforts for the election of your brother and your obliging attentions to the Elector, you have pleased that nice old man and us as well. That business is now ended for the best, our neighbor* is much annoyed at it and will try, on another occasion, to take his revenge and make the falsest, most dangerous insinuations. He says we want all the bishoprics and all the electorates; he makes all

* Frederick II.

Leopold's children, though they range in age from nine to one, bishops since everyone must be sure that the two eldest ones are not destined to be churchmen. God knows what he will invent about the trip to Russia! The Emperor seems very pleased with it but not blinded. I can assure you that nothing was negotiated, but apparently the wrongful preventions against us, which were strong, have been dispelled. . . .

The Emperor came back in very good health, and his suite too, but since then three of them have caught fevers. There are many fevers here, but they are not dangerous; I would not like you to catch one, but I do wish you an alteration in your health; I care about it a great deal.

Everything you have done for the memory of your dear uncle honors you greatly and touched me deeply. We are far removed from it here, and his regiment, which I so hoped could keep his name, has been named for Charles, his namesake in Tuscany, but is commanded by a very mediocre general. I must say it really upset me.

The Emperor expects to leave for Bohemia on the eighteenth, to see the two fortresses. The mornings and evenings are already becoming very cool; I think that we will have an early winter and that I will not stay here more than three weeks. Even so, your sister's departure for the Netherlands will only be next spring. She expects to come back after a few months, and then she means to go and see you so as to come and give me your news and those of my dear goddaughter. This is only an idea; you see that it is almost two years off, and it will all depend mostly on you; but in the meantime the idea pleases me, consoles me for the departure of the others because they would be coming straight back to you, to my dear Queen, whom I kiss lovingly.

P.S. What you did for the abbé de Vermond pleases me infinitely and does you honor.

Marie Antoinette to Maria Theresa, 19 September 1780

Madame my very dear Mother,

It is a great joy for me to see that my dear Mama approves of my behavior; but I am ashamed to be getting so much praise when I have already been rewarded by success and my love for my brother. I am not surprised at our enemy's bad temper; but it seems to me that if he looked to his glory and his pride, he would no longer show it over a finished business. If he goes on compromising himself, his impotent rage will finally look ridiculous and unimportant.

After the joy I have had at the Emperor's happy return, which for me is the main thing, I share the satisfaction of his success over there. It will be a great good in the future if intrigues and politics do not change the good dispositions of a Court like that one. In the meantime we must be pleased to see them come around. . . .

I have settled in Trianon for eight or ten days so I can take walks in the morning; this is essential for my health and was not possible at Versailles. Trianon is only ten minutes away in a carriage, and one can easily walk there. The King seems to like it a great deal; he comes here for supper every day and visits me in the morning just like in my Versailles apartment. I chose this moment for my stay here because it is the month when the King hunts almost every day and needs me the least. My health and that of my daughter are very good. As for a pregnancy, I do not dare to talk about it, although the way we live must give me every hope.

I would be very sorry about my arrangement, particularly concerning the regiment, if it did not answer to the affection and respect we owe the memory of our dear uncle. May I kiss my dear Mama very lovingly? . . .

Madame my very dear Mother,

I have been occupied and a little worried by my daughter's health for the last three weeks. Several teeth which came out all at once gave her great pain and caused a fever which turned tertiary. Lassone is sending the details to my dear Mama and assures me there is no danger. Since yesterday the fever has stopped; God grant that it is over! I am touched by the sweetness and patience of the poor child in the midst of her sufferings, which at times were very acute.

The King has gone hunting for three days at Compiègne; I am spending that time at Trianon. On the thirteenth we will go to Marly; the company will be larger so there will be much more etiquette, and on All Saints Day* I will take up Court functions, which can be completed here only during the winter. We have slept separately for a long time. I thought my dear Mama knew it. It is the customary way here between husband and wife, and I did not think I should torment the King on that point, which would go very much against his way of being and his own tastes. I would be all the more wrong to insist that we are living together very much as husband and wife.

Peace would be good; but if the enemies do not ask for it, I would be very sorry that we agreed to a humiliating treaty. I am delighted with what my dear Mama tells me about Maximilian's health and his trip; it is very proper that he show his gratitude to the Elector, who behaved so well to him. The Emperor wrote me just as he was leaving. I hope that the winter at least will end his traveling. I wish it will not be contrary to my dear Mama's health. May I kiss her with all my soul?

Lassone is sending my dear Mama a detailed account of

* October 31.

my daughter's illness; the fever started again this afternoon, but it is so slight I hope it may not amount to anything.

Maria Theresa to Marie Antoinette
Vienna, 3 November 1780

Madame my dear daughter,

Yesterday I spent the time more in France than Austria, and I remembered all the happy times in the past, which is indeed gone. Just the memory consoles me; I am very pleased that your little girl, whom you say is so sweet, should be getting better, and about everything you tell me about your relation with the King. We must hope for consequences. I must admit that I did not positively know that you didn't sleep together, I just suspected it. . . .

I am very glad that you intend to resume a full Court life at Versailles; I know how dull and empty it is, but, believe me, without it the drawbacks are far more important than the little inconveniences of public ceremonies, especially in your country, with such a lively people. Like you, I wish the winter ended the Emperor's trips; but he is planning to go to the Netherlands at the beginning of March and then will stay abroad all summer. This gets worse every year and increases my work and my worries, when at my age one needs help and consolation, and I lose all those I love one after the other; I am quite overcome. The Emperor, after a stay in Brussels, will see the country and then go to Holland and will perhaps visit you, which I would prefer to his crossing the sea, even if it makes his trip last longer.

I am worried about Marianne; she suffers from a hardness of the stomach caused by the terrible way she is set up. It makes her throw up everything she eats, quite effortlessly, but it cannot go on forever. She has caught a cold, which inconveniences [her] greatly; there is nothing to be done with these stomach disorders because of their cause. I see her sufferings with sorrow, and her courage, which you know, is beginning to weaken. I myself have suffered from a rheumatism in the right arm for four weeks, which is why this letter is even less well written than usual, and it makes me end, assuring you of all my love.

T HE EMPRESS MARIA THERESA died on November 29, 1780. The news reached Versailles some eight days later. Louis XVI, who knew how attached Marie Antoinette was to her mother, insisted on breaking the news to her himself, and he did so with remarkable kindness and tact.

Marie Antoinette to Joseph II, 10 December 1780

Crushed by the most dreadful misfortune, I cannot stop crying as I write you. Oh, my brother, oh, my friend! You only are now left to me in a country which is, which will always be, dear to me! Take care of yourself, watch over yourself; you owe it to all. . . . Adieu, I no longer see what I write. Remember we are friends, allies; love me.

AFTERWORD

With her mother's death, Marie Antoinette lost the only person capable of restraining her, the only one to whose advice she might listen. Although she corresponded with the Emperor, her brother, often in a tone of contempt for the French, it was on equal terms. The "scoldings," as she called them, which she had received from Vienna were well and truly at an end.

In some ways no doubt her behavior after 1780 would have pleased her mother. She paid attention to her children—a Dauphin was born in 1781; he was followed by a Princess, who died soon after birth, and by a second son in 1785. She gave less of her time to keeping up with the latest fashion, although she went on spending just as much money. She grew less fond of amusements like gambling, horse races, and dancing. In other respects, however, her faults intensified. More and more she shunned the kind of public display she had always disliked. As Trianon grew more and more charming, she retreated to the fantasyland she had created. To her English-style park, she added a hamlet complete with cottages, dairy, and stables. There she could play at being just a private person surrounded by her friends and forget the mounting problems which beset the Monarchy.

That alone would have sufficed to make her unpopular,

especially since the cost of all these embellishments, never low, was widely thought to be ruinous. Far worse was the Queen's undisguised involvement in the government. She made and unmade ministers, often at the behest of the Polignac coterie, and her appointees, with one exception, proved to be incompetent, indeed dangerous: she was responsible for the two Finance Ministers, Calonne and Loménie de Brienne, who so mismanaged the already ominous public debt that they brought on the Revolution.

The results of Marie Antoinette's behavior are too well known to need retelling here. Certainly Maria Theresa would have been surprised and horrified at the extent of her daughter's fall: in all probability she feared no more for the Queen than an early retreat to some lonely château or a return to Austria, but she saw clearly that her daughter was preparing a grim future for herself.

It would obviously be absurd to make Marie Antoinette wholly responsible for the onset of the Revolution; the ancien régime, briefly reformed by Louis XV but returned to its old errors by Louis XVI, was paralyzed, inefficient, and crumbling; the very society that sustained it because it guaranteed its privileges was the first to attack it. Nor can that irretrievable mistake, the recall of the Parlement, be blamed on Marie Antoinette: it was purely the King's idea and probably made the Revolution inevitable.

That the Queen hastened events—especially after 1780—cannot, however, be doubted. And in her hatred of the changes brought about by the National Assembly in 1789 and 1790, she may well have sealed the Monarchy's doom. Without her influence on Louis XVI, a constitutional regime headed by a King might well have been possible: the Assembly and the people wanted it, but the King did not; and without him no liberal government could be sustained. Revolutions are often thought to develop their own irresistible momentum: in this case it owed much to the King's obvious loathing for the reforms which he might have accepted if he had not listened to Marie Antoinette's advice, or more exactly, to her demands.

At least one member of the royal family supported the reforms of 1789. All through the 1780s, the comte de Provence had been one of the leaders of the liberal opposition to his brother's government. Remaining in Paris during the early phases of the Revolution, he was involved in a plot to assassinate Louis XVI so that he could replace him; the plot was discovered and Monsieur found himself generally discredited, but he was in fact much the cleverest of the family. He fled Paris at the same time as the King and Queen; but, unlike them, he managed to cross the border instead of being stopped at Varennes. In the end he got his wish and lived long enough to become King Louis XVIII by the grace of God and the Allies who had vanquished Napoléon in 1814.

As for the Queen's friends—Coigny, Guines, Vaudreuil, Besenval, the Polignacs—all, with the single exception of the princesse de Lamballe, deserted her when the Revolution started: along with the comte d'Artois, they left France on July 15, 1789. Most died in exile, but two survived to provoke yet another revolution: Artois, who became King Charles X in 1824 and Jules de Polignac, the duchesse's son, who became his Prime Minister in 1829. Together, in an effort to bring back the ancien régime, they suspended the constitution and were swiftly punished: the people of Paris rose in July 1830 and finally drove the Bourbons from the throne.

Of all the people who had surrounded Marie Antoinette, only one remained faithful: in 1790 Mme de Lamballe, who had already left France, came back to Paris when she realized that the Queen was left without a friend. It was a noble gesture, since she was widely hated as one of the Queen's favorites. When in August 1792 the royal family was imprisoned and the Republic declared, Mme de Lamballe was arrested; in September, like most of the other inmates of the prison of L'Abbaye, she was massacred by an enraged mob, who paraded her head at the end of a pike before Marie Antoinette's window.

Alone of the Queen's children, her eldest daughter, Marie Thérèse Charlotte, survived the Revolution because she was exchanged for French prisoners of war. Married to her impotent cousin, the duc d'Angoulême, Artois's son, she lived to see the Restoration in 1814, the Revolution of 1830 which sent her back into exile, the enthronement of the younger branch of the Bourbons, the Orléans, and their fall in 1848. From the first she was a proud, embittered woman who never forgot that the Revolution had killed her parents, her brother, and her aunt; but, although she worshiped her father, she never mentioned her mother, whose frivolity she thought was responsible for much of the catastrophe which befell her family.

It is the fashion these days to look at history in terms of large economic and sociological forces and to downgrade the role of the individual accordingly. Why then publish Marie Antoinette's letters? She was after all only a King's consort and certainly neither responsible nor even aware of the great movements shaping France in the 1780s. Still, we can never understand the past if we confine ourselves to graphs and statistics. Marie Antoinette's letters provide us with just that feeling of reality which general histories so often lack. As we read her correspondence and Mercy's reports, we begin to understand what it was like to live at Versailles, what people cared about, how they spoke, what they did; and we are also shown how France was ruled after 1770.

That Marie Antoinette modified the course of history directly and personally can hardly be denied by anyone who reads the correspondence. Without her nagging, for instance, France would not have given Austria any support in resolving the War of the Bavarian Succession, and the Peace of Teschen would have reflected that. And if, after all, the Queen had been the sober and thoughtful Princess her mother hoped for, France might even have been spared the Revolution: another Maria Theresa, another Catherine II might well have reformed the Monarchy and avoided the worst.

For all these reasons the correspondence makes interesting reading; but of course there is more. Because of her disastrous end and her earlier glamour, Marie Antoinette still fascinates a very wide public. Like Mary Queen of Scots, whom she resembles in some ways, she has cast her magic over a group of endlessly renewed devotees; and indeed her story is exemplary. Faced with so spectacular a fate, we cannot resist wondering how and why it happened, how and why it wasn't avoided. The letters give us our answer, even as they provide the intimate story of a fascinating woman. We understand few living people as well as the Dauphine, then the Queen.

Still, much remains in the shadow: while a glance at Maria Theresa's constant criticism makes her daughter's shortcomings plain enough, we never get to see the side of her that entranced courtiers and foreigners alike. When it was pointed out to Horace Walpole, who was watching her dance, that the Queen was in fact out of step with the music, he answered, "In that case then, it is the rhythm that is wrong"—as eloquent a testimonial to her charm as can be imagined, especially since it came from someone who normally took the most negative view possible. This sort of admiration, indeed, became commonplace; more extraordinary, however, was her ability to fascinate even the people who opposed her violently. Time and time again during the Revolution, stalwart Republicans who had been clamouring for her head found themselves, upon meeting her, weak-kneed and starry-eyed, so that in the end Marie Antoinette made more converts to her cause than the massive bribes handed out by the King.

The Queen had other talents as well. Of course she cared nothing for intellectual pursuits—few rooms at Versailles can have remained more unused than her library—and spent much of her time listening to the silliest sort of gossip, but she understood at least two of the arts as well as any of her contemporaries. As she often told the Empress, she liked playing the harp; more important, she appreciated good music when she heard it. When Gluck's *Iphigénie en Aulide* was first performed at the Paris Opera, Marie Antoinette attended performance after performance, clapping vigorously, and thus prevented it from being hissed out of town. The French, who thought music had stopped with Rameau, did not understand that Gluck had abandoned the brilliant but sterile idiom of his predecessors only so as to improve it by expressing emotion directly in his music. Marie Antoinette realized this; in short order, after listening to *Iphigénie* solely in order to please the Queen, the public came to the conclusion that here indeed was a masterpiece.

Important as her role may have been, however, it was not creative; Gluck would have written his music even if the French had not liked it; there is another field in which Marie Antoinette has left us a far more important legacy. Decor in the eighteenth century had become one of the arts, and all Europe looked to France for the lead. Already at Schönbrunn, the Archduchess Antoinette had had a taste of what a determined monarch could achieve, but it was only when she came to Versailles that she began to see masterpieces. She caught on very quickly. All through her reign, she patronized the greatest ébénistes and bronze makers then working, men like Riesener, Jacob, Weisweiler, Séné, and Gouthière, and worked directly with them so as to achieve a series of extraordinary pieces and environments.

Here we need no contemporary source: we have the great

good luck of being able to see most of it directly for ourselves. Whether at Versailles, Compiègne, or Fontainebleau, the Queen's rooms reflect the grace and sophistication typical of the Louis XVI style, while a closer look at the details —the carving of a boiserie, the chasing of a bronze—show just why the French artisans were universally admired. Nor was it merely a question of ordering a new decor: the Queen planned it all carefully with her architects and cabinet makers. Conference followed conference, and the result was invariably a triumph. If today we still marvel at a desk or a commode which looks as rich, as graceful, and as carefully finished as a piece of jewelry, if we know just how beautiful life could be in the 1770s and 1780s, it is because Marie Antoinette was the most enlightened of connoisseurs.

To this already very considerable achievement, yet another must be added. Although she designed its gardens with her architect, Richard Mique's, help, the Petit Trianon is the most personal, most direct expression of Marie Antoinette's taste and the one which, from that day to this, has enchanted the greatest number of people. The house itself predates 1774: it was commissioned by Louis XV from Jacques-Ange Gabriel at the suggestion of Mme de Pompadour, completed in 1770 and used frequently by the King until his death in May, 1774. Then, when the new Queen asked for a country house, Louis XVI gave her the Petit Trianon and the park surrounding it. Leaving the house much as it was, she proceeded to remodel the gardens in the new English style. Soon there were hills and streams, a lake complete with its island, a grotto, a Temple of Love, a little octagonal summer pavillion, even a Chinese carousel; and then, as if it wasn't enough, she added a proper hamlet, with thatch-roofed cottages, wooden balconies, and even a real farm house. It was all a game of course, but a curiously magical one: even today, as we walk through the hamlet, we cannot help being caught up in the fantasy. It is no wonder that two English visitors in the 1920s were convinced that they had seen the Queen: nowhere else does her spirit survive so strongly, so closely to our own.

All this must be remembered as well as her faults. More than anyone Marie Antoinette embodied all the allure of that time when life could indeed be sweet; but then, as the storm broke and she left Trianon forever, the Queen went on to reveal another dimension of herself. As the Revolution progressed and she was beset by rapidly worsening crises, she showed that in one respect at least she was really Maria Theresa's daughter: nothing, not bloodthirsty crowds, not the execution of her husband, not even the loss of her son, could ever break her indomitable courage. During her trial, when she was accused (among other horrors) of having had sexual relations with the six-year-old Dauphin, in the darkest of prisons, at the foot of the guillotine, she remained always true to herself and asked for no pity.

That of course is all a matter of public record—as is her steadfastly reactionary influence on her weak husband. The more intimate matters to be found in the correspondence, on the other hand, were carefully hidden from contemporaries. As, after two centuries, we discover her private thoughts and worries, we cannot help seeing the victim of a cruel and unavoidable fate. Already by 1775, we can watch— as did Maria Theresa—the shadows closing in around the oblivious Queen. Because she suffered so greatly and so courageously, because she paid for her mistakes with her life, she has earned our ever-renewed attention. More than anyone, she is the incarnation of the ancien régime with all its faults and all its attractions. There perhaps is the truest secret of Marie Antoinette: as we study the Queen, it is the century which in all its glory comes back to dazzling life.

INDEX

All page references from material in correspondence are in italics. Names that include "Du" or "La" are indexed under D and L respectively.

Adélaïde, 13, 14, 20, *46, 56–57, 75–76, 79,* 129, *134, 138–39,* 140n., *147,* 153, 180n., *213*
  See also Mesdames de France
Aiguillon, duc d', 16, 29, *63n., 68, 69, 80, 90, 100, 101, 110, 142, 147–48, 156, 281*
  exile of, *165, 166, 168, 195*
Aiguillon, duchesse d', *86, 94*
Albert, Prince, *34*
Amelot, M., *188*
American Revolution, *209, 243, 269n., 275n., 283, 299, 300*
Andlau, comtesse d', *180*
Anecdotes of the Court of Philip-Augustus (Lussan), *95*
Angivilliers, comte d', *91, 93*
Angoulême, duc d' (nephew of Marie Antoinette), *191, 194,* 311
Aremberg, Duke and Duchess, *53*
Arenberg, duc d', *198*
Arpajon, chevalier d', *93*
Artois, comte d' (*later* Charles X), 27, *86, 99, 103–5, 107, 108,* 125, *148, 150, 162–64, 199, 295*
  character of, 27, *86,* 217
  friction between Louis and, 126
  Lamballe backed by, *180*
  measles of, *191, 193, 194*
Artois, comtesse d', 110n., *126,* 144
  pregnancies of, *153, 156, 165, 169–70, 173–75, 191, 193–96, 220, 221*
Austrian Netherlands,
  Hapsburg possession of, 5, 17n., *171, 296n.*

Belderbush, M. de, *297*
Belgium. *See* Austrian Netherlands
Bellevue (chateau), 11, *38*
Bernis, cardinal de, *289*
Bertin, Mlle, 130
Bertrand (painter), *155*
Besenval, baron de, *180,* 270, *271,* 310
Bohemia and Moravia, *303*
  crop failure in, *82*
  Hapsburg possession of, 5
  serfdom in, 162n.
Boufflers, Mme de, *79*
Bourbon, duc de, *96, 102*
Bourbon, duchesse de, *96*
Bourbon, Mlle de, *96, 178*
Boynes, Bourgeois de, *105*
Braganza, Duke of, *232*
Brancas, Mme de, *85, 86*
Brandis, Countess, *107, 108*
Breteuil, baron de, *151–52, 182, 185, 258, 259, 278, 280–81, 283*
Brissac, maréchal de, *80*
Broglie, maréchal de, *72, 74, 77, 79,* 255

Calonne, Charles Alexandre de, 309
Campan, Mme, 26, 131
Card playing
  in court etiquette, 21, *36, 40, 70*

Machault d'Arnouville, Jean
    Baptiste, 128
Madame. *See* Provence, comtesse
    de
Madame Royale (Marie
    Antoinette's first daughter),
    *267, 274, 277, 279, 282–84,
    287, 288, 291–93, 295, 305–6,*
    311
Mailly, M. de, *185*
Mailly, Mme de, *175*
Malesherbes, Chrétien Guillaume
    de Lamoignon de, *168, 188*
Mandoux, abbé, *39*
Maria Amalia (Infanta; Duchess
    of Parma), *91, 99, 110, 121,
    123*
Maria Carolina (Queen of
    Naples), *34, 39, 81–83, 230,
    248, 279, 288, 291*
    pregnancies of, *90, 99, 107–9,
        112, 116, 118, 120, 123, 223–
        25, 238, 284, 289, 293, 296*
Marianne (archduchess), *95, 306–7*
Maria Theresa (Empress of
    Austria)
    advice of, to Marie Antoinette.
        See specific persons and topics
    calamities predicted by, *171*
    children of, 4–7
    death of, 307
    on failings of French court, 48–
        49
    hypocrisy of, 8, 24–25, *35n.*
    jeweled-flower gift of, *122, 123*
    Marie Antoinette prepared for
        marriage by, 2–4
    written instructions, 7, *31–34*
    Marie Antoinette's fear of, *98*
    medals in praise of charity of,
        93
    nature of correspondence
        between Marie Antoinette
        and, 22–24, 29
    nuptial alliances of, 3, 10
    popularity of, *115*
    portrait of, *95, 120*
    possessions of, 5
    source for correspondence

between Marie Antoinette
    and, 30
War of the Bavarian
    Succession and, 233–34,
    235–67, 272–74
Marie-Anne (archduchess), *49, 50*
Marie Antoinette (Queen of
    France)
    as "Austrian" or "German," 24,
        57, 64, 74, 116*n.,* 132, 138,
        159, 260*n.*
    children of, 308
        first daughter (Madame
            Royal), *267, 274, 277, 279,
            282–84, 287, 288, 291–93,
            295, 305–6,* 311
    control of Louis XVI by, 19, *42,
        43, 45,* 138, *189, 217,* 244–
        45, *271*
    as Dauphine
        balls and dances arranged, *56,
            58, 85,* 100
        corset controversy, 29, *44, 46–
            48, 50*
        description of her life, *39–41*
        Du Barry and. *See under* Du
            Barry, comtesse
        entry into France, 1
        married by procuration, 2*n.*
        at masked ball, *102, 106*
        nonconsummation of
            marriage, 18–19, 27, *43, 45,
            66, 80, 84, 87, 94, 95, 105–7*
        official entry into Paris, *109–
            10, 113–15, 118–19*
        popularity, 2, *46, 111,* 112–13,
            113–14, 118–19, 125
    description of, 18
    education of, 4–7
    illnesses of, *102, 152–53, 164,
        180, 198, 199, 202, 222, 232,
        241, 285, 287, 288*
        measles (guarded by men),
            270, 271, 272, 274
    Louis' loving behavior toward,
        *115, 125, 213, 217, 219, 277,
        289*
    Maria Theresa's advice to. *See
        specific persons and topics*